Implementing Sustainable Development Goals in Europe

Implementing Sustainable Development Goals in Europe

The Role of Political Entrepreneurship

Edited by

Charlie Karlsson

Professor Emeritus of the Economics of Technological Change, Jönköping International Business School, Jönköping University and Professor Emeritus of Industrial Economics, Blekinge Institute of Technology, Sweden

Daniel Silander

Associate Professor, Department of Political Science, Linnaeus University, Sweden

Edward Elgar
PUBLISHING

Cheltenham, UK • Northampton, MA, USA

Published by
Edward Elgar Publishing Limited
The Lypiatts
15 Lansdown Road
Cheltenham
Glos GL50 2JA
UK

Edward Elgar Publishing, Inc.
William Pratt House
9 Dewey Court
Northampton
Massachusetts 01060
USA

A catalogue record for this book
is available from the British Library

Library of Congress Control Number: 2020942943

This book is available electronically in the **Elgar**online
Social and Political Science subject collection
http://dx.doi.org/10.4337/9781789909975

ISBN 978 1 78990 996 8 (cased)
ISBN 978 1 78990 997 5 (eBook)

Printed by CPI Group (UK) Ltd, Croydon CR0 4YY

Contents

Contributors

Nino Berishvili is consultant to non-governmental organizations, policymaker on the strategy for sustainable development goals in Georgia and an international development specialist. She has worked within civil society organizations, and her research interests mainly involve rural–urban interactions, regional economic development, European Union integration and sustainable development goals.

Darlene Budd is Professor of Political Science at the University of Central Missouri, United States. Her main areas of interest are comparative climate change policy, women in politics and globalization.

Akis Kalaitzidis is Professor of Political Science at the University of Central Missouri, United States, with particular expertise in international and comparative politics with a focus on United States foreign policy and government, the European Union, international organizations and international relations and conflict resolution.

Charlie Karlsson is Professor of Economics at Jönköping International Business School, Sweden. In his research, he has focused on infrastructure economics, urban economics, the economics of technological change, regional economics, spatial industrial dynamics, entrepreneurship and small business economics.

Anna Parkhouse is Senior Lecturer of Political Science at Dalarna University, Sweden. Her research interests include the European Union as a regional and global actor, the impact of the European Union membership incentive on rule adoption in minority rights legislation and the impact of European policies on asylum seekers and refugees.

Charlotte Silander is Senior Lecturer of Political Science in the Department of Education, Linnaeus University, Sweden. Her research focuses on European Union education policy, gender equality in higher education, systems of higher education and university research policies.

Daniel Silander is Associate Professor of Political Science at Linnaeus University, Sweden. His main areas of interest are political entrepreneurship on domestic and international levels, international politics, democracy and state and human security.

Don Wallace is Professor of Criminal Justice at the University of Central Missouri, United States. He conducts research on the United Nations, global governance and international organizations, state policies on security and climate change challenges to state and human security.

Henry Kiragu Wambuii is Professor of Political Science at the University of Central Missouri, United States. His areas of expertise are international development and public policy formulation, comparative politics and human rights and democratization in developing countries.

1. The EU and Agenda 2030

Daniel Silander

We, the Heads of State and Government and High Representatives, meeting at United Nations Headquarters in New York from 25 to 27 September 2015 as the Organization celebrates its seventieth anniversary, have decided today on new global Sustainable Development Goals. On behalf of the peoples we serve, we have adopted a historic decision on a comprehensive, far-reaching and people-centred set of universal and transformative Goals and targets. We commit ourselves to working tirelessly for the full implementation of this Agenda by 2030.
(United Nations, 2015: 4)

About 70 years ago, state leaders around the globe decided to create the United Nations (UN) to emphasize the importance of global solidarity and collaboration to provide for peace and prosperity. Today, a new generation of state leaders have decided to work towards sustainable peace and prosperity to safeguard our planet and human dignity. On 25–27 September 2015, the heads of states, at a special UN Summit, which included 193 member states, debated and adopted *Transforming Our World: The 2030 Agenda for Sustainable Development* (see Chapter 2). The Agenda became operational in 2016, with a lifespan of 15 years, in the context of the Paris Climate Agreement, the Addis Ababa Action Agenda and the Sendai Framework for Disaster Risk Reduction (European Commission, 2016: 1; European Commission, 2019: 6). The 2030 Agenda consists of four sections: (i) a political declaration, (ii) 17 sustainable development goals (SDGs) and 169 targets, (iii) means of implementation and (iv) a framework for follow up and review of the Agenda. Into the Agenda are embedded different dimensions of sustainable development – economic, social, cultural, political and environmental – and it stresses how all of these dimensions and goals are interlinked and must be approached together to promote global sustainability. The Agenda explicitly stresses a shared global responsibility and the necessity of a global partnership to promote a better world (United Nations, 2015).

Agenda 2030 is the result of a long political process, which started in June 2012 with the Rio-20 Conference on Sustainable Development, where participating states agreed to develop global SDGs based on the previous Millennium Development Goals and the 2005 World Summit Outcome. The Agenda 2030 is, however, also guided in its foundation by the UN Charter and the Universal

Table 1.1   Summary of Agenda 2030

Goals	Content
1. End Poverty	Reduction and, in the long term, eradication of poverty
2. Food Security	End hunger and promote sustainable agriculture
3. Health and Well-Being	Health systems, health coverage and countermeasures for diseases
4. Quality Education	Inclusive and equitable education, as well as life-long learning opportunities
5. Gender Equality	Girls' and women's empowerment, plus social and economic participation
6. Clean Water and Sanitation	Sustainable management of water to provide safe water and sanitation
7. Sustainable Energy	Sustainable energy services, and sure access to affordable, reliable and modern energy
8. Works and Growth	Promote decent work and full employment through inclusive and sustainable economic growth
9. Industries and Innovation	Sustainable industrialization and fostered innovation
10. Reduced Inequalities	Structural transformation to address income inequalities
11. Sustainable Community	Sustainable urbanization to enhance effective local development
12. Responsible Consumption and Production	Responsible supply chains and business practices, as well as promotion of green economy
13. Climate Action	Combat climate change and its impacts
14. Life below Water	Conservation and sustainable use of oceans, seas and marine resources
15. Life on Land	Protect and promote sustainable terrestrial ecosystems on land, and combat unsustainable management of forests, desertification and land degradation
16. Peaceful Societies and Strong Institutions	Promote inclusive societies based on strong institutions and the rule of law
17. Global Partnerships and Implementation	Strengthen and monitor means of implementation of development goals based on global partnerships

Declaration of Human Rights and is influenced by various historical decisions and instruments.[1] The established 17 SDGs (see Table 1.1) and the 169 targets of the Agenda are to be applied globally and highlight the four Ps – people, planet, prosperity and peace:

1. People – actions aimed at ending poverty and hunger by promoting a healthy environment.
2. Planet – actions aimed at protecting the world from degradation by fostering sustainable consumption and production, as well as the sustain-

able management of natural resources with a focus on combating climate change.

3. Prosperity – actions aimed at ensuring sustainable economic, social and technological progress.

4. Peace – actions aimed at fostering peaceful, just and inclusive societies, free from fear and violence, and based on enduring institutions and the rule of law (United Nations, 2015: preamble).

The UN has stated that billions of citizens continue to face global challenges. Although progress has been made on many goals, the Agenda calls for enforcement of crucial new global reforms to fight the numerous and complex challenges. The focus must be on countries steeped in poverty and despair, as well as on conflict or post-conflict status, people with special vulnerability, such as children, youth, women, the elderly, persons with disabilities and diseases, refugees and indigenous groups. Some alarming and global challenges are poverty and unsafe drinking water, hunger and diseases, social and economic inequalities within and among countries, gender inequality, unemployment, social marginalization and discrimination, illiteracy and poor education, conflicts and wars, human rights abuses and humanitarian crises, and unjust societies. In addition, global challenges present in natural disasters and climate change in desertification, drought, land degradation, loss of biodiversity, sea level rise and ocean acidification and unsustainable energy. In sum, the Agenda 2030 is a far-reaching agenda that addresses SDGs in the political, economic, social, cultural and environmental spheres, including all geographical areas and intended for every global citizen.

The UN urges a global commitment to address challenges and reach the development goals by 2030 (see Goal 17). It does not only address the crucial importance of state engagement in the developed and developing world, but also of local, sub-regional, regional and global engagement, in addition to private-sector actorness and civil society. The Preamble of Agenda 2030 clearly argues that only through partnerships can necessary means be mobilized to address the many and highly interrelated SDGs. As stated in the Preamble of Agenda 2030:

> All countries and all stakeholders, acting in collaborative partnership, will implement this plan. We are resolved to free the human race from the tyranny of poverty and want and to heal and secure our planet. We are determined to take the bold and transformative steps which are urgently needed to shift the world on to a sustainable and resilient path. (United Nations, 2015: preamble)

EU GOVERNANCE AND POLITICAL ENTREPRENEURSHIP ON AGENDA 2030

The Agenda identifies state governments as primary actors to promote the 17 goals, and to monitor the implementation of measures taken on all levels of governance. The Agenda also calls upon individual states to develop national responses implementing measures intended to obtain the development goals, and to set up tools to conduct reviews of past progress and future challenges on each goal. The states are addressed as the engines driving the reforms, but, as stated, their efforts must be complemented by work at the regional/international level as a potential opportunity for increased capacity.

Today, the UN Agenda 2030 is the blueprint for Europe's push for sustainable development and the European Union (EU) has stressed its position as a frontrunner to implement sustainable development throughout Europe (European Commission, 2016: 3), but also through its external actions. Based on the identified SDGs, the European Commission has set out priorities to work on, as key challenges for Europe (see also Chapter 3). As stated by the Commission,

> The SDGs, together with the Paris Agreement on Climate Change, are the roadmap to a better world and the global framework for international cooperation on sustainable development and its economic, social, environmental and governance dimensions. The EU was one of the leading forces behind the United Nations 2030 Agenda and has fully committed itself to its implementation. (European Commission, 2019: 6)

In 2016, the European Commission published the Communication *Next Steps for a Sustainable European Future – European Action for Sustainability*. The Commission stressed that 'a life of dignity for all within the planet's limits that reconciles economic prosperity and efficiency, peaceful societies, social inclusion and environmental responsibility is at the essence of sustainable development' (European Commission, 2016: 2). The Communication confirmed that Europe, compared to many places in the world, is in a beneficial starting position to implement sustainable reforms based on a historically good track record within the EU institutions and Treaties of committing to sustainable development (European Commission, 2016: 2). Despite the favourable position in a global context, the Communication also addressed challenges that exist in Europe. It highlighted the extent to which European societies face many sustainability challenges, in unemployment, aging populations, climate change, pollution, unsustainable energy, migration, inequalities, healthcare shortages, resource inefficiency, the demand for research and innovation and an old-fashioned economy in need of becoming greener (European Commission,

2016: 2). It further highlighted that existing challenges needed to be solved to protect and develop the European social economic model that had been developed successfully since the 1950s (Silander, 2019: 36–53). Hard work on sustainable development would occur in cross-cutting projects, sectoral policies and initiatives, based on the previous records in the EU Sustainable Development Strategy of 2001, revised in 2006 and reviewed in 2009.

In Europe, the UN Agenda 2030 was preceded by the European Agenda 2020, which was already initiated in 2010 by the Commission (see Chapter 3). The Agenda 2020 was an official communication by the European Commission titled *Europe 2020: A Strategy for Smart, Sustainable and Inclusive Growth* and represented a direct response to the global recession of 2008–2009. The Commission called for a European partnership similar to the commitments cited by the UN in Agenda 2030; this partnership was conceived in a European context, however, to coordinate all EU institutions, member states, regional and local authorities and the private sector to address the economic crisis (Wandel, 2016: 10; Zeitlin & Vanhercke, 2014: 8–9). Together, the European partnership would promote and implement measures aimed at smart, sustainable and inclusive growth: smart growth, in terms of promoting an economy based on knowledge and innovation; sustainable growth, in terms of economic growth based on resource efficiency and a greener economy; and inclusive growth, in terms of growth that provides for social integration.

It then argued that the ongoing recession, which had severe political (rising nationalism and populism), economic (unemployment and declining growth) and social (marginalization, exclusion and poverty) consequences, and which jeopardized European integration and collaboration, had to be solved through sustainable development. Based on the strategy of Agenda 2020 and a political system of European governance, the Commission described how the European Council had to play the role of guiding the EU member states towards the objectives set out in the agenda. The European Council was expected to steer the work on Agenda 2020, as the political body capable of promoting integration and collaboration and ensuring member state interdependence and collaboration between the EU and member states. On the other hand, the Council of Ministers would be responsible for the implementation of Agenda 2020, making sure that all objectives were met. The progress made by member states with regional and local authorities would be monitored and assessed annually by the European Commission to ensure implementation. It was also the role of the Commission to set out policy recommendations, warnings and proposals based on these assessments of individual member states. The European Parliament would be co-legislator with the Council of Ministers, as well as integrator of European citizens into the agenda; it would compel national parliaments to engage in debate concerning the best possible ways to implement Agenda 2020 on a national level, as well as on regional and local levels, including domestic authorities in relation to private actors and civil society (Silander, 2018).

In 2010, the fulfilment of Agenda 2020 in Europe not only required coordinated actions throughout the system of European governance, but arguably, it also demanded the pursuit of European political entrepreneurship, leadership, innovative ideas and bold measures. The previous economic crisis was a wake-up call for the EU and an alarming signal that European politics as usual would lead the EU, along with member states, into further recession and the second rank in the new global economic order. However, a European crisis could also serve as a window of opportunity for European integration, as had been the case throughout the many decades of European politics (see Cross, 2017). The EU had to engage new, innovative politics and be bold and ambitious, by showing leadership and entrepreneurship, to determine Europe's socioeconomic future. In 2010, the former chair of the Commission, José Manuel Barroso, called for new innovative measures taken by politicians, bureaucrats, officers and institutions within the publicly funded sector (this study refers to such behaviour as European political entrepreneurship). With innovative approaches, political entrepreneurship encourages entrepreneurship towards a goal of growth and employment for the common good (see Karlsson et al., 2016, 2018; Silander & Silander, 2015). As stated by the former chair of the Commission,

> The condition for success is a real ownership by European leaders and institutions... European leaders have a common analysis of the lessons to be drawn from the crisis. We also share a common sense of urgency on the challenges ahead. Now we jointly need to make it happen... We must have confidence in our ability to set an ambitious agenda for ourselves and then gear our efforts to delivering it. (Barroso, 2010: preface)

In a similar fashion, the next chair of the Commission, Jean-Claude Juncker, stated, in reference to the complexity of global sustainable development challenges as set out in Agenda 2030, that Europe had to tackle such challenges through new, bold and innovative political measures to provide for sustainable development in Europe and globally. Based on the successful work to tackle the economic crisis of 2008, and on smart, sustainable and inclusive growth and forward movement, Juncker stressed that the wind was back in Europe's sails and that this was the moment for bold leadership, changes and reforms, and to stand strong for present and future challenges. As he argued,

> Europe was not made to stand still. It must never do so. Helmut Kohl and Jacques Delors, whom I had the honour to know, taught me that Europe only moves forward when it is bold. The single market, Schengen and the single currency: these were all ideas that were written off as pipe dreams before they happened. And yet these

three ambitious projects are now a part of our daily reality. Now that Europe is doing better, people tell me I should not rock the boat. But now is not the time to err on the side of caution. We started to fix the European roof. But today and tomorrow we must patiently, floor by floor, moment by moment, inspiration by inspiration, continue to add new floors to the European House. We must complete the European House now that the sun is shining and whilst it still is. Because when the next clouds appear on the horizon – and they will appear one day – it will be too late. So let's throw off the bowlines. Sail away from the harbour. And catch the trade winds in our sails. (Juncker, 2017)

POLITICAL ENTREPRENEURSHIP

The Juncker Commission statements on UN 2030 reflected on the need for European political entrepreneurship to build a better Europe. The bulk of the studies in economics have, for more than half a century, stressed the extent to which entrepreneurship and entrepreneurs are vital aspects of growing and dynamic societies (see Schumpeter, 1934; Carroll, 2017). In the academic literature, the focus is on the crucial role that entrepreneurship plays in development, identifying entrepreneurs as the important risk takers, innovators and responders to socioeconomic challenges. Although research on entrepreneurs and entrepreneurship has taken place mostly within economics, there has been a growing pool of studies on entrepreneurial activity in the public sector. This growing body of literature has been inspired by core elements of entrepreneurs and entrepreneurship from the business sector, such as the importance of knowledge, innovation, opportunity, implementation and risk taking (Carroll, 2017: 115–19).

Although the concept of a public entrepreneur had already been identified in 1965 (see Ostrom, 1965), it took about three more decades for the concept of entrepreneurship in the public sector to be developed further in academia (Baumol, 1990). Studies have identified public entrepreneurs as innovative and creative actors within municipalities and public corporations, who seek implementation of innovations in public-sector practice (Ostrom, 1965; Roberts & King, 1991). Studies have also identified social entrepreneurs as innovative and goal-oriented citizens who have an objective of promoting a normative good that may not be economically oriented; rather, they may have social goals in cooperative associations, interest organizations and movements and so on (Gawell et al., 2009; Borzaga et al., 2008). In addition, policy entrepreneurs have often been used to exemplify actors beyond the formal positions of government, who seek to introduce and implement new ideas in the public sector (Roberts & King, 1991) or for politicians and/or government employees who act upon what they see as a window of opportunity to improve government policies. Policy entrepreneurs may or may not be formally or directly engaged in legislative policymaking, but their know-how, reputation,

Table 1.2   Types of entrepreneurs – European political entrepreneurs

Types of entrepreneurs	Common definitions
Economic/business entrepreneurs	Actors within the business sector acting as risk takers, innovators and responders to market disequilibria to seek economic gains for their companies/organizations
Social entrepreneurs	Actors within civil society who seek societal changes within cooperative associations, interest organizations, aid branches and rights and liberties movements
Policy entrepreneurs	Actors inside or outside the formal positions of government/politics who seek to introduce and implement new ideas in the public sector for development of the public good rather than for individual profit
Public entrepreneurs	Actors within public corporations from the public sector who seek implementation through innovations in public-sector practice
Bureaucratic entrepreneurs	Actors who gain power from policymakers to influence the policy process and/or the public sector by initiating a political process, setting priorities or interpreting the implementation phase
Political entrepreneurs (traditionally applied)	Actors (politicians) within the political arena, driven by the common good or individual profit from the political system, acting to receive political support, votes, campaign contributions or improved political status
Political entrepreneurs – theoretically defined in this study	Actors and institutions (politicians, bureaucrats, officers and institutions) within the publicly funded sector that act with innovative approaches to encourage entrepreneurship/business and for which the goal is growth and employment for the common good
European political entrepreneurs – empirically applied in this study	European actors and institutions (European and EU politicians, bureaucrats, officers and institutions) within the publicly funded sector that act with innovative approaches to encourage entrepreneurship/ business and for which the goal is growth and employment for the common good; i.e. Agenda 2030 Goals

money and time puts them in a position to develop and present alternative policy solutions to existing problems that face policymakers (Kingdon, 1995). Finally, bureaucratic entrepreneurs have been referred to as acting as public servants or similar who gain power from policymakers to influence the policy process by initiating a political process, setting priorities and interpreting the implementation phase and so on (Silander, 2016: 11–12; Carroll, 2017; Roberts & King, 1991).

There is a growing body of studies on different types of entrepreneurs. Some of the most commonly used are summarized in Table 1.2.[2]

More recent studies embody the developing multidisciplinary approach to entrepreneurship, which has focused on political entrepreneurs and political entrepreneurship (Silander, 2016, 2018; Silander & Silander, 2015; Scheingate, 2003).[3] Recent research on political entrepreneurship has been based on a few core aspects. First, studies on political entrepreneurship have focused on political entrepreneurs from an actor-oriented perspective by analysing individual motives and perceptions, using institutions as a forgotten dimension. Second, such studies have often started from the assumption that political entrepreneurship is aimed at individual profit-seeking activities within the political/public system, rather than at the common good. Third, it has also been argued that fuzzy distinctions have been made between what actually defines political entrepreneurship; that is to say there is still some ambiguity surrounding the nature of political entrepreneurship, compared to regular, day-to-day political/public activities in the public sector. From a political entrepreneurship perspective, studies have focused on the ways that politicians and bureaucrats may change tax distribution, regulations and implementation procedures, but have forgotten to make compelling arguments about whether regular activities in politics can be defined as political entrepreneurship (Scheingate, 2003; Holcombe, 2002; Schneider & Teske, 1992). Fourth and last, political entrepreneurship has also been studied in a domestic setting of societal actors, a perspective that fails to account for the potential importance of these actors on the international scene, such as within international organizations like the EU.

Following recent studies on political entrepreneurs and political entrepreneurship (see Karlsson et al., 2016, 2018; Silander & Silander, 2015), *our perspective focuses on politicians, public servants, bureaucrats and institutions that seek to create new, innovative and favourable formal and informal institutional conditions* (see North, 1990; Kingdon, 1995). Political entrepreneurship is about approaching and challenging traditional formal institutions in political steering, leadership, strategies, policies, rules, regulations, laws and budgets for entrepreneurial activities and/or in the ideas, attitudes, values, perceptions, images and symbols of traditional informal institutions in ways that structure day-to-day public activities and culture around entrepreneurship (North, 1990; Morgan, 1986; Putnam, 1993). Political entrepreneurship in this book occurs when traditional EU/European institutions, formal and/or informal, are challenged and changed by new institutions, formal and/or informal, better suited to promote entrepreneurial activity on the SDGs of the Agenda 2030. As argued in a previous study, 'The political entrepreneur operates beyond traditional and routinized procedures and is innovative and creative in using formal and informal institutions and networks to improve the public sector's activities towards entrepreneurs and entrepreneurship by developing and promoting new norms that have not been embedded in traditional day-to-day public activities' (Silander, 2016: 10).

The implementation of Agenda 2030 and the SDGs began in 2016 and governments, institutions, organizations, businesses, universities and individuals started to work on the realization of the goals. At the global level, the sustainable goals are meant to be transformed into national, regional and local ones, and they are therefore translated into national legislation. This allows for a broad range of cooperation and coordination among the various countries and regions. The entire world seems to work towards the realization of the SDGs, thereby involving many actors at all levels of governance, who shape the goals and influence the implementation and achievement of Agenda 2030. This offers a wide area and a huge platform for political entrepreneurs to shape the policy process and the outcomes.

AIM AND STRUCTURE OF THE STUDY

This study focuses on European political entrepreneurship in the EU's approach towards the Agenda 2030 strategy, adding an international perspective on entrepreneurship to a discussion of the European context. The aim of the study is to analyse the 2030 Agenda, its SDGs and the role of European political entrepreneurs in shaping, influencing and realizing these goals at all levels of European governance. Based on studies of political entrepreneurship in a European context, the book adds to our conceptual insights regarding the role of political entrepreneurship and its potential to shape policies. In contrast to other studies, this study broadens the area of political entrepreneurship at an international level and explains how European political entrepreneurs, at various governance levels, act and interact to push their policies through. The aim of the study is therefore twofold: first, to analyse the 2030 Agenda and its SDGs, as well as the role of EU political entrepreneurship in debating, shaping and implementing the agenda at all levels of governance; and second, to provide conceptual insights regarding the role of political entrepreneurship and the political entrepreneur at an international level.

CONCLUSION

This book on EU governance and political entrepreneurship in Agenda 2030 explores the role of EU actors in debating, shaping and implementing Agenda 2030 in Europe. It explores several EU actors in the context of numerous development goals to see how the EU overall has downloaded the UN SDGs in a European context. This chapter has asserted that the EU constitutes a system of governance, and that the European Commission has a prior record of accomplishment as an engine driving the promotion of sustainable development in Europe. The initiation of Agenda 2020 for smart, sustainable and inclusive growth was a major reform within Europe between 2010 and 2020 and yielded great results within most EU member states (see Silander, 2019). Such efforts within Europe have influenced the debate and decisions leading up to the UN Agenda 2030. The UN Agenda represents a complex set of goals that includes most areas of society: social, economic, environmental, cultural and political. The development goals are devised to protect and promote the people, planet, prosperity and peace through a global partnership. This book explores the content of Agenda 2030, the many actors involved in European governance to promote such goals and the ways that these UN goals are embedded in a European context through European political entrepreneurship.

NOTES

1. These include the following: the World Summit on Sustainable Development, the World Summit for Social Development, the Programme of Action of the International Conference on Population and Development, the Beijing Platform for Action, the UN Conference on Sustainable Development, the Fourth UN Conference on the Least Developed Countries, the Third International Conference on Small Island Developing States, the Second UN Conference on Landlocked Developing Countries and the Third UN World Conference on Disaster.
2. Many different types of entrepreneurs and entrepreneurship are described in the literature, and the definitions of these types have differed from one study to another. This has led scholars to argue that 'perhaps the largest obstacle in creating a conceptual framework for the entrepreneurship field has been its definition. What the many different studies on types of entrepreneurship have in common is the main focus on how entrepreneurship includes knowledge, innovation, opportunity, implementation and risk taking as core elements' (see Carroll, 2017: 115). However, the primary distinction between private/business and public-sector entrepreneurs and entrepreneurship has been the lack of entrepreneurial profit (see Boyett, 1996: 49) in public-sector entrepreneurship.
3. Such conceptualization was introduced by Robert Dahl, who focused on resourceful and masterful political leaders and argued that the political entrepreneur was 'the epitome of the self-made man' (1974: 25, 223–7, 282). According to Dahl, Homo politicus are people formally engaged in politics. Political entrepreneurs may be driven by the common good and the provision of collective benefits to the many, but they may also be oriented towards individual profit seeking from the political system through, for instance, receiving political support and votes, campaign contributions or improved political status (see Dahl, 1974). In Dahl's discussions, individual leaders are often referred to as entrepreneurial politicians (Scheingate, 2003), but others have used political entrepreneurship to refer to

individuals trying to profit individually from the political system (see McCaffrey & Salerno, 2011).

REFERENCES

Barroso, J.M. (2010). 'Preface' in *Com* 2020. *Communication from the Commission: Europe 2020: A Strategy for Smart, Sustainable and Inclusive Growth*. Brussels, 3 March. Brussels: European Commission.

Baumol, W.J. (1990). 'Entrepreneurship: Productive, unproductive and destructive'. *Journal of Political Economy*, **98**(5): 893–921.

Borzaga, C., G. Galera & R. Nogales (eds) (2008). *Social Enterprise: A New Model for Poverty Reduction and Employment Generation: An Examination of the Concept and Practice in Europe and the Commonwealth of Independent States*. UNDP Regional Bureau for Europe and the Commonwealth of Independent States.

Boyett, I. (1996). 'The public sector entrepreneur: A definition'. *International Journal of Public Sector Management*, **9**(2): 36–51.

Carroll, J.J. (2017). 'Failure is an option: The entrepreneurial governance framework'. *Journal of Entrepreneurship and Public Policy*, **6**(1): 108–26.

Cross, D.M.K. (2017). *The Politics of Crisis in Europe*. Cambridge: Cambridge University Press.

Dahl, R.A. (1974). *Who Governs? Democracy and Power in an American City*. New Haven, CT: Yale University Press.

European Commission (2016). *Next Steps for a Sustainable European Future: European Action for Sustainability*. Accessed 12 October 2018 at https://ec.europa .eu/europeaid/commission-communication-next-steps-sustainable-european-future _en

European Commission (2019). *Europe in May 2019 Preparing for a more united, stronger and more democratic Union in an increasingly uncertain world: The European Commission's contribution to the informal EU27 leaders' meeting in Sibiu (Romania) on 9 May 2019*, January. Luxembourg: Publications Office of the European Union, 2019.

Gawell, M., B. Johannisson & M. Lundqvist (2009). *Samhällets Entreprenörer – En Forskarantologi om Samhällsentreprenörskap* [Social Entrepreneurs: A Research Anthology on Social Entrepreneurship]. Stockholm: KK-stiftelsen.

Holcombe, R.G. (2002). 'Political entrepreneurship and the democratic allocation of economic resources'. *Review of Austrian Economics*, **15**(2/3): 143–59.

Juncker, J.C. (2017). *State of the Union 2017*, Brussels, 13 September. Accessed 13 October 2019 at http://eurireland.ie/assets/uploads/2017/09/SOTEU-Address.pdf

Karlsson, C., C. Silander & D. Silander (eds) (2016). *Political Entrepreneurship: Regional Growth and Entrepreneurial Diversity in Sweden*. Cheltenham, UK and Northampton, MA, USA: Edward Elgar Publishing.

Karlsson, C., C. Silander & D. Silander (eds) (2018). *Governance and Political Entrepreneurship in Europe: Promoting Growth and Welfare in Times of Crisis*. Cheltenham, UK and Northampton, MA, USA: Edward Elgar Publishing.

Kingdon, J. (1995). *Agendas, Alternatives, and Public Policies*. New York: HarperCollins.

McCaffrey, M. & J.T. Salerno (2011). 'A theory of political entrepreneurship'. *Modern Economy*, **2**(4): 552–60.

Morgan, G. (1986). *Images of Organizations*. Los Angeles: Sage.

North, D.C. (1990). *Institutions, Institutional Change and Economic Performance.* Cambridge: Cambridge University Press.

Ostrom, E. (1965). *Public Entrepreneurship: A Case Study in Ground Water Basin Management.* Los Angeles: University of California, Los Angeles.

Putnam, R. (1993). *Making Democracy Work: Civic Traditions in Modern Italy.* Princeton, NJ: Princeton University Press.

Roberts, N.C. & P.J. King (1991). 'Policy entrepreneurs: Their activity structure and function in the policy process'. *Journal of Public Administration Research and Theory*, 1(2): 147–75.

Scheingate, A.D. (2003). 'Political entrepreneurship, institutional change and American political development'. *Studies in American Political Development*, 17(2): 185–203.

Schneider, M. & P. Teske (1992). 'Toward a theory of the political entrepreneur: Evidence from local government'. *American Political Science Review*, 86(3): 737–47.

Schumpeter, J.A. (1934). *The Theory of Economic Development: An Inquiry into Profits, Capital, Credit, Interest, and the Business Cycle.* Cambridge, MA: Harvard University Press.

Silander, D. (2016). 'The political entrepreneur', in C. Karlsson, C. Silander and D. Silander (eds), *Political Entrepreneurship: Regional Growth and Entrepreneurial Diversity in Sweden.* Cheltenham, UK and Northampton, MA, USA: Edward Elgar Publishing, pp. 7–20.

Silander, D. (2018). 'European governance and political entrepreneurship in times of economic crisis'. In C. Karlsson, C. Silander and D. Silander (eds), *Governance and Political Entrepreneurship in Europe: Promoting Growth and Welfare in Times of Crisis.* Cheltenham, UK and Northampton, MA, USA: Edward Elgar Publishing.

Silander, D. (2019). 'The European Commission and Europe 2020: Smart, sustainable and inclusive growth'. In Charlie Karlsson, Daniel Silander & Brigitte Pircher (eds), *Smart, Sustainable and Inclusive Growth: Political Entrepreneurship for a Prosperous Europe.* Cheltenham, UK and Northampton, MA, USA: Edward Elgar Publishing, pp. 36–53.

Silander, D. & C. Silander (eds) (2015). *Politiskt Entreprenörskap – Den Offentliga Sektorns Sätt att Skapa Bättre Förutsättningar för Entreprenörskap Lokalt, Regional och Nationellt* [Political Entrepreneurship: The Public Sector and Measurements to Improve Conditions for Entrepreneurship on Local, Regional and National Levels]. Stockholm: Santérus förlag.

United Nations (2015). *Transforming Our World: The 2030 Agenda for Sustainable Development.* Accessed 12 October 2018 at https://sustainabledevelopment.un.org/post2015/transformingourworld

Wandel, J. (2016). 'The role of government and markets in the strategy "Europe 2020" of the European Union: A robust political economy analysis'. *International Journal of Management and Economics*, 49(January–March): 7–33.

Zeitlin, J. & B. Vanhercke (2014). *Socializing the European semester? Economic governance and social policy coordination in Europe 2020.* Brown University, Watson Institute for International Studies Research Paper No. 2014–17.

2. The UN regime and sustainable development: Agenda 2030

Don Wallace

The groundbreaking ambition in the international agreement on Agenda 2030 was immediately recognized when it was approved by heads of state and governments of all member states of the United Nations (UN) on September 25, 2015. Optimistic observers (e.g. Dodds et al., 2016) viewed the 2030 Agenda for Sustainable Development as a twenty-first-century blueprint providing 17 Sustainable Development Goals (SDGs) for the development of humanity and the planet (see Chapter 1 for further information on Agenda 2030). In a single global agreement, the world was summoned to confront the major challenges of the time, *inter alia*, eliminating poverty, providing affordable and clean energy, implementing climate action, and sustainably managing natural resources. By contributing to the creation of conditions for sustainable economic growth (Dodds et al., 2016), these goals were anticipated to "stimulate action over the next 15 years in areas of critical importance for humanity and the planet" (UNGA, 2015, preamble). The adoption of these goals was seen as "embarking on the greatest public policy experiment of human society of our time" (Xue et al., 2017: 150). These SDGs are far more integrated, broad, and complex than the Millennium Development Goals (MDGs), which were sublimated by the SDGs. The SDGs represent a significant increase in the breadth of coverage of the economic as well as social and environmental dimensions of sustainable development across the 17 SDGs' 169 targets and 232 indicators (Allen et al., 2018). While the MDGs were supposed to be achieved by 2015, an extended process was needed to continue development goals for the years 2015–30 (Wallace, 2018). Hope was expressed that the 2030 Agenda could build upon the "fragile platform of the MDGs," presenting an opportunity to reverse some of the damage caused by the global recession that resulted from the two decades' experience of "market fundamentalism" (McCann, 2015). Agenda 2030 with its SDGs and targets came into effect on January 1, 2016.

This chapter provides an overview of the UN regime and sustainable development with its focus on the developments of Agenda 2030. First, a brief background is given on the UN's activities leading to approval of Agenda 2030. The content of Agenda 2030 is examined in the second part, with some description provided of the 17 goals of sustainable development. The notion of global governance in the Agenda 2030 context is discussed in the third part of the chapter. The fourth part considers the role of regional actors for Agenda 2030. In the conclusion, there is an overview of the progress of Agenda 2030 reported at the 2019 SDG Summit.

BACKGROUND TO AGENDA 2030

The UN has a long track record, in constructing specific strategies with the goal to create the fundamental conditions for equitable and environmentally sustainable forms of development. These aspirational initiatives include a series of international conferences linking environment and development. These conferences include the first UN Conference on the Human Environment held in Stockholm in 1972; the 1992 UN Conference on Environment and Development held in Rio de Janeiro; the World Summit on Sustainable Development 2002 held in Johannesburg; and the 2012 UN Conference on Sustainable Development, also known as Rio+20. Formative documents arose from these events (Bebbington & Unerman, 2018), such as the Brundtland Report of the World Commission on Environment and Development (WCED, 1987) and Agenda 21 (UN Division, 1992), a non-binding, unimplemented agenda for sustainable development and climate change agreed to at Rio in 1992.

Providing a set of broad objectives for poverty eradication to guide the international community for the first years of the twenty-first-century, 189 UN member states adopted the Millennium Declaration in September 2000 (UNGA, 2000). Eight specific goals were presented by UN Secretary-General Kofi Annan in his report, "Road Map Towards the Implementation of the Millennium Declaration" (UNSG, 2001). This global and outcome-oriented policy provided a framework for development during the period of 2000 to 2015 (Tosun & Leininger, 2017).

Shawki (2016) observed that though originally intended to be universal in their scope, the MDGs became limited addressing only forms of absolute poverty and thus becoming irrelevant for nations without people experiencing this sort of extreme indigence. The accomplishments of the MDGs were uneven and in some areas fell short. Reductions in extreme poverty were seen in China and India, but the 2015 Millennium Development Goals Report showed that in sub-Saharan Africa, more than 40 percent of the population still suffered from extreme poverty (Nanda, 2016: 395–6) A major blow to progress under the MDGs came from the financial crisis beginning in 2008, and prior to this the terrorist attacks on 9/11 hindered member states' focus on sustainable development with concerns of security and counter-terrorism (Dodds et al., 2016).

Apart from these externalities, there were intrinsic challenges for the MDGs. One critique regarding the shortcomings of the MDGs was that they were a direct result of a lack of understanding of the structural contexts of poverty and underdevelopment (McCloskey, 2015). The underlying assumption of the MDGs was that poverty was a factor primarily of internal domestic factors and could be largely eliminated by domestic reform supported by foreign aid (Bello, 2015). The objective of the MDGs for reducing poverty according to Nanda (2016) focused on the symptoms of poverty and failed to address the underlying causes. Additionally, the poverty standard did not address the severity and depth of poverty, rather as observed by Shetty (Amnesty International, 2013) the MDG framework's focus was on statistical averages and aggregated data.

Additionally, Dodds et al. (2016) observed that under the MDGs there had been insufficient attention paid to providing for an arrangement for monitoring of implementation and for financing. Similarly, Nanda (2016) noted that one of their shortcomings was the lack of transparency in the formulation of the MDGs in that the responsibility for the drafting process was placed upon a group of staff members from the UN, International Monetary Fund, World Bank, and Organisation for Economic Co-operation and Development (UN System Task Team, 2012) without broader participation, especially from non-governmental organizations and other parts of civil society.

In September 2007, in a speech before the UN General Assembly (UNGA), Lula da Silva, the president of Brazil, proposed a new sustainable development summit for 2012, coinciding on the 20-year anniversary of the first Rio Conference. This second Rio summit would become known as Rio+20. At the 2012 Rio+20 conference, nations agreed to establish SDGs that reached beyond the MDGs. It was further agreed that these new goals should apply to all countries, both developing and developed, and an anticipated 2030 target date was noted (Griggs et al., 2014). Dodds et al. (2016) identified contributions from Rio+20 that continue to impact the agenda of the current environment of SDGs. In particular, Rio+20 established:

- The Open Working Group, established on January 22, 2013 by decision of the UNGA (2013a), constituted an intergovernmental process for obtaining the desired broad consensus for the SDGs.
- The High-Level Political Forum (HLPF) is a subsidiary body of both the UN General Assembly and the UN Economic and Social Council responsible for the entire organization's policy on sustainable development. Its establishment was mandated in 2012 by the outcome document and now provides a conduit for monitoring implementation of the eventual SDGs (UN, 2019a).

- The Technology Facilitation Mechanism facilitates meaningful and sustained capacity building and technical assistance. ¶70 of the 2030 Agenda announced the launch of a Technology Facilitation Mechanism in order to support the implementation of the SDGs (UN, 2019b).
- The Intergovernmental Committee of Experts on Sustainable Development Finance led the Third International Conference on Financing for Development. The outcome of the 2015 Third International Conference on Financing for Development at Addis Ababa was to be called the Addis Ababa Action Agenda (AAAA). Among the announcements at Addis Ababa of new funding was the acceptance of an increased position of the private sector in development finance (Dodds et al., 2016).

At the request of Secretary-General Ban Ki-moon, world leaders agreed to hold a high-level summit in September 2015 to address the phase after 2015 that would improve upon the record of the MDGs (Nanda, 2016: 394–5). In this, the MDGs provided an agenda for aligning development with sustainability (Tosun & Leininger, 2017). The overriding objective was for a new global partnership, working toward a range of time-bound targets, that would reduce by half the number of people living in extreme poverty (Bello, 2015).

Two other important multilateral agreements had a landmark year in 2015. In addition to the 2030 Agenda, the Paris Agreement on climate change joined in identifying pathways for a more sustainable future (UNSG, 2019). Additionally, the 2015 AAAA provides a blueprint to support the implementation of the 2030 Agenda by providing a global framework for financing sustainable development that aligns all financing flows and policies with economic, social, and environmental priorities (UNSG, 2019). Four years later, the UN Economic and Social Council (UNESC, 2019a) looked upon the achievements in 2015 as a "moment of great hope and promise, when the light of an inclusive multilateralism shone brightly." Governments were seen responding to their common challenges by uniting behind what appeared to be a "forward-looking, yet urgent, plan to end poverty and create shared prosperity on a healthy and peaceful planet" (UNESC, 2019a: ¶3).

CONTENT OF AGENDA 2030

The 2030 Agenda for Sustainable Development came into force in January 2016 as the UN strategy of "unprecedented scope and significance" for achieving "integrated and indivisible" goals and targets "which involve the entire world" (UNGA, 2015: ¶5) covering "a wide range of economic, social and environmental objectives" (UNGA, 2015: ¶17). The 17 SDGs, adopted to implement the 2030 Agenda for Sustainable Development, include 169 Targets and 232 Indicators, which provide for programs of action, along with a measurement and performance framework (Bebbington & Unerman, 2018). While the goals are intended to satisfy high aspirations, the targets are specific and measurable and contribute to attaining one or more goals (Shulla et al., 2019). There was a striking difference in the process of developing the SDGs, where instead of being formulated by the staff of the UN and a few other international organizations, there was outreach and openness in the creation of the SDGs (Nanda, 2016).

Compared to their predecessors, the MDGs, the SDGs are more integrated, broad, and complex with considerable coverage of the economic, social, and environmental dimensions of sustainable development (Allen et al., 2018: 421). The innovative approach of enriching the concept of sustainable development allows these three dimensions to be integrated coherently into the framework of sustainable development (Xue et al., 2017). The indivisibility or integrated nature of the SDG targets means that progress towards one target will be linked through complex feedbacks to other targets (Allen et al., 2018). The 2030 Agenda declares, "Governments have the primary responsibility for follow-up and review, at the national, regional and global levels" (UNGA, 2015: ¶47). The 2030 Agenda recognizes the necessity of "[q]uality, accessible, timely and reliable disaggregated data to help with the measurement of progress" (UNGA, 2015: ¶48) With these parameters, the 2030 Agenda requires a focus on policy coherence with monitoring and evaluation for effective implementation (Tosun & Leininger, 2017).

A key feature of the SDGs, which contrasts with previous understandings of global development, particularly with the MDGs, is the notion of universalism, in that the goals are to be implemented by all states – rich and poor – signing up to the 2030 Agenda (Tosun & Leininger, 2017). In introducing the plan the 2030 Agenda declares that "no one will be left behind" and there is a desire "to see the Goals and targets met for all nations and peoples and for all segments of society" (UNGA, 2015: ¶4). Thus, the policy process will be inclusive enough to have both developed and developing countries, working together under this set of goals to address a variety of development challenges that impact the entire international community (Xue et al., 2017).

To assess the interlinkages underscoring the 17 SDGs, observers have attempted to use various classification schemes to arrange the individual goals in groups to observe commonalities. Several have relied upon the elements addressed by the World Commission on Environment and Development (WCED) report, *Our Common Future* (WCED, 1987). In this Mignaqui (2014) observed that the WCED report did not explicitly identify these elements as the "three pillars" of economic, environmental, and social sustainability as the World Bank would do 25 years later (World Bank, 2012: xi). Though not invoking the term "pillars," in its 2030 Agenda for Sustainable Development, the UNGA in 2015 would announce the goals and targets as balancing the "three dimensions of sustainable development: the economic, social and environmental" (UNGA, 2015: preamble). Because each of these dimensions is independently crucial and the pillars are interlinked, a successful implementation of sustainable development must refer to economic, social, and environmental systems, all of which must be sustainable at the same time (Drastichová & Filzmoser, 2019).

At a December 2012 event for the Overseas Development Institute, Jeffrey Sachs, then special adviser to UN Secretary-General Ban Ki-moon on the MDGs, shared his perspective on a post-2015 development agenda. Sachs proposed four pillars for a set of post-2015 goals. The first three restate the essentials of the pillars identified by the World Bank. His addition of a fourth pillar focused on governance to support the first three goals. He recommended that governance objectives focus on both the public and corporate sectors (Wahlén, 2012). Other observers have similarly referred to an "institutional dimension" as the fourth pillar of sustainable development because of its "necessity in supporting progress in the previous three pillars" and in sustainable development generally (Drastichová & Filzmoser, 2019).

To ensure that the momentum of the multilateral achievements of 2015 would not dissipate, the subsequent challenge has been in the implementation of Agenda 2030 and the subsequent reviews of progress. In this the HLPF, meeting under the auspices of the UN Economic and Social Council (ECOSOC) every year and under the authority of the UNGA once every four years, would have a significant task of oversight responsibility for implementing Agenda 2030. The comprehensive overviews conducted by the HLPF will be critical in supporting member states in their efforts to implement the SDGs (Dodds et al., 2016).

With its follow-up and review mechanisms, the 2030 Agenda for Sustainable Development encourages the member states to engage in regular and inclusive country-led and country-driven reviews of progress at the national and sub-national levels. These national reviews should serve as a basis for the regular reviews by the HLPF. Under ¶84 of the 2030 Agenda document, regular reviews conducted by the HLPF are voluntary, state-led, undertaken by both developed and developing countries, and involve multiple stakeholders (UN DESA, 2019). Under ¶82 of the 2030 Agenda document (UNGA, 2015), the HLPF facilitates the sharing of experiences, including successes, challenges, and lessons learned, and political leadership, guidance, and recommendations for follow-up and promotes the system-wide coherence and coordination of sustainable development policies (UNESC, 2019b). The aim of these voluntary national reviews (VNRs) is to facilitate the sharing of experiences with a view to accelerating the implementation of the 2030 Agenda. The VNRs seek to strengthen policies and institutions of governments and to mobilize multi-stakeholder support and partnerships for the implementation stakeholders (UN DESA, 2019). Of the 110 VNRs submitted during the 2016, 2017, and 2018 sessions of the HLPF, 35 mentioned explicit measures to link the SDGs to their national budgets or were considering such action (UNGSDR, 2019: xx).

ORGANIZING THE 17 GOALS: FOUR DIMENSIONS

To begin to ascertain the interlinkages of the SDGs, some observers have used these four pillars or dimensions of sustainable development, economic, social, environmental, and governance, to categorize the 17 goals. Recently Niklasson (2019) provided examinations of the SDGs by dividing the goals among these four groupings. There is considerable overlap or interaction among the SDGs within and between these dimensions; the dimensions cannot be considered in isolation. There are important economic and social development aspects to the environmental goals; economic growth serves as an important conduit for the goals of the social and environmental dimensions.

Economic Dimension

Goal 1: End poverty in all its forms everywhere.

Goal 8: Promote sustained, inclusive, and sustainable economic growth, full and productive employment, and decent work for all.

Goal 9: Build resilient infrastructure, promote inclusive and sustainable industrialization and foster innovation.

Goal 10: Reduce inequality within and among countries.

There are four goals that are primarily focused on the economy, highlighting the task of reducing the levels of poverty. These four goals speak about the means of increasing wealth for impoverished societies (Niklasson, 2019). Ending poverty (Goal 1) is connected with the goal of reducing inequality (Goal 10) (Meuleman, 2019). The various targets for these goals include provisions for objective measures of success, such as an ambition to halve the amount of poverty, providing for a minimum growth of gross domestic product per capita of 7 percent in the least developed countries. There are interrelationships between goals that are identified, for example, Goal 9, with its emphasis on building sustainable industrialization, is seen to be closely linked to the aims of promoting economic growth under Goal 8 (Niklasson, 2019). Meuleman (2019) observed that these goals are applicable to developed as well as developing countries, such as Goal 9 with its emphasis on the use of sustainable approaches for industry and technology. As summarized by Niklasson (2019) these four goals on the economic dimension emphasize economic growth, specifying increased industrialization, trade, productivity, and implementation of technology. Underpinning this is an emphasis on ensuring that all share in the benefits of this growth on an equal footing.

Social Dimension

Goal 2: End hunger, achieve food security and improved nutrition and promote sustainable agriculture.

Goal 3: Ensure healthy lives and promote well-being for all at all ages.

Goal 4: Ensure inclusive and equitable quality education and promote lifelong learning opportunities for all.

Goal 5: Achieve gender equality and empower all women and girls.

Goal 6: Ensure availability and sustainable management of water and sanitation for all.

Goal 7: Ensure access to affordable, reliable, sustainable, and modern energy for all.

Goal 11: Make cities and human settlements inclusive, safe, resilient, and sustainable.

For Niklasson (2019) this category of goals involves welfare issues where countries make decisions on essential services to be provided to their inhabitants. The social dimension goals focus on specific areas of concern for individuals living in poverty as well as in rich nations. Several of these are demanding financial resources to pay for basic investments that will support these goals. There are seven goals that are identified under this dimension. Goal 2 provides the objective for ending food insecurity and malnutrition for all. Goal 3 identifies a need for all societies, but particularly for the poorest individuals (Niklasson, 2019); its targets provide details on certain aspects of the quality of health care rather than on systemic concerns (Meuleman, 2019). Goal 4 and its targets expand upon the objectives to be achieved for the goal of increased educational opportunities; priority is identified for increasing education facilities, the supply of educators, and the number of scholarships (Meuleman, 2019). Achieving gender equality under Goal 5 is stated as a general principle (Niklasson, 2019), but will require strenuous efforts to counter deeply held social norms (Meuleman, 2019). The objective of requiring proper management of water and sanitation under Goal 6, as seen in its targets, will necessitate support for capacity building in developing countries and for strengthening participation of the local communities in these critical services (Meuleman, 2019). The efforts required under Goal 7 regarding sustainable energy will need to be made by both developing and developed societies; its targets aim to enhance access to related research and technology, particularly for least developed countries (Meuleman, 2019). Niklasson (2019) sees Goal 11 as a bridge between the social and environmental dimensions as it seeks to make cities and human settlements inclusive, safe, and sustainable.

Environmental Dimension

Goal 12: Ensure sustainable consumption and production patterns.

Goal 13: Take urgent action to combat climate change and its impacts.

Goal 14: Conserve and sustainably use the oceans, seas, and marine resources for sustainable development.

Goal 15: Protect, restore, and promote sustainable use of terrestrial ecosystems, sustainably manage forests, combat desertification, and halt and reverse land degradation and halt biodiversity loss.

Though several goals in other dimensions can be linked to environmental issues, four goals are identified to come within this dimension that relate to traditional environmental concerns. Goal 12 aims to ensure sustainable consumption and production patterns by formulating features of sustainable development in placing limitations on consumption and production and in supporting corporate social responsibility (Meuleman, 2019). Goal 13 focuses on climate change, explicitly making reference to the efforts of the work within the UN Framework Convention on Climate Change as the primary international, intergovernmental forum for negotiating the global response to climate change; noting the specific commitments made under the 2015 Paris Agreement, this goal calls for urgent action. Goals 14 and 15 address the needs for sustainable development of marine and terrestrial resources and to halt the degradation and loss of biodiversity (UNGA, 2015).

Governance Dimension

Goal 16: Promote peaceful and inclusive societies for sustainable develop-ment, provide access to justice for all and build effective, accountable, and inclusive institutions at all levels.

Goal 17: Strengthen the means of implementation and revitalize the Global Partnership for Sustainable Development.

These goals highlight concerns of implementation of the SDGs, especially for the role of governance (Goal 16) and of international support (Goal 17) (Niklasson, 2019). Goal 16 goes beyond the first three dimensions of sustain-able development and focuses on governance and the process of achieving the goals in the first three dimensions (Niklasson, 2019). Various challenges for a nation are considered in this goal: maintaining peace, addressing corruption, creating viable institutions, and assuring access to information, among others (Meuleman, 2019). The second governance goal, Goal 17, covers the means for implementation, both nationally and transnationally, for the SDGs, involv-ing issues on finance, technology transfer, development assistance, capacity building, trade, and other concerns, addressed in a broad array of targets. There is a call to consider systemic issues such as policy and institutional coherence, multi-stakeholder partnerships, monitoring, and accountability (Meuleman, 2019).

The 2030 Agenda places great emphasis on the role of multi-stakeholder partnerships as a way to enhance cooperation (Shulla et al., 2019). This is explicitly stated in Goal 17, "Strengthen the means of implementation and revitalize the global partnership for sustainable development," and Target 17.16 "Enhance the global partnership for sustainable development, comple-mented by multi-stakeholder partnerships that mobilize and share knowledge, expertise, technology, and financial resources, to support the achievement of the sustainable development goals in all countries, in particular developing countries" (UNGA, 2015).

With this, as Atapattu (2019) noted, sustainable development has evolved as a concept that embodies both substantive and procedural components. Agenda 2030 is not an exception to this observation. This fourth, procedural, dimension is emphasized because of the necessity for supporting the more substantive goals of the previous three dimensions. There is a recognition that proper governance and institutions are critical to the success of sustainable development in all economies (Drastichová & Filzmoser, 2019). The interac-tions among the SDGs of the first three elements are context dependent and their impacts will be greatly influenced by implementation of apposite govern-ance under the fourth element (Nilsson et al., 2018).

ORGANIZING THE 17 GOALS: ENTRY POINTS AND LEVERS

The Global Sustainable Development Report (GSDR) serves as a provider of scientific information to the HLPF on Sustainable Development. This responsibility was established by the UN in the 2012 outcome document for Rio+20, and in the UNGA Resolution for the 2030 Agenda (UNGA, 2015, ¶83). A GSDR, titled *The Future Is Now: Science for Achieving Sustainable Development*, that evaluated the progress on the 2030 Agenda, authored by a team of experts in social and natural sciences, was made available for the September 2019 SDG Summit (UNGSDR, 2019). The report concluded that the SDGs could be clustered to promote synergistic exchanges that would promote increased effectiveness, noting that the most efficient, or even the only, way to make progress on a given target is to take advantage of positive synergies with other targets while resolving or ameliorating the negative trade-offs with yet others. In this recognition, this GSDR identified six "entry points" into underlying systems, not into an individual goal or clusters of goals. An exclusive focus on goals and targets, not attending to the interlinkages, would, according to the GSDR, imperil progress across multiple elements of the 2030 Agenda. These identified entry points are:

1. human well-being and capabilities
2. sustainable and just economies
3. food systems and nutrition patterns
4. energy decarbonization with universal access
5. urban and peri-urban development
6. global environmental commons.

The GSDR (UNGSDR, 2019) identified four levers that accommodate the multiple, complementary roles that individual actors and entities play in bringing about change. These levers can be deployed through each of the six entry points to bring about the necessary transformations. They are seen as related to, but different from, the means of implementation detailed in Goal 17. These levers consist of:

1. governance
2. economy and finance
3. individual and collective action
4. science and technology.

This GSDR does not explicitly purport to rewrite the 17 goals or their 169 targets (Crossette, 2019). Yet, this report presents an alternative approach that adds a new layer of analysis for detailing strategies that utilize the SDGs, or even treats them as secondary in importance. This report stresses the need to see that advancing the 2030 Agenda must involve an urgent and intentional transformation of socioenvironmental-economic systems, that are seen as differentiated across countries, but will lead to the desired regional and global social, economic, and environmental outcomes (UNGSDR, 2019: xxi). This GSDR stresses that it is seeking the interactions between goals and targets to be carefully taken into account (UNGSDR, 2019: xxi).

An observation has been made that the 17 goals and 169 targets that comprise the SDGs are diverse, complex, and interconnected; as such this beckons an "implementation nightmare" (Xue et al., 2017: 151). When interlinkages are identified among different combinations of goals, the result can be that progress in one goal will reinforce progress in others thus enhancing the effectiveness of implementation and reducing the related costs. The converse will also hold where a lack of progress for one goal could impede improvement in others (Xue et al., 2017). How the GSDR for the 2019 SDG Summit advances the success of the implementation of the SDGs remains an open question until some further experience is obtained.

GLOBAL GOVERNANCE

The goal-setting approach to global governance was popularized with the MDGs (Piselli & Pavoni, 2017). Key to this form of goal-setting global governance for the SDGs is: "advancing the idea that a set of limited, time-bound, measurable goals can constitute a normative and policy framework for guiding the public's understanding of complex challenges, mobilizing stakeholders and resources, facilitating the assessment of progress, supporting integrated thinking, and fostering accountability" (Piselli & Pavoni, 2017: 551). For global governance to be successful in today's context of profound challenges to humanity and for the Earth itself, there is a need for the current international system to transcend its anarchic power structures. Compounding these challenges is the set of tasks made explicit in the set of SDGs, where Agenda 2030 is now half a decade past its starting point. For successful implementation of the 2030 Agenda, there is an aspect of global governance that stems from a recognition that the indivisibility of the SDGs means that human development and prosperity are interlinked across national boundaries (Shulla et al., 2019). Where the primary task will be to assess how well the SDG targets are met, observers have noted that various types of auditing technologies are themselves instruments of a new form of governance and power, designed to engender new forms of conduct (Abrahamsen, 2004; Death & Gabay, 2015).

The oversight should avoid being overbearing from the global level. With coordination at a global level, there is a risk that the development of the administration of the efforts remains at this level, excluding the important contributions and connections that could arise from other, localized levels (Shulla et al., 2019). Since implementation will take place largely at the national level, countries will need to set their own priorities and target values (Allen et al., 2018: 421). Yet, a major problem is that many governments have weak state capacity, being unable to carry out the activities which are needed to fulfill the SDGs. For most developing countries, it is governance failures that play a significant role in impeding sustained economic development (Xue et al., 2017). The global governance mechanisms that rely principally on traditional forms of intergovernmental negotiation and rigid implementation have difficulty in combating the new global challenges to sustainable development (Xue et al., 2017). Though humanitarian services can be provided by the international community in the form of aid in the short run, for longer-term prospects of success all governments, even those of developed countries, will need to develop the needed state capacities as indicated by the SDG goals and targets (Niklasson, 2019). To meet these challenges alternative governance mechanisms must be explored and developed for policy coordination within and across national boundaries (Xue et al., 2017).

There are global governance and implementation concerns that emerge from having Agenda 2030 placing responsibility at a state level. A level which, for some states, is subject to ongoing challenges from the processes of globalization in a context of poorly regulated transnational flows of capital and limited protections for ecosystems and transnationally mobile labor. Concerns are raised that this enhancement of a state-centric model of development accountability could exacerbate the lives of rural populations and labor. Though national governments can claim to be operating under the Agenda 2030 approach, under claims of internationalized standards, individual states may offer only limited protections for vulnerable migrant labor and small landholding classes (Sexsmith & McMichael, 2015).

The call for the international system to transcend business as usual will present challenges for the UN itself. The policy framework of the 2030 Agenda requiring that its indivisible goals and targets be implemented in an integrated manner runs counter to the customary way of operating the organization, which generally encompasses sectors and processes that operate in isolation from each other (Dodds et al., 2016). The current UN system, including its intergovernmental bodies, such as the UNGA and the UN Economic and Social Council (ECOSOC), has insufficiently promoted integration of its many operations and has not adequately attended on the implementation of policy. Compounding this situation is the way funding is distributed, also fostering more fragmentation of efforts (Dodds et al., 2016). With the adoption of the 2030 Agenda, momentum to evaluate these shortcomings in UN processes has been renewed.

The decentralized nature of the UN system is underscored by the UN Charter's call for coordination through "consultation and recommendation." There exists no central authority to compel compliance by organizations of the UN system to act in a concerted manner. Thus, coordination and cooperation become contingent upon the willingness of the system's organizations to work together in pursuit of common goals (UNCEB, 2016). Despite these seemingly organic limitations on the possibility of coordinating the roles of the various implicated bodies of the UN system to better achieve the multi-faceted tasks of Agenda 2030, the Chief Executives Board, which is the highest-level coordination body at the UN, is evaluating how to implement this new vision (Dodds et al., 2016). Additionally, since becoming the UN Secretary-General on January 1, 2017, António Guterres indicated in the 2019 UN annual report his understanding that current global challenges require global solutions, where the UN must continuously demonstrate the merits of multilateral cooperation (UN News, 2019a).

REGIONAL ACTORS FOR AGENDA 2030

There is a recognition, which predates Agenda 2030, of the role of regional actors for the coordination and implementation of sustainable development policies (see Chapter 3 for more information on the role of the European Commission on Agenda 2030). As noted at Rio+20, the 2012 UN Conference on Sustainable Development, regional frameworks could complement and facilitate the effective translation of sustainable development policies into concrete action at the national level. It was emphasized that regional and subregional organizations, including the regional commissions and their sub-regional offices, play a significant role in promoting the balanced integration and operationalization of the economic, social, and environmental dimensions of sustainable development in their respective regions (UNESC, 2019c). Additionally, in its Resolution 67/290 (UNGA, 2013b) the UN General Assembly, in deciding on the format and organizational aspects of the HLPF on sustainable development, acknowledged the importance of the regional dimension of sustainable development and invited the regional commissions to contribute to the work of the HLPF.

The value of follow-up and review at the regional level was also recognized in the 2030 Agenda for Sustainable Development: "We acknowledge also the importance of the regional and subregional dimensions, regional economic integration and interconnectivity in sustainable development. Regional and subregional frameworks can facilitate the effective translation of sustainable development policies into concrete action at the national level" (UNGA, 2015: ¶21). In the 2030 Agenda, member states are encouraged to identify the most suitable regional forum in which to engage, so that such forums can contribute to the global follow-up and review process, including at the HLPF. More recently, as the UN Department of Economic and Social Affairs (UN, 2018) has recognized, the 2030 Agenda and the SDGs require coordinated implementation across the different levels of governments. This multi-level governance involves linkages and exchanges between institutions at the local regional (subnational), national, and transnational levels. The Secretariat Economic and Social Council observed that the regional commissions have initiated consultative processes leading to the establishment of regional forums on sustainable development, where the forums have generally been organized in collaboration with partners of the regional commissions. The 2019 forums included the following: (a) Europe region, Geneva; (b) Asia-Pacific region, Bangkok; (c) Arab region, Beirut; (d) Africa region, Marrakech; (e) Latin America and the Caribbean region, Santiago.

CONCLUSION

In September 2019, the opening days of the 74th session of the UN General Assembly provided the setting for what was promoted as the "High-level Week" (UN DGC, 2019), consisting of five important high-level summits and meetings covering many of the major challenges facing the international com-munity (UN News, 2019a). These high-level events considered many related themes for sustainable development issues. These included the Climate Action Summit convened by UN Secretary-General António Guterres. Additionally, the UN hosted the first ever High-Level Meeting on Universal Health Coverage, which was seen as the best opportunity to secure political commit-ment from heads of state and government to prioritize and invest in universal health provision. The remaining three events included two summits, the High-Level Midterm Review of the SAMOA Pathway, focusing on supporting small island developing states, and the High-Level Dialogue on Financing for Development. These four events seemed to underscore the week's broadly encompassing fifth high-level event, the 2019 Sustainable Development Goals Summit, which was the first of its kind since the 2030 Agenda for Sustainable Development was adopted in 2015. This SDG Summit provided an opportunity to accelerate progress on the 17 Goals and their targets of the 2030 Agenda (UN News, 2019a).

Assessing the outcomes of the 2019 SDG Summit, the Deputy Secretary-General Amina Mohammed acknowledged that though the present progress towards the Goals appeared off track, the high-level meeting provided an opportunity for a renewed commitment to implementing the Agenda and a determination to accelerate efforts to achieve them (UN News, 2019b). The incoming president of the General Assembly, Tijjani Muhammad-Bande, identified the broad challenges for the next decade for meeting the goals of the

2030 Agenda, which include ensuring more integration of the 2030 Agenda into National Development Plans, mobilizing resources and investing in programs and sectors that are more likely to result in "greater acceleration" (UN News, 2019b). The General Assembly president took the opportunity to look ahead to the 2020 Summit of the UN, when member states and relevant partners will report, again, on the contributions they are making towards achieving the SDGs (UN News, 2019b). There might have been much effort placed in drafting these hopeful statements made by UN officials, where there was a need to find optimism in the light of some very sobering assessments of the progress being made on the 2030 Agenda.

For the 2019 SDG Summit, the HLPF adopted a political declaration, entitled "Gearing Up for a Decade of Action and Delivery for Sustainable Development: Political Declaration of the Sustainable Development Goals Summit" (UNHLPF, 2019). The declaration reaffirmed the principles in the 2030 Agenda. It took note of the UN Secretary-General's SDG Progress Report and the GSDR, reviewing the progress, and the political declaration expressed concern in the following areas:

• progress is slowing in many areas, including poverty eradication, hunger, gender equality, and wealth inequality;
• biodiversity loss, environmental degradation, plastic litter in the oceans, climate change, and disaster risk continue at rates that bring potentially disastrous consequences for humanity;
• violent extremism, terrorism, organized crime, corruption, illicit financial flows, global health threats, humanitarian crises, and forced displacement of people threaten to reverse decades of development progress; and conflicts and instability have endured, or intensified, and natural disasters have become more frequent and intense in many parts of the world, causing untold human suffering.

In its turn, the GSDR made clear that the world is at risk of irreversibly degrading the natural systems that sustain life and further observed that the international community is off track in "leaving no one behind." More ambitious, more transformative, and more integrated responses are urgently needed (UNGSDR, 2019: xiii). The GSDR examined the progress being made towards the numerical targets associated with the SDGs as illustrated in Table 2.1. The rate of progress towards each target was used to estimate whether that target will be achieved or, if not, how closely it will be approached by 2030. The table (UNGSDR, 2019: 10) of the GSDR shows the current state of progress at the global level for some selected indicators for which adequate data are currently available. At current rates of progress, several of the objectives of the 2030 Agenda should be attainable by 2030. Other goals may also be reached

Table 2.1   Agenda 2030, SDGs and progress

Goal	Within 5%	5–10%	>10%	Negative long-term trend
Goal 1	1.1 Eradicating extreme poverty		1.3 Social protection for all	
Goal 2	2.1 Ending hunger (undernourishment)		2.2 Ending malnutrition (stunting) 2.5 Maintaining genetic diversity 2.a Investment in agriculture*	2.2 Ending malnutrition (overweight)
Goal 3	3.2 Under-5 mortality 3.2 Neonatal mortality		3.1 Maternal mortality 3.4 Premature deaths from non-communicable diseases	
Goal 4	4.1 Enrolment in primary education	4.6 Literacy among youth and adults	4.2 Early childhood development 4.1 Enrolment in secondary education 4.3 Enrolment in tertiary education	
Goal 5			5.5 Women and political participation	
Goal 6		6.2 Access to safe sanitation (open defecation practices)	6.1 Access to safely managed drinking water 6.2 Access to safely managed sanitation services	
Goal 7		7.1 Access to electricity	7.2 Share of renewable energy* 7.3 Energy intensity	
Goal 8			8.7 Use of child labor	
Goal 9		9.5 Enhancing scientific research (research and development expenditure)	9.5 Enhancing scientific research (number of researchers)	
Goal 10			10.c Remittance costs	Inequality in income*
Goal 11			11.1 Urban population living in slums*	

Goal	Within 5%	5–10%	>10%	Negative long-term trend
Goal 12				12.2 Absolute material footprint, and domestic material consumption*
Goal 13				Global greenhouse gas emissions relative to Paris targets*
Goal 14				14.1 Continued deterioration of coastal waters* 14.4 Overfishing*
Goal 15				15.5 Biodiversity loss* 15.7 Wildlife poaching and trafficking*
Goal 16			16.9 Universal birth registration**	

Notes: Selected indicators only. SDG 17 is not included as it consists of a wide range of indicators that cannot easily be captured using the methodology for assessing distance from reaching targets. Estimates of the distance from the target by 2030 are based on forecasted value of the corresponding indicator in 2030, relative to target. Forecasts based on best-fit trends of individual indicators, given the available data range.
* Quantitative target for 2030 is not specified in the SDG indicator framework; targets are estimated. ** Assessment is based on indicators outside the SDG indicator framework; inequality in income is based on data from household surveys.

with some additional effort, such as eradicating extreme poverty, ending hunger, ensuring universal access to electricity, eliminating open defecation, literacy among youth and adults, and desirable levels of expenditure on scientific research and development. However, recent trends along several dimensions have been moving in the wrong direction. Four in particular fall into that category: rising inequalities, climate change, biodiversity loss, and increasing amounts of waste from human activity that are overwhelming capacities to process them. Even more troubling is the recognition that the inherent indivisibility of these SDGs means these four goals have cross-cutting impacts across the entire 2030 Agenda (UNGSDG, 2019).

The 2019 SDG Summit was to be the event to launch a decade of accelerated delivery and action. However, progress on the 2030 Agenda and its SDGs was seen as not only inadequate, but in the words of one GSDR scientist the world is "going backwards" in some areas, including equality, climate, and biodiversity. The message from the GSDR scientists, speaking at the Summit, could not be stronger: "we seem to find it easier to imagine the end of humanity, than changing our systems" (Earth Negotiations Bulletin, 2019: 6).

Governance of the sustainable development framework is proving to be not sufficient by itself. The enthusiasm leading up to establishing the 2030 Agenda has not been paralleled by the requisite political will to move away from a posture of governance-as-usual and devise and implement the innovative arrangements needed to achieve sustainable management of global resources. There are anthropogenic factors, which increasingly exacerbate the planet's biosystems that also impede progress. Compounding these aggravating aspects is the escalating general impasse for the institutions and processes of global governance (Piselli & Pavoni, 2017). In the first few years of Agenda 2030, the process seems to have lost ground for significant SDGs. Clearly for the coming decade, the "stakes could not be higher" for the success of developmental governance and the implementation of the Agenda 2030 process (Death & Gabay, 2015: 4).

REFERENCES

Abrahamsen, R. (2004). "The Power of Partnerships in Global Governance." *Third World Quarterly*, 25(8): 1453–67.
Allen, Cameron, Graciela Metternicht, & Thomas Wiedmann (2018). "Prioritising SDG Targets: Assessing Baselines, Gaps and Interlinkages." *Sustainability Science*, 14: 421–38.
Amnesty International (2013). *UN Millennium Development Goals: Human Rights Must Not Be Marginalized in Post-2015 Agenda Amnesty Int'l*, September 23. Accessed November 30, 2019 at www.amnesty.org/en/latest/news/2013/09/un-millennium -development-goals-human-rights-mustnot-be-marginalized-post-agenda/

Atapattu, Sumudu (2019). "From 'Our Common Future' to Sustainable Development Goals: Evolution of Sustainable Development under International Law." *Wisconsin International Law Journal*, 36: 215–46.

Bebbington, Jan & Jeffrey Unerman (2018). "Achieving the United Nations Sustainable Development Goals." *Accounting, Auditing and Accountability Journal*, 31(1): 2–24.

Bello, Walden (2015). "Post-2015 Development Assessment: Proposed Goals and Indicators." In Gerard McCann & Stephen McCloskey (eds) *From the Local to the Global: Key Issues in Development Studies* (3rd ed.). London: Pluto Press.

Crossette, Barbara (2019). *Salvaging the SDGS: New Thinking to Spur Action Takes Shape*. Inter Press Service, October 28, 2019. Accessed November 28, 2019 at www.ipsnews.net/2019/10/salvaging-sdgsnew-thinking-spur-action-takes-shape/

Death, Carl & Clive Gabay (2015). "Doing Biopolitics Differently? Radical Potential in the Post-2015 MDG and SDG Debates." *Globalizations*, 12(4): 597–612.

Dodds, Felix, David Donoghue, & Jimena Leiva Roesch (2016). *Negotiating the Sustainable Development Goals*. London: Routledge.

Drastichová, Magdaléna & Peter Filzmoser (2019). "Assessment of Sustainable Development Using Cluster Analysis and Principal Component Analysis." *Problems of Sustainable Development*, 14(2): 7–24.

Earth Negotiations Bulletin (2019). "SDG Summit Highlights: 24–25 September 2019." *IISD Reporting Services*, 33(56), September 26: 1–6.

Griggs, David et al. (2014). "An Integrated Framework for Sustainable Development Goals." *Ecology and Society*, 19(4): 49.

McCann, G. (2015). "Neoliberal Decline and International Development Post-2015." In Gerard McCann & Stephen McCloskey (eds), *From the Local to the Global: Key Issues in Development Studies* (3rd ed.). London: Pluto Press.

McCloskey, Stephen (2015). "Introduction: Creating New Paradigms for Development." In Gerard McCann & Stephen Mccloskey (eds), *From the Local to the Global: Key Issues in Development Studies*. London: Pluto Press.

Meuleman, Louis (2019). *Metagovernance for Sustainability: A Framework for Implementing the Sustainable Development Goals*. London: Routledge.

Mignaqui, Vera (2014). "Sustainable Development as a Goal: Social, Environmental and Economic Dimensions." *International Journal of Social Quality*, 4(1): 57–77.

Nanda, Ved (2016). "The Journey from the Millennium Development Goals to the Sustainable Development Goals." *Denver Journal of International Law and Policy*, 44: 389–412.

Niklasson, Lars (2019). *Improving the Sustainable Development Goals: Strategies and the Governance Challenge*. London: Routledge.

Nilsson, M. et al. (2018). "Mapping Interactions between the Sustainable Development Goals: Lessons Learned and Ways Forward." *Sustainable Science*, 13(6): 1489–503.

Piselli, Dario & Riccardo Pavoni (2017). Governing through Goals: Sustainable Development Goals as Governance Innovation. *Transnational Environmental Law*, 6(3): 551–60.

Sexsmith, Kathleen & Philip McMichael (2015). "Formulating the SDGs: Reproducing or Reimagining State-Centered Development?" *Globalizations*, 12(4): 581–96.

Shawki, Noah (2016). "Norm Evolution and Change: Analyzing Negotiation of the Sustainable Development Goals." In Noah Shawki (ed.), *International Norms, Normative Change, and the UN Sustainable Development Goals*, pp. 1–15. Lanham, MD: Lexington Books.

Shulla, Kalterina, Walter Filho, Lardjane, Leal, Sommer, Salim, Jan Henning, Amanda Lange Salvia, Lange, & Christian Borgemeister (2019). "The Contribution of

Regional Centers of Expertise for the Implementation of the 2030 Agenda for Sustainable Development." *Journal of Cleaner Production*, 117(117809).

Tosun, Jale & Julia Leininger (2017). "Governing the Interlinkages between the Sustainable Development Goals: Approaches to Attain Policy Integration." *Global Challenges*.

UN (2018). "Working Together: Integration, Institutions and the Sustainable Development Goals." *World Public Sector Report*. Department of Economic and Social Affairs.

UN (2019a). "High-Level Political Forum on Sustainable Development." *UN Sustainable Development Goals Knowledge Platform*. Accessed November 30, 2019 at https://sustainabledevelopment.un.org/hlpf/2019

UN (2019b). *Technology Facilitation Mechanism: UN Sustainable Development Goals Knowledge Platform*. Accessed November 30, 2019 at https://sustainabledevelopment .un.org/tfm

UN DGC (2019). *The Sustainable Development Goals Summit: UN Department of Global Communications*. Accessed September 23, 2019 at www.un.org/en/summits2019/pdf/SDGSummit.pdf

UN Division for Sustainable Development (1992). *Agenda 21: United Nations Conference on Environment and Development Rio de Janerio, Brazil, 3 to 14 June 1992*. Accessed October 25, 2019 at https://sustainabledevelopment.un.org/content/documents/Agenda21.pdf

UN News (2019a). *UN General Assembly: Here Are the 5 Big Summits to Watch Out For*, September 15. Accessed September 23, 2019 at https://news.un.org/en/story/2019/09/1045782

UN News (2019b). *Sustainable Development Summit: A Reminder of "the Boundless Potential of Humanity"*, September 25. Accessed September 28, 2019 at https://news.un.org/en/story/2019/09/1047562?utm_source=UN+News++Newsletter&utm _campaign=fa673971d3-EMAIL_CAMPAIGN_2019_09_28_12_06&utm

UN System Task Team on the Post-2015 UN Development Agenda (2012). *Discussion Note, Review of the Contributions of the MDG Agenda to Foster Development: Lessons for the Post-2015 UN Development Agenda*, March. Accessed November 30, 2019 at www.un.org/en/development/desa/policy/untaskteam_undf/mdg _assessment.pdf

UNCEB (2016). *Chief Executives Board for Coordination – Mandate*. Accessed November 29, 2019 at www.unsystem.org/content/ceb

UNDESA (2019). *Voluntary National Reviews Database: Sustainable Development Knowledge Platform*. UN Department of Economic and Social Affairs. https://sustainabledevelopment.un.org/vnrs/

UNESC (2019a). *Special Edition: Progress Towards the Sustainable Development Goals. Report of the Secretary-General*. E/2019/68 UN Economic and Social Council, May 8.

UNESC (2019b). *Note by the Secretariat. Synthesis of Voluntary Submissions by Functional Commissions of the Economic and Social Council and Other Intergovernmental Bodies and Forums*, May 10. E/HLPF/2019/4 Accessed November 25, 2019 at https://undocs.org/pdf?symbol=en/E/HLPF/2019/4

UNESC (2019c). *Reports of the Regional Forums on Sustainable Development, Note by the Secretariat*. E/HLPF/2019/3, July 9–18. Accessed November 25, 2019 at https://sustainabledevelopment.un.org/content/documents/22664E_HLPF_2019_3 _Note_by_the_Secretaiat_on_reports_of_the_regional_forums.pdf

UNGA (2000). *United Nations Millennium Declaration: Resolution Adopted by the General Assembly*. A/RES/55/2, September 18.

UNGA (2013a). *Open Working Group of the General Assembly on Sustainable Development Goals. Draft Decision Submitted by the President of the General Assembly*. A/67/L.48/Rev.1, January 15. Accessed November 29, 2019 at www.un.org/ga/search/view_doc.asp?symbol=A/67/L.48/Rev.1&Lang=E

UNGA (2013b). *Format and Organizational Aspects of the High-Level Political Forum on Sustainable Development*. A/RES/67/290, July 9. Accessed November 27, 2019 at www.un.org/ga/search/view_doc.asp?symbol=A/RES/67/290&Lang=E

UNGA (2015). *Transforming Our World: The 2030 Agenda for Sustainable Development. Resolution Adopted by the General Assembly on 25 September 2015*. A/RES/70/1.

UNGSDR (2019). *Independent Group of Scientists Appointed by the Secretary-General, Global Sustainable Development Report 2019: The Future Is Now – Science for Achieving Sustainable Development*. New York: United Nations.

UNHLPF (2019). *Gearing Up for a Decade of Action and Delivery for Sustainable Development: Political Declaration of the SDG Summit. Political Declaration of the SDG Summit*. Accessed November 25, 2019 at www.un.org/pga/73/wp-content/uploads/sites/53/2019/05/Zero-draft-Political DeclarationHLPF-17.5.19_.pdf

UNSG (2001). *Road Map towards the Implementation of the United Nations Millennium Declaration. Report of the Secretary-General A/56/326*, September 6. Accessed November 28, 2019 at www.preventionweb.net/files/13543_N0152607.pdf

UNSG (2019). *Roadmap for Financing the 2030 Agenda for Sustainable Development. Executive Summary*. Accessed November 28, 2019 at www.un.org/sustainabledevelopment/wpcontent/uploads/2019/07/EXEC.SUM_SG-Roadmap-Financing-SDGs-July-2019.pdf

Wahlén, Catherine Benson (2012). *UN Adviser Proposes Four Pillars for Post-2015 Goals. SDG Knowledge Hub*. IISD, December 11. Accessed November 26, 2019 at http://sdg.iisd.org/news/unadviser-proposes-four-pillars-for-post-2015-goals/

Wallace, Donald H. (2018). "The UN Regime on Climate Change." In Don Wallace & Daniel Silander (eds), *Climate Change, Policy and Security: State and Human Impacts* (pp. 41–66). London: Routledge.

WCED (1987). *Our Common Future*. World Commission on Environment and Development. United Nations. Accessed November 25, 2019 at https://sustainabledevelopment.un.org/content/documents/5987our-common-future.pdf

World Bank (2012). *Inclusive Green Growth: The Pathway to Sustainable Development*. Washington, DC: World Bank. Accessed November 30, 2019 at http://siteresources.worldbank.org/EXTSDNET/Resources/Inclusive_Green_Growth_May_2012.pdf

Xue, Lan, Linfei Weng, & Hanzi Yu (2017). "Addressing Policy Challenges in Implementing Sustainable Development Goals through an Adaptive Governance Approach: A View from Transitional China." *Sustainable Development*, 26, 150–58.

3. The European Commission on Agenda 2030

Daniel Silander

On 25–27 September 2015, the United Nations (UN) adopted *Transforming Our World: The 2030 Agenda for Sustainable Development* (see Chapter 2). The UN stressed the importance of a global stand on sustainable development. In 2010, the European Commission released an official communication titled *Europe 2020: A Strategy for Smart, Sustainable and Inclusive Growth*.[1] The Commission then called upon European Union (EU) institutions, member states, regional and local authorities and the private sector to address the global socioeconomic crisis that started in 2008, by pushing for EU governance to promote sustainable development in Europe (Wandel, 2016: 10; Zeitlin & Vanhercke, 2014: 8–9). Then, the Commission assumed the position of a driving engine in a time of crisis. Through political entrepreneurship in new, bold and fundamental reforms, the Commission described how to protect Europe from deeper recession, and how to build a stronger and more prosperous Europe, with the protection of the socioeconomic model, democratic stability and integration (see Silander, 2018). The Agenda 2020 explicitly embedded SDGs by referring to smart, sustainable and socially inclusive growth (see Silander, 2018; Barbier, 2011; European Commission, 2010: 12–13).

In 2016, the European Commission explicitly addressed the new UN Agenda 2030 in the Communication *Next Steps for a Sustainable European Future: European Action for Sustainability*. The Communication was based upon the progress made on Europe 2020 and the international work on Agenda 2030, in which the EU, along with member states, was actively engaged. The UN Agenda 2030 is, in its content, strongly related to the Europe 2020 Strategy. Agenda 2030 calls upon the global community to promote and protect sustainable development through the identified Sustainable Development Goals (SDGs) (see Chapter 1), by calling upon all actors to pursue any measures possible. From an EU perspective, the UN approach towards sustainable development was an urgent and necessary step to promote sustainable development in Europe and globally. As an active force behind the creation of Agenda

2030, the EU saw such global commitment as a new window of opportunity to provide for a better region and world. As stated,

> Action is needed at all levels. EU institutions, Member States and regions will have to be on board. Cities, municipalities and rural areas should all become drivers of change. Citizens, businesses, social partners and the research and knowledge community will have to team up. The EU and its Member States will have to work together with international partners. If we are to succeed, we must pull in the same direction at all levels. (European Commission, 2019a: 15)

The EU institutions and member states have all recognized the Agenda 2030 for global sustainable development. Once again, the European Commission has acted upon such global agendas as a European driving engine to promote such goals within Europe and through its external actions, globally. This chapter seeks to explore the role of the European Commission in the promotion and implementation of Agenda 2030. Moreover, the activities by the Commission on Agenda 2020 led to the logical next step taken by the Commission to download norms and values from Agenda 2030 and, from 2016 forward, to seek new European reforms on sustainable development. The Commission operates as an active political entrepreneur in European politics, and has a historical track record of fostering sustainable development in the political, economic, social and environmental fields.

On December 11, 2019, the Commission also presented the European Green Deal as a roadmap for further promoting sustainable development. The new roadmap declared how the EU will strive to become the first climate-neutral continent in the world in 2050. The Commission highlighted how climate and environmental challenges could become opportunities for change; a window of opportunity for European transformation and progress in a spirit of true European political entrepreneurship (European Commission, 2019b).

THE EUROPEAN COMMISSION, NORMS AND POLITICAL ENTREPRENEURSHIP

The idea of European sustainable development has, historically, been integral to the process of European integration. The Commission has also recently argued that 'The EU and the United Nations are natural partners in the efforts to shape a safer and better world for all' (European Commission, 2019b: 31). The different European Treaties from the 1950s onward have recognized economic, social and environmental dimensions of development and stressed the importance of peace and cooperation as fundamental cornerstones of European progress. Over the last two decades, sustainable development has officially become a European objective. The EU embedded sustainable development in the Treaty of Amsterdam, stressing the overall objective to promote a European social-economic model of economic growth and price stability as well as full employment, social progress and inclusiveness, along with protection of the quality of the environment. Since then and based on the Treaty of Amsterdam, sustainable development has been mainstreamed into EU policies, legislations, norms and values.

There is a large body of research on the nature of European politics and what constitutes European norms and values. Rooted in a somewhat limited discussion in the 1970s, on the nature of European norms and values, scholars explored Europe's ability to exist as one coherent community (Sjöstedt, 1977; Hill, 1993). One of the most heated debates concerned the foreign and security policy area and whether Europe was able to speak with one voice in international politics (Bull, 1982: 151; Hill, 1993; Kagan, 2003). Different perspectives on political actorness and the nature of European integration resulted in numerous conceptualizations of what Europe is. In the early 1970s, François Duchêne argued in favour of Europe as a coherent civilian actor (Duchêne, 1972, 1973), by focusing on European political and economic relations. It was argued that Europe consisted of like-minded political states and economic entities that provided for a coherent Europe in international politics (Smith, 2000; Whitman, 1998). From early 2000 onwards, articles written by Ian Manners strengthened the notion of a European community of like-minded states by arguing for Europe's existence as a normative community (Manners, 2002) and stressed Europe's capacity to become an 'idée force' (Manners, 2002: 239). His main argument was that Europe symbolized a normative actor, embedding norms, such as democracy, the rule of law, common institutions and treaties guiding Europe towards a constitutional order (see Chapter 10).

The notion of Europe as one coherent normative community also included a socioeconomic dimension. Manners argued for a socioeconomic dimension in Europe, including social freedom, equality, solidarity and sustainability. First, by social freedom, Manners referred to a union of freedom in the sense of a free movement of persons, goods, services, capital and establishment (the Charter of Fundamental Rights). Second, social equality referred to the adoption of countermeasures against social exclusion, discrimination and social injustice, due to sex, race, colour, ethnic or social origin, genetic features, language, religion or belief. Third, social solidarity was emphasized as a European norm that linked economic growth in full employment, social cohesion and progress and eradication of poverty. Fourth and last, Manners also argued for the norm of sustainable development. Sustainable development referred to the objective of promoting improved quality of the environment, sustainable management of global natural resources and a greener economic growth.

FROM EUROPE 2020 TO UN 2030

The Commission has acted as a driving engine for European norms and values. This is not a surprise due to its main functions assigned within the EU. The European Commission has important functions as the promoter and protector of the European community. The official role of the Commission consists of

1. initiating legislation by proposing European laws that are to be amended and approved by the Council and European Parliament;
2. guarding EU treaties by ensuring that member states follow EU legislation;
3. acting as an executive body to manage policies and the annual budget; and
4. representing the EU in external relations and actions by negotiating trade and development cooperation agreements with third-party states.

The European Commission is a powerful actor within the EU with the duty to represent European norms and values beyond individual member states' interests. The Commission has an embedded role as political entrepreneur. In the early 2000s, the Commission successfully, through years of political entrepreneurship, managed to set democratic, market-oriented and social issues on the official agenda and pushed for sustainable development within European member states. In 2010, after a few years of economic recession globally and in Europe, the European Commission officially published *Europe 2020: A Strategy for Smart, Sustainable and Inclusive Growth*. Europe 2020 was a strategic concept from the Commission on how to promote and protect European growth, jobs and social integration in times of political, economic and social challenges (Walburn, 2010: 699). The Europe 2020 strategy stressed the importance of developing and consolidating a European social market economy model. This model had previously been stressed within the EU, but Europe 2020 re-emphasized the importance of such a model by focusing on smart, sustainable and inclusive growth (Budd, 2013: 274–6; Gros & Roth, 2012: 1–2).

First, *smart growth*, in developing an economy based on knowledge and innovation, referred to new knowhow and technology as being the main drivers of a prosperous future European economy. The main themes identified are innovation, education and digital society. Smart growth requires improved education, research and innovations to provide a skilled workforce and new products and services, but also innovative entrepreneurship and financial investments to identify new needs, demands, markets and so on. The Commission argued for greater spending on research and development and for principally targeting private investments by facilitating improved conditions for private-sector research and development in Europe. The Commission further identified the importance of improving education, training and lifelong learning by promoting better reading competences and increased numbers of people with university degrees, improving the standards and status of European universities, and matching education with labour market demands. In addition, Europe had to improve its competitiveness in the digital society by reaching out to the fast-expanding demands for communication technologies and increasing investment of European societies in the Internet and providing for more Internet-based goods and services (European Commission, 2010: 9–10). Smart growth was planned to be implemented through targets on thematic areas, one for research and development and two for education. These targets were to increase public and private investments in research and development to 3 per cent of gross domestic product, reduce school drop-out rates to less than 10 per cent and increase the share of the population in the 30–34 age group having completed tertiary education to 40 per cent or more (Eurostat, 2018).

Second, *sustainable growth*, through a transition to a greener economy, refers to building a European economy of resource efficiency and sustainability, as well as staying globally competitive based on new, greener technologies. The main themes in focus are climate, energy, mobility and competitiveness. This requires innovative European political entrepreneurship to foster competitive entrepreneurship and new businesses and networks, as well as promoting a consumer culture that values resource efficiency and a greener low-carbon economy. The Commission stated the importance of continued open trade of exports and imports, but also that Europe had to become more competitive and partner states needed to increase productivity. Europe must also continue its early initiatives to become a global green economic actor by pushing for green technologies to safeguard resource efficiency. The push for green technologies would lead to fulfilled climate change goals, with significantly decreased emissions, but would also open the way for a transition to a new environmentally friendly economy of new innovations, products and services that all together would create new jobs and a growing economy. A transition to a greener economy would also lead to lowered costs for the import of expensive oil and gas and would be beneficial for European security because of lowered dependency on specific foreign governments (European Commission, 2010: 12–13). Sustainable growth would be approached based on three climate change and energy targets. The so-called 20-20-20 targets set out by the EU include reducing greenhouse gas emissions by 20 per cent, increasing renewable energy in gross final energy consumption by 20 per cent and increasing energy efficiency by 20 per cent. Such targets not only provide important measures against ongoing climate change, but also provide new jobs in a transformed, greener economy with green products and services and help the EU become a green, global competitive actor (Eurostat, 2017: 15).

Third, *inclusive growth*, with a high-employment economy providing economic, social and territorial cohesion and integration, refers to empowering

Europeans by offering job opportunities, an improved labour market, lifelong training, education and social protection from poverty and marginalization to all of Europe and all Europeans regardless of age and gender, etc. The main themes to prioritize are employment and skills and fighting poverty. The Commission clearly outlined in 2010 the challenge of demographic change in Europe, with a future limited workforce beside an unemployment rate that is higher than in the United States – about two-thirds of Europe's working-age citizens are employed compared to about 70 per cent in the United States. The Commission further stressed challenges in the economic and social marginalization of women, older workers and young people, all facing different hindrances to entering the labour market and/or finding opportunities for education and financial support for building and developing businesses and so forth. The Commission estimated that about 80 million Europeans had only low or basic skills, 80 million Europeans faced the serious risk of poverty (among them 19 million children) and the grave consequences of unemployment and poverty in social exclusion and health inequalities. The Europe 2020 strategy should focus on growth and jobs to sustain and develop Europe's social market economy (European Commission, 2010: 16). Inclusive growth would be approached based on targeting employment, poverty and social exclusion. These targets were established to increase the employment rate to 75 per cent in the 20–64 age group and to prevent at least 20 million people from living under the threat of poverty and/or social exclusion (Eurostat, 2017: 15).

In 2016, based on the UN Agenda 2030, the Commission set out the Communication *Next Steps for a Sustainable European Future: European Action for Sustainability*, aiming to transform the EU into a sustainable actor in international relations (European Commission, 2016a). The Communication embedded visions and strategies on how to commit the EU to sustainable development. The EU would, as a normative actor, push for a 'life of dignity for all within the planet's limits that reconciles economic prosperity and efficiency, peaceful societies, social inclusion and environmental responsibility' (European Commission, 2016a: 1).

The development of Agenda 2030 was influenced by the EU. The European Commission was active in the debates on Agenda 2030, which was visible in the 2013 Communication *A Decent Life for All: Ending Poverty and Giving the World a Sustainable Future*, in the 2014 Communication *A Decent Life for All: From Vision to Collective Action* and in the 2015 *A Global Partnership for Poverty Eradication and Sustainable Development after 2015*. The 2016 Communication set out how the EU is fully embracing Agenda 2030 and includes two work streams. The first work stream includes all 17 goals in the European policy framework and a European stand on each goal and what priorities need to be done, while the second track focuses on how to implement reforms on these goals in the long run using sectoral policies and the allocation of financial means to fulfil the objectives.

The EU decided to focus on ten priorities between 2014 and 2019, both within Europe as well as in its external actions. These priorities included many of the UN SDGs, but also indicate how the EU decided to prioritize sustainable development. The main areas of focus can be summarized in terms of jobs, growth, fairness and democratic change. These priorities are:

1. Jobs, growth and investment – boosting investment and creating jobs.
2. Digital single market – bringing down barriers to unlock online opportunities.
3. Energy union and climate – making energy more secure, affordable and sustainable.
4. Internal market – creating a deeper and fairer internal market.
5. A deeper and fairer economic and monetary union – combining stability with fairness and democratic accountability.
6. A balanced and progressive trade policy to harness globalization – supporting open trade without sacrificing Europe's standards.
7. Justice and fundamental rights – stepping up cooperation on security and justice in the EU and preserving the rule of law.
8. Migration – moving towards a European agenda on migration.
9. A stronger global actor – strengthening the global role of Europe.
10. Democratic change – making the EU more transparent and democratically accountable.

On 30 January 2019, the Commission presented a reflection paper, *Towards a Sustainable Europe by 2030* (European Commission, 2019a). It stressed the EU's strong commitment to Agenda 2030 and explored in what ways Europe could reach the SDGs and how Europe could be a leading actor in the world. It set out that the EU had become a frontrunner in promoting sustainable development, with the best social and environmental conditions globally. As stated by the Commission, 'Europe has all that it takes to tackle the greatest of challenges. We can do this, together. What we need is everyone's engagement and the political will to follow through' (European Commission 2019a: Foreword). The Commission paper also, however, acknowledged the many challenges ahead of Europe in climate change, demographic change, migration, inequality, economic and social convergence and pressure on public finances. It argued that individual states are unable to tackle our shared global challenges and noted how the Agenda 2030 highlighted the importance of a shared commitment among all actors to handle sustainable development. As argued by the Commission:

> No one state or nation can effectively deal with these challenges alone. We need the scale of the European Union, which – when unified and determined – is a global force to be reckoned with. However, ultimately even a European scale will not be enough; we need an agenda that has a global impact, and that agenda is best captured by the 17 SDGs 193 states signed up to, including the European Union and its Member States. These SDGs plot out a route on how to overcome the challenges we face, and to improve our habitat, our economy and our lives. (European Commission, 2019a: Foreword)

In addition, the paper also highlighted the challenge of nationalism and argued that the latest trends in Europe of isolationism, nationalism (see Chapter 10) and anti-European integration rhetoric are major challenges to a united Europe on sustainable development. The new negative trend of 'my country first' (European Commission, 2019a: 8) is a major challenge to Europe and could disrupt ongoing integration, leading to political strife and conflict within Europe and a challenged global commitment within Europe and elsewhere to the Agenda 2030. The Commission has urged the EU to step up its efforts on Agenda 2030 and lead the way towards global sustainable development (European Commission, 2019a: 9). The European Commission has also tried to foster a European debate among all actors on how to promote Agenda 2030 within Europe. It set out three scenarios outlining different ways for the EU to work on sustainable development within Europe and to become a global leading actor. These scenarios were supposed to become triggering factors to a European debate and discussion, from which clear actions on sustainable development could develop. Overall, the UN SDGs could be reached by aiming for three scenarios within the EU (European Commission, 2019a: 33–9), as summarized in Table 3.1:

1. To provide for an overarching strategy within the EU.
2. To continue to mainstream SDGs within EU policies by the Commission and to make recommendations of action to member states.
3. To promote external actions on these goals, besides the efforts taken within the EU.

A SUSTAINABLE EUROPE? STATE OF THE UNION 2016–19

Each year in September, the president of the European Commission announces the State of the Union speech to the European Parliament. The annual statement addresses progress made in Europe over the preceding year, the challenges that are ahead of Europe, and how EU institutions, member states and other core

Table 3.1   European Commission proposal of three scenarios on the sustainable development goals

Scenario 1: An overarching EU sustainable development goal strategy to guide actions of the EU/ member states.	– Endorse at the highest EU political level the globally agreed sustainable development goals as the overarching strategic policy objectives for the EU and its member states. – The UN 2030 Agenda and the goals become compass and map and determine the strategic framework for the EU and its member states. – Strategic action by the EU and the member states would be pursued and effectively coordinated. A joint approach at all levels of government would be stimulated, in close cooperation with all stakeholders. – This would include a strong component in the EU's relations with third countries to further international sustainability action. – This would also imply the establishment of a 'European process for sustainable development goals policy coordination' to assess and monitor progress in implementation.
Scenario 2: Continued mainstreaming of sustainable development goals in all relevant EU policies by the Commission, but without enforcing member states' actions.	– The goals will inspire our political decision making with regard to the EU's policy making and guide the development of the post-EU 2020 strategy, while not binding EU member states to achieving collectively the sustainable development commitments in the EU. – A member of the European Commission is granted a broad responsibility for sustainability and the commissioner could continue working together with other commissioners in a project team involving all the commissioners. – To ensure policy coherence, close cooperation with other project teams of commissioners would have to be sought. – This approach would leave more freedom to member states and regional and local authorities as to whether and how they adjust their work to delivering in a consistent manner on the SDGs.
Scenario 3: Putting enhanced focus on external action and consolidating sustainability ambition at EU level.	– External action would be prioritized in the context of the SDGs. – Europe's social market economy has become an EU trademark. – Europe has some of the world's highest environmental standards. – European businesses are ahead of the curve compared to global competitors. – Europe is seen as a stronghold for freedom and democracy, with stable institutions based on the rule of law and a vibrant civil society. – The EU could therefore decide to promote more strongly its current environmental, social and governance standards through multilateral negotiations and trade agreements and intensify collaboration with key international organizations and forums to advance the EU's values-based external policy agenda.

Source: Copied from European Commission, 2019a, but slightly modified to fit into the table.

actors within the system of European governance should tackle these. The State of the Union is followed by a plenary debate that is the platform for a dialogue with Parliament and Council to begin to prepare the Commission Work Program for the coming year. On 14 September 2016, in the context of the new UN Agenda 2030, Jean-Claude Juncker, the former president of the European Commission, delivered the State of the Union *Towards a Better Europe: A Europe that Protects, Empowers and Defends*. He described numerous challenges to Europe and called upon all European actors to show leadership and strength to meet such challenges. As stated, 'Is this not the time to pull ourselves together? Is this not the time to roll up our sleeves and double, triple our efforts? Is this not the time when Europe needs more determined leadership than ever, rather than politicians abandoning ship?' (Juncker, 2016: 11). President Juncker addressed urgent challenges in (1) high unemployment, social inequality and mountains of public debt; (2) integration of refugees; (3) threats to our security at home and abroad; (4) capacity regarding signing trade deals with third states; (5) the fight for human rights and fundamental values; and (6) the efforts to reach European consensus in numerous areas to speak with one voice. President Juncker called upon EU member states to seek out consensus to strengthen the EU and help it become an improved international actor on both European and global challenges. He also urged European leaders to contribute to a better Europe: 'a Europe that protects; a Europe that preserves the European way of life; a Europe that empowers our citizens, a Europe that defends at home and abroad; and a Europe that takes responsibility' (Juncker, 2016: 10). Such efforts had to be based on and serve the founding European norms and values: the European way of life in peace, freedom, democracy, the rule of law, free movement, anti-discrimination and anti-racism, valuing human life and anti-death penalty, open trade, international trade agreements and a social market model, security both within the EU as well as externally and the importance of global responsibility against further climate change (Juncker, 2016: 10–13).

On 13 September 2017, President Jean-Claude Juncker launched the State of the Union Address 2017, *Roadmap for a More United, Stronger and More Democratic Union*, readdressing the many challenges Europe had in 2016, but how 2017 had been a year with wind in the European sails. Stressing a European climate of 2016 of disintegration, Juncker announced in 2017 how the European Parliament and individual member states had shown unity based on the European ground of shared norms and values. Juncker announced a continued economic recovery in all member states with increased employment, declining public deficits and ongoing work to strive for the completion of an Energy Union, a Security Union, a Capital Markets Union, a Banking Union and a Digital Single Market. The State of the Union of 2017 re-emphasized some of the priorities laid out in 2016 as ongoing priorities where more work had to be done. This work should focus on the European trade agenda with more trade agreements signed around the world, reforms to strengthen, make more competitive and greener the European industry based on innovation, digitization and decarbonization and to become the number one leader on climate change based on the Paris Agreement. Other priorities mentioned were the security of Europe from cyberattacks to terrorism and external threats, as well as unity on how to approach and handle integration and refugee flows both within the EU and across European external borders (Juncker, 2017).

President Juncker once again stressed the importance of a union of shared values. The shared European values 'are our compass', he argued, pointing out freedom, equality and the rule of law as the cornerstone of European integration. As stated,

> Freedom from the kind of oppression and dictatorship our continent knows all too well – sadly none more than the central and Eastern European countries. Freedom to voice your opinion, as a citizen and as a journalist – a freedom we too often take for granted. It was on these freedoms that our Union was built. But freedom does not fall from the sky. It must be fought for. In Europe and throughout the world…
>
> Equality between its Members, big or small, East or West, North or South… Otherwise our continent will struggle for air. In a Union of equals, there can be no second class citizens… In a Union of equals, there can be no second class consumers either…
>
> The rule of law means that law and justice are upheld by an independent judiciary. Accepting and respecting a final judgement is what it means to be part of a Union based on the rule of law. Our Member States gave final jurisdiction to the European Court of Justice. The judgements of the Court have to be respected by all. To undermine them, or to undermine the independence of national courts, is to strip citizens of their fundamental rights. The rule of law is not optional in the European Union. It is a must…
>
> These three principles – freedom, equality and the rule of law – must remain the foundations on which we build a more united, stronger and more democratic Union. (Juncker, 2017: 5)

In the State of the Union of 2018, *On Efforts That Are Bearing Fruit*, President Juncker acknowledged the economic progress since the global recession a decade earlier and how Europe showed great signs of economic and financial stability and improvements, 70 trade agreements signed around the world and the Paris Agreement on climate change as a platform for providing for a healthier planet by reducing CO_2 emissions. The statement stressed the importance of global responsibility also in the area of security, from the Western Balkans and neighbouring states in the east to Syria. He emphasized the importance of building a European defence capable of providing for independence and security at home and fulfilling global responsibilities abroad. As argued, 'I want Europe to get off the side-lines of world affairs. Europe can no longer be a spectator or a mere commentator on international events. Europe must be an active player, an architect of tomorrow's world. There is strong demand for Europe throughout the world. To meet such high demand, Europe will have to speak with one voice on the world stage. Our solidarity must be all-embracing' (Juncker, 2018).

On 9 May 2019, the EU leaders met in Sibiu, Romania to discuss a strategic agenda for Europe between 2019 and 2024. The Commission and President Juncker presented recommendations ahead of the meeting to influence and shape the agenda and the future policies which would be decided. The Commission addressed the areas of most concern for the EU, with member states, to address for a better Europe 2019–24 (European Commission, 2019b: 22–6):

Digitalization: A first addressed challenge was technological change and how digitalization and new technologies will transform societies and our daily lives regarding health, mobility, industry and science and how Europe both could be an engine for growth and competitiveness, as well as provide risks with the widening of the digital skills gaps between groups of people and regions within Europe.

Climate change and environment: A second challenge mentioned was how Europe fosters many of the biggest clean tech companies in the world and has acted upon climate change challenges politically to address the growing concern that exists in Europe and around the world. It was, however, also stated that to meet the Paris Agreement requires very much more European effort and at a faster speed. Climate actions are necessary for our survival and for social health, but should also be seen as a window of opportunity for a transformed economic sector.

Demography and society: A third identified challenge concerned the effects of demographic change, including high quality of life, overall wellbeing and increased European life expectancy as positive symbols, but that comes with demands on the health care and welfare systems. In addition, the overall lower birth rate in Europe creates a related challenge of a limited workforce that is to provide tax income to a welfare system that needs to provide for more elderly people than ever before in history. In addition, the Commission also raises concerns over existing welfare gaps between urban areas and rural and centrally located regions versus remote regions, creating demands on European leaders to promote inclusion and integration within and between regions and states.

An increasingly multipolar world: A fourth challenge addressed by the Commission focused on the transformation of the international landscape regarding security, with increasing competition over power between states and the rising insecurity in neighbouring areas to the EU. Linked to digitalization and new technology, security risks in hybrid threats, threats to critical infrastructure, malicious cyber activities and disinformation campaigns are alarming challenges to our democratic society. In addition, terrorism, domestic as well as international, fuelled by technological tools and radical ideologies, is a present danger to Europe. On the economic scene, multipolarity also comes with economic competition, scarcity of resources and the striving for new strategic resources and geopolitical alliances in both favour and disfavour of European interests.

In 2019, the Commission was an active player to guide Europe forward towards a prosperous and sustainable Europe. There have been policy recommendations to EU institutions and member states on how to protect and promote European norms and values both within Europe, as well as externally on the global scene (see European Commission, 2019b: 29–35). The Commission has argued for a *protective Europe*; Europe has for decades provided peace and security as a unique international actor in both military and civilian measures. The Commission outlined how the EU must continue to fulfil the role of European integration and collaboration and act globally to promote European norms and values. Internal and external security are interwoven and require a European stand on a European Security Union against terrorism, organized crime, cybercrime and hybrid threats, but also a European Defence Union focusing on a defence industry and research, cyber-defence, military mobility, hybrid crisis management and missions and operations abroad, together within the North Atlantic Treaty Organization as well as among EU member states. The Commission also stated the importance of a well-functioning asylum system, protecting human rights and EU external borders by fulfilling international obligations and safeguarding European cohesive and inclusive societies.

The Commission also emphasized the importance of a *competitive Europe*, focusing on research and innovation for promoting ecological, social and economic transformations in European societies to meet challenges in diseases, dangerous emissions and material harmful to our environment. The Commission stresses the importance of partnerships between member states and industry to push for strategic investments to boost new innovative projects that contribute to regional development throughout Europe. One important area mentioned is the promotion of key European digital capacities to become competitive in digital transformation through joint measures. In addition, an up-to-date European policy needs to address the importance of infrastructure, innovations and new technologies, and a smart regulatory ecosystem, as well as providing support to industry overall based on the single market and the Economic and Monetary Union.

A third issue raised by the Commission has been the push for a *fair Europe*, addressing the European Pillar of Social Rights, emphasizing the importance of tackling inequalities and social challenges across and within member states, regions and different economic areas. This is about creating jobs to lower unemployment rates and promote inclusion, but is also about creating quality jobs, social protection and improved access to health care and high-quality education and training. Europe faces inequalities and injustices based on regional development levels, minorities' needs, gender inequality, challenges of an ageing population and limitations regarding rights and liberties and the rule of law in some member states.

The Commission also addressed, as a fourth issue, the importance of a *sustainable Europe*, both within Europe as well as globally. The Commission in particular mentioned the importance of Agenda 2030 and how to fulfil the development goals detailed there. The Commission highlighted the importance of sustainable consumption and production patterns, energy use and energy supply, building and infrastructure and promoting a transition into a green economy. Europe needs to fight climate change on land and in water and air to reverse environmental degradation, biodiversity loss and climate-related disasters and diseases.

Fifth and finally, the Commission set its focus on an *influential Europe*, referring to the importance of the EU strengthening its role in international politics to safeguard European norms and values. In a multipolar order consisting of different powerful actors and interests, the EU must seek greater unity among member states in order to remain a normative power by influencing the international agenda in a European direction to preserve the European way of life. The EU should continue to speak out for a multilateral, rules-based international order, global governance and universal rights and liberties. The Commission also called upon the EU to use its power globally to promote European interests in a multilateral trading system, the importance of the UN, integration and collaboration with and within EU neighbouring territory to the east and south, and to enhance collaboration with the African continent both politically and economically in order to handle common interests, changes and challenges regarding trade, education, rights and liberties and migration, etc.

A GLOBAL OUTREACH

The Commission addresses the many linkages between European and global progress and development. To build a protected, competitive, fair, sustainable and influential Europe requires a global engagement and commitment by Europe. The Commission has also emphasized the important role of the EU as a global actor on sustainable development. In *Shared Vision, Common Action: A Stronger Europe – A Global Strategy for the European Union's Foreign and Security Policy* (Mogherini, 2016), the Commission addressed the importance of the EU, in collaboration with member states, coordinating policies and being comprehensive and coherent in addressing global challenges. It argues that European and global sustainability challenges are highly interlinked and that peace and prosperity in our part of the world is dependent on the rest of the world and vice versa.

On 22 November 2016, the Commission launched a proposal for a new *European Consensus on Development: Our World, Our Dignity, Our Future* (European Commission, 2017). The new proposal was an update and development of the original *European Consensus on Development* of 2005. The proposal included a blueprint for linking the existing development policy to the UN Agenda 2030. It was suggested that a new development policy would address the main objectives in the Agenda 2030 by focusing on people, planet, prosperity, peace and partnership. The proposal also aimed at stressing the importance of the EU's external actions and complementing the *Global Strategy on the EU's Foreign and Security Policy* from June 2016 (Mogherini, 2016). The overall ambition was to make EU actions on development more efficient by promoting a comprehensive and universal approach that explicitly acknowledged the complexity of development by focusing on cross-cutting themes in gender equality, youth empowerment and participation, sustainable energy and climate action, investment, renewable energy, migration and forced mobility and peace. The Commission highlighted how the EU is a global leader in promoting certain norms and values and how the EU would continue to strive for economic and social empowerment for everyone. As stated by the commissioner for international cooperation and development, Neven Mimica:

> The proposal for a new European Consensus on Development is the EU's response to an increasingly interconnected and challenging world. I aim for a genuine consensus, under the shared ownership of EU Institutions and all Member States that will help us spearhead global action to implement the Sustainable Development Goals. Together with our proposals for our future partnership with the African, Caribbean and Pacific countries, it unequivocally confirms the EU's readiness to engage with our partners across the world to build a better common future. (Mimica, 2016)

The new consensus should always refer to the five core themes of the Agenda 2030 and mutually and in a coordinated matter set up shared analysis, strategies, programmes, actions and reports to promote economic, social and environmental development for people, planet, prosperity, peace and partnership as integrated areas of action. The Commission clearly argued for the promotion of development cooperation as:

> 'Do more': The new Consensus should integrate more systematically the economic, social and environmental dimensions. This requires giving more prominence to key drivers such as gender equality, youth, sustainable energy and climate action, investments, migration and mobility. It also means demonstrating the contribution

of development policy to tackle global interconnected challenges, such as conflict, migration, economic growth and jobs and climate change.

'Do it better': The new Consensus should foster a more coordinated approach to development between the EU and its Member States, promoting joint programming and joint actions and making the most of tools such as budget support, trust funds and blending. It should also demonstrate a real cultural shift from inputs to outputs when it comes to measuring the effectiveness of our development actions, focusing on results. It will support greater efforts for policy coherence for development.

'Do it differently': The EU and its Member States together continue to be the world's largest development and humanitarian aid donor. The new Consensus should put forward a package that combines Official Development Assistance with domestic resource mobilisation and private sector investment, supported by sound policies. It also requires differentiated, better-tailored partnerships with partner countries at different levels of development – to combine a focus on the poorest and most fragile partners with innovative partnerships with Middle Income Countries – and with a broad range of other stakeholders. (European Commission, 2016b)

CONCLUSION

This chapter has addressed the role of the European Commission in promoting the Agenda 2030 and its SDGs in a European context. In 2016, the Commission addressed the new UN Agenda 2030 in the Communication *Next Steps for a Sustainable European Future: European Action for Sustainability*. After a decade of political entrepreneurship on Agenda 2020, to deal with a severe global recession, the Commission now addressed another global crisis: the urgent need for sustainable development. Based on the progress made on smart, sustainable and socially inclusive growth in Europe, between 2010 and 2020, the Commission called upon all actors within the EU system of governance, and especially the EU member states, to begin a European partnership on the 17 SDGs in the Agenda 2030.

Based on the goals, the Commission specifically addresses ten priorities: jobs, growth and investment, the digital single market, energy union and climate, internal market, a deeper and fairer economic and monetary union, a balanced and progressive trade policy to harness globalization, justice and fundamental rights, migration, a stronger global actor and democratic change. Such priorities must be addressed by a coherent and comprehensive approach by EU actors based on shared norms and values. There are serious challenges to development in contemporary Europe and only a shared European stand can respond to such challenges and provide for a better Europe. In recent years' States of the Union, delivered by the chair of the European Commission, shared norms and values, as well as challenges, have been pointed out, with the explicit emphasis on how Europe is a strong Europe based on European norms and values, how Europe only can meet existing challenges together and how the rest of the world is in need of a coherent EU on sustainable development.

NOTE

1. It succeeded the European Single Market programme (1986–92) and the Lisbon Strategy (2000–10), with the European Council deciding on it at a meeting on 26 March 2010.

REFERENCES

Barbier, J.C. (2011). *Changes in Political Discourse from the Lisbon Strategy to Europe 2020: Tracing the Fate of 'Social Policy'*. Brussels: ETUI.

Budd, L. (2013). EUROPE 2020: A strategy in search of a regional policy rationale? *Policy Studies*, 34(3): 274–90.

Bull, H. (1982). Civilian power Europe: A contradiction in terms? *Journal of Common Market Studies*, 21(2), 149–64.

Duchêne, F. (1972). Europe's role in world peace. In R. Mayne (ed.), *Europe Tomorrow: Sixteen Europeans Look Ahead*. London: Fontana, 32–47.

Duchêne, F. (1973). The European Community and the uncertainties of interdependence. In M. Kohnstamm & W. Hager (eds), *A Nation Writ Large? Foreign Policy Problems before the European Community*. Basingstoke: Macmillan, 17–45.

European Commission (2010). *Communication from the Commission: Europe 2020: A Strategy for Smart, Sustainable and Inclusive Growth*. Brussels, 3 March. Brussels: European Commission.

European Commission (2016a). *Next Steps for a Sustainable European Future: European Action for Sustainability*. Accessed 12 October 2018 at https://ec.europa .eu/europeaid/commission-communication-next-steps-sustainable-european-future _en

European Commission (2016b). *A Proposal for a New European Consensus on Development*. Accessed 23 January 2019 at https://ec.europa.eu/commission/ presscorner/detail/en/MEMO_16_3884

European Commission (2017). *The New European Consensus on Development: 'Our World, Our Dignity, Our Future'*. European Commission. Accessed 11 December 2019 at https://ec.europa.eu/international-partnerships/european-consensus -development_en

European Commission (2019a). *Europe in May 2019 Preparing for a More United, Stronger and More Democratic Union in an Increasingly Uncertain World: The European Commission's Contribution to the Informal EU27 Leaders' Meeting in Sibiu (Romania) on 9 May 2019*, January. Luxembourg: Publications Office of the European Union.

European Commission (2019b). *The European Green Deal Set Out How to Make Europe the First Climate-Neutral Continent by 2050, Boosting the Economy, Improving People's Health and Quality of Life, Caring for Nature, and Leaving No One Behind*, 11 December. Accessed 28 January 2020 at https://ec.europa.eu/ commission/commissioners/2019-2024/president/announcements/european-green -deal-sets-out-how-make-europe-first-climate-neutral-continent-2050-boosting -economy_en

Eurostat (2017). *Smarter, Greener, More Inclusive? Indicators to Support the Europe 2020 Strategy*. Luxembourg: Publications Office of the European Union.

Eurostat (2018). *Smarter, Greener, More Inclusive? Indicators to Support the Europe 2020 Strategy*. Luxembourg: Publications Office of the European Union.

Gros, D. & F. Roth (2012). *The Europe 2020 Strategy: Can It Maintain the EU's Competitiveness in the World?* Brussels: Centre for European Policy Studies.

Hill, C. (1993). The capability-expectations gap, or conceptualizing Europe's international role. *Journal of Common Market Studies*, 31(3), 305–28.

Juncker, J.C. (2016). *State of the Union 2016.* Brussels, 14 September. Accessed 13 October 2019 at https://op.europa.eu/en/publication-detail/-/publication/c9ff4ff6 -9a81-11e6-9bca-01aa75ed71a1/language-en/format-PDF/source-30945725

Juncker, J.C. (2017). *State of the Union 2017.* Brussels, 13 September. Accessed 13 October 2019 at http://eurireland.ie/assets/uploads/2017/09/SOTEU-Address.pdf

Juncker, J.C. (2018). *State of the Union 2018: The Hour of European Sovereignty.* Accessed 13 October 2018 at https://ec.europa.eu/commission/news/state-union -2018-hour-european-sovereignty-2018-sep-12_en

Kagan, R. (2003). *Paradise and Power: America and Europe in the New World Order.* London: Atlantic Books.

Manners, I. (2002). Normative power Europe: A contradiction in terms? *Journal of Common Market Studies*, 40(2): 235–58.

Mimica, N. (2016). Policy Forum on development: *Sustainable development: EU sets out its priorities*, press release. Accessed 15 January 2020 at https://europa.eu/ capacity4dev/policy-forum-development/blog/sustainable-development-eu-sets-out -its-priorities-press-release

Mogherini, F. (2016). *Shared Vision, Common Action: A Stronger Europe – A Global Strategy for the European Union's Foreign and Security Policy.* Accessed 3 November 2019 at https://op.europa.eu/en/publication-detail/-/publication/3eaae2cf -9ac5-11e6-868c-01aa75ed71a1

Silander, D. (2018). 'European governance and political entrepreneurship in times of economic crisis'. In C. Karlsson, C. Silander & D. Silander (eds), *Governance and Political Entrepreneurship in Europe: Promoting Growth and Welfare in Times of Crisis.* Cheltenham, UK and Northampton, MA, USA: Edward Elgar Publishing.

Sjöstedt, G. (1977). *The External Role of the European Community.* Farnborough: Saxon House.

Smith, K. (2000). The end of civilian power EU: A welcome demise or cause for concern? *International Spectator*, 23(2), 11.28.

Walburn, D. (2010). Europe 2020. *Local Economy*, 25(8): 699–702.

Wandel, J. (2016). The role of government and markets in the strategy 'Europe 2020' of the European Union: A robust political economy analysis. *International Journal of Management and Economics*, 49(January–March): 7–33.

Whitman, R. (1998). *From Civilian Power to Superpower? The International Identity of the European Union.* Basingstoke: Palgrave.

Zeitlin, J. & B. Vanhercke (2014). 'Socializing the European semester? Economic governance and social policy coordination in Europe 2020'. Brown University, Watson Institute for International Studies Research Paper No. 2014-17.

4. Agenda 2030 and the EU on gender equality

Charlotte Silander

In 2015, the United Nations (UN) adopted 17 Sustainable Development Goals (SDGs) as a part of the 2030 Agenda for Sustainable Development, which should meet urgent environmental, political and economic challenges of the world (United Nations, 2015) and which have been adopted by all UN member states. These goals build upon the earlier Millennium Development Goals (MDGs) which were set out by the UN in 2000 and expired in 2015. Goal number 5 deals with gender equality and seeks to "achieve gender equality and empower all women and girls" (United Nations, 2015: 14). The UN states that "women and girls represent half of the world's population and therefore also half of its potential. But, today gender inequality persists everywhere and stagnates social progress" (United Nations, 2017a: 1).

Unlike its predecessors the MDGs, the SDGs do not represent a "one-size-fits all" approach, but are instead universal and expected to be adapted to different national and local contexts and relate to existing problems and policies. The concept of political entrepreneurship (see Chapter 1) captures new and innovative ways to address political problems. Seeking global change through global goal setting can represent a new and innovative way of policymaking (Biermann et al., 2017), although successful fulfilment of the SDGs will depend on the effectiveness of the network of implementation.

It is often repeated how gender equality is one of the fundamental values of the European Union (EU) (European Commission, 2016b). Work to support gender equality in the EU dates back to 1957 and the principle of equal pay for equal work in the Treaty of Rome, but it is also an area of contradictions and, as argued by Young (2000), a policy in line with the neoliberal model of capitalism, as improvements have come as part of trade-offs in the form of large packages serving to integrate the European market and risking the weakening of social protection at the national level (Rossilli, 1999). Gender equality has been analyzed in terms of a move from the strategy of equal treatment, with a strong focus on equal rights for workers resulting in a number of directives and pieces of legislation that have influenced the member states, followed by the use of positive action and to the current situation with a focus on mainstreaming (Rees, 1998, 2006). The first two phases are intimately connected to women's participation in the workforce, where the legal basis for action in the area of gender equality is anchored. The third phase, mainstreaming, argues for widening the scope of gender equality by also addressing representation, decision making and private spheres of life. Mainstreaming is now the main strategy of gender equality in the EU, which means that gender equality should be integrated into all policy areas (Council of Europe, 1998).

The EU played an important part in shaping the Agenda 2030, which "is fully consistent with Europe's vision" (European Commission, 2016a: 3). The EU aims to be a leading force in adopting the Agenda and the SDGs and proudly refers to its member states as top SDG performers (European Commission, 2016a). In relation to the goal on gender equality, the Commission states that "gender equality is enshrined in the EU political and legal framework since the very start of European integration and new policies are being developed to address persistent gender inequalities" (European Commission, 2016b: 21).

The responsibility for the implementation of the 2030 Agenda is at the national level. This means that the EU member states need to formulate national measures to translate the SDGs into action. The Commission has launched a two-stream strategy for the implementation of the Agenda, in which the first step is to integrate the SDGs into the European policy framework and current Commission priorities, and the second is to shape a longer-term policy that will focus on sectoral policies after 2020 for the long-term implementation of the SDGs. The first step was presented in the Commission document of 2016 (European Commission, 2016a), while the second has not yet taken form.

This chapter sets out to investigate the gender equality policy of the EU and how it is related to and can be expected to be influenced by the SDG goal on gender set in the Agenda 2030. The chapter will be guided by the following research questions:

• How does EU gender equality policy relate to the global SDGs on gender equality?
• How can the SDGs expect to influence the direction of EU gender equality policy?
• What is the role of the EU in implementing the goal on gender equality in relation to its stated strategy of mainstreaming?

The EU strategy in relation to Agenda 2030 does in many ways focus on external action. Externally, the EU addresses gender equality issues through *external relations* and its *development cooperation policy*. The EU also has a *Global Strategy on Foreign and Security Policy* emphasizing the importance of mainstreaming human rights and gender issues across policy sectors and institutions. The *European Neighbourhood Policy* applies a gender mainstreaming policy and gender equality is included as one of the requirements and present in *the EU humanitarian aid policy* (European Commission, 2016b). The focus in this chapter will be on the relation between the SDGs and EU gender equality policy *internally* in the Union. In the first part, the SDGs on gender equality will be described. In the second part, the EU policy on gender equality will be described and analyzed. In the third part, the implementation of the SDGs in relation to the EU will be discussed.

SUSTAINABLE DEVELOPMENT AND GENDER EQUALITY

UN support for the rights of women is originally based on the founding Charter, where article 1 states the ambition to achieve international co-operation "in promoting and encouraging respect for human rights and for fundamental freedoms for all without distinction as to race, sex, language, or religion" (UN Charter of Human Rights). The UN has since 1970 been active in advancing women's rights on a global level, marked by the adoption of the Convention on the Elimination of All Forms of Discrimination Against Women in 1979 and the World Conferences on Women (Mexico City in 1980; Copenhagen in 1985; Nairobi in 1990; and Beijing in 1995), each of which resulted in action platforms serving as a basis on which to hold governments and national policymakers responsible to make efforts for the development of women's rights. The overall goal on gender equality is to "achieve gender equality and empower all women and girls" (United Nations, 2015). To reach the goal, nine targets are formulated, which will be assessed using 14 indicators (Table 4.1).

The SDGs are in many ways different from the previous MDGs in terms of number of goals and targets, purpose and the political process that developed them (Fukuda-Parr, 2016).

First, the goal to "achieve gender equality and empower all women and girls" (United Nations, 2015: 14) is stronger than the previous MDG "to promote gender equality and empower women" (www.un.org). The goal represents a "rights based" approach to gender equality, meaning that the starting point is that gender equality is a fundamental right. This is a dual strategy consisting of both a standalone goal on gender equality and women's rights, as well as specific gender-equality targets in other goals (Bidegain Ponte & Rodrigies Enríquez, 2016).

Second, the SDGs have a broader scope than the MDGs. Although the MDGs were admired by some for their simplicity, Fukuda-Parr (2016) argues that life is complicated and problems are multifaceted and the simplicity of the MDGs limits their ability to bring about change. The MDGs were more modest in their ambition and only covered a few areas, derisively referred to by some as "Minimum Development Goals" (Harcourt, 2005). The MDGs,

Table 4.1   *Indicators for targets on goal 5 to achieve gender equality and empower all women and girls*

Targets	Indicators
5.1 End all forms of discrimination against all women and girls everywhere	5.1.1 Whether or not legal frameworks are in place to promote, enforce and monitor equality and non-discrimination on the basis of sex
5.2 Eliminate all forms of violence against all women and girls in the public and private spheres, including trafficking and sexual and other types of exploitation	5.2.1 Proportion of ever partnered women and girls aged 15 years and older subjected to physical, sexual or psychological violence by a current or former intimate partner in the previous 12 months, by form of violence and by age 5.2.2 Proportion of women and girls aged 15 years and older subjected to sexual violence by persons other than an intimate partner in the previous 12 months, by age and place of occurrence
5.3 Eliminate all harmful practices, such as child, early and forced marriage and female genital mutilation	5.3.1 Proportion of women aged 20–24 years who were married or in a union before age 15 and before age 18 5.3.2 Proportion of girls and women aged 15–49 years who have undergone female genital mutilation/cutting, by age
5.4 Recognize and value unpaid care and domestic work through the provision of public services, infrastructure and social protection policies and the promotion of shared responsibility within the household and the family as nationally appropriate	5.4.1 Proportion of time spent on unpaid domestic and care work, by sex, age and location
5.5 Ensure women's full and effective participation and equal opportunities for leadership at all levels of decision making in political, economic and public life	5.5.1 Proportion of seats held by women in national parliaments and local governments 5.5.2 Proportion of women in managerial positions
5.6 Ensure universal access to sexual and reproductive health and reproductive rights, as agreed in accordance with the Programme of Action of the International Conference on Population and Development and the Beijing Platform for Action and the outcome documents of their review conferences	5.6.1 Proportion of women aged 15–49 years who make their own informed decisions regarding sexual relations, contraceptive use and reproductive health care 5.6.2 Number of countries with laws and regulations that guarantee women aged 15–49 years access to sexual and reproductive health care, information and education

Targets	Indicators
5.a Undertake reforms to give women equal rights to economic resources, as well as access to ownership and control over land and other forms of property, financial services, inheritance and natural resources, in accordance with national laws	5.a.1 (a) Proportion of total agricultural population with ownership or secure rights over agricultural land, by sex; and (b) share of women among owners or rights bearers of agricultural land, by type of tenure 5.a.2 Proportion of countries where the legal framework (including customary law) guarantees women's equal rights to land ownership and/or control
5.b Enhance the use of enabling technology, in particular information and communications technology, to promote the empowerment of women	5.b.1 Proportion of individuals who own a mobile telephone, by sex
5.c Adopt and strengthen sound policies and enforceable legislation for the promotion of gender equality and the empowerment of all women and girls at all levels	5.c.1 Proportion of countries with systems to track and make public allocations for gender equality and women's empowerment

for example, lacked a target regarding violence against women and girls (Stuart & Woodroffe, 2016). In comparison, the targets of goal number 5 are more expansive and include a number of areas such as ending discrimination; ending violence against women (including trafficking and sexual forms of exploitation); ending child, early and forced marriage and female genital mutilation; recognition of unpaid care and domestic work; promoting women's participation and opportunities for leadership; providing universal access to sexual health and reproductive rights; increasing ownership of land and other property, including natural resources; and expanding access to intermediate technology (United Nations, 2015).

Third, goal 5 set out to change the underlying structures causing inequalities. The MDGs were criticized for mainly focusing on poverty, with a donor agenda where ending poverty was understood as meeting "basic needs" and the targets were limited to ending extreme poverty in "poor countries" (Fukuda-Parr, 2016). Many of the goals and targets were focused on developing countries only (for example, universal primary education). The SDGs are instead about sustainable development. Instead of emphasizing outcome or results, the SDGs seek to address the structural causes of inequality (Esquivel, 2016). This incorporates ending poverty as a core objective, but the goals and targets set out a broader agenda. On principal grounds, the MDGs were criticized for not being aligned with human rights principles such as equality, participation, non-discrimination and transparency and for a technocratic implementation, based on an assumption that resources and technology are the answer to poverty (OHCHR, 2008).

Fourth, the process of negotiation of the SDGs took place through a relatively open negotiation process (Bidegain Ponte & Rodrigies Enriquez, 2016), in contrast to the MDGs which had been drafted by technocrats with limited consultations with other groups (Fukuda-Parr, 2016). Fukuda-Parr and Hulme (2011) argue that the MDG agenda was driven by development ministers and heads of development agencies and drafted by the office of the UN Secretary-General and a handful of UN staff. In sum, there are several ways in which the SDGs seek to address several of the key shortcomings of the MDGs and incorporate a broader and more transformative agenda (Fukuda-Parr, 2016).

Another way in which the SDGs are innovative is in the way they build on a few key principles which differ from the MDGs and which indicate a new form of global government very much in line with EU strategies. First, the goals are *universal*, stressing that the Agenda 2030 is applicable to all countries. The preamble of the Agenda 2030 document states that these are universal human rights, which hold the possibility to hold governments responsible for development. On the other hand, although the human rights framing is clear in the preamble, the goals are linked to targets and monitoring indicators, which are not framed as rights, but instead allow every country to develop its own approach to implementation (European Parliament, 2019b). The goals are *interconnected*, which means that development in one area will influence other areas. Gender equality is one of the goals that are considered to be strongly connected to other goals. "Realizing gender equality and the empowerment of women and girls will make a crucial contribution to progress across all the goals and targets" (United Nations, 2015: 6). This means that the 17 SDGs need to be considered in their entirety, which also requires a strong level of policy integration, coherence and coordination, as well as connections between internal and external policies implementing the SDGs. The principle of *Inclusiveness* ("Leave no one behind") calls for the participation of all parts of society, but also all countries and relevant stakeholders. The principle of *partnerships* means that the Agenda seeks to establish multistakeholder partnerships in order to mobilize and share knowledge, technology and other resources to support the work on the SDGs.

MOTIVES FOR GENDER EQUALITY

The UN argument for gender equality rests on three legs. First, gender equality is viewed as a basic human right (the rights-based approach). The commitment to human rights is present in the Agenda preamble, based on the principles of the Charter of the United Nations, grounded in the Universal Declaration of Human Rights, international human rights treaties and the Millennium Declaration:

> We envisage a world of universal respect for human rights and human dignity, the rule of law, justice, equality and non-discrimination; of respect for race, ethnicity and cultural diversity; and of equal opportunity permitting the full realization of human potential and contributing to shared prosperity. (United Nations, 2015: 5)

Taken as a whole, the SDGs reflect a wider definition of gender that includes a range of inequalities and considers men as well as women.

Second, the goal of gender equality is based on a view that gender equality is not only a fundamental human right, but also necessary for a peaceful, prosperous and sustainable world. The liberalist perspective is embedded in the Agenda 2030 with the underlying assumption that social development fundamentally lies in generating employment through growth (Utting, 2013). This growth rationale forms a base for women's economic empowerment (Esquivel, 2016). The main argument for gender equality is really as a means to prosperity. The UN's website states:

> Women and girls represent half of the world's population and, therefore, also half of its potential. Gender equality, besides being a fundamental human right, is essential to achieve peaceful societies, with full human potential and sustainable development. Moreover, it has been shown that empowering women spurs productivity and economic growth. (www.un.org)

Hence, the economic case for gender equality is strong and emphasizes the economic benefits at the macro level making gender equality an investment. The main argument is the need to exploit the full potential of the labor force (Cuberes & Teignier-Baque, 2011; OECD, 2012). "Women's and girls' empowerment is essential to expand economic growth and promote social development. The full participation of women in labor forces would add percentage points to most national growth rates double digits in" (United Nations, 2018). This is in line with research showing strong evidence of positive and increasing benefits from gender equality on economic growth (Maceira, 2017; Kabeer & Natali, 2013). In comparison to labor market and education policies, gender equality policies have been proven to have a strong impact on gross domestic product, which makes it a highly relevant policy measure to foster economic growth (Maceira, 2017). Agenda 2030 has also been criticized by feminist scholars for not challenging the economic model of development based on resource-intensive economic growth as a pre-condition for policies (Gupta & Vegelin, 2016; Bidegain & Enríquez 2016; Razavi, 2016). Industrialization is seen as the main driver of growth, and countries should aim to "significantly raise industry's share of employment and gross domestic product" (Target 9.2) as economic growth is perceived as the most important generator of domestic resources needed to achieve the SDGs (Esquivel, 2016). Critics also comment on the unwillingness of the Agenda to deal with power. Inclusiveness is indeed highlighted, but there are few suggestions about how power differences can be addressed. As argued by feminists, growth does not automatically translate into gender equality, but will depend on growth patterns (Esquivel, 2016).

The third leg is the importance of gender in relation to interconnectivity. Ending all forms of discrimination against women and girls also has a multiplier effect across all other development areas. The Agenda states that "Realizing gender equality and the empowerment of women and girls will make a crucial contribution to progress across all the goals and targets" (United Nations, 2015: 6). SDGs are interconnected, in the sense that success in one area is expected to give success in other areas. For example, achieving gender equality or better health is expected to contribute to the eradication of poverty, and fostering peace and inclusive societies will reduce inequalities and help develop economies.

GENDER EQUALITY POLICY IN THE EU

Gender equality is recurrently emphasized as a fundamental value of the EU. It is stated in article 2 of the Treaty of the European Union (TEU) that:

> The Union is founded on the values of respect for human dignity, freedom, democracy, equality, the rule of law and respect for human rights, including the rights of persons belonging to minorities. These values are common to the Member States in a society in which pluralism, non-discrimination, tolerance, justice, solidarity and equality between women and men prevail.

This strong commitment to gender equality is repeated in policy documents in all areas (European Commission, 2011, 2015). Gender equality policy is often taken as an example of one of the most developed areas of the EU's social dimension (Hyman, 2008; Hix, 2005), as the EU has since the 1970s put pressure on individual member states through gender-related directives in the area of working life (Walby, 1999; Rees, 2006).

Gender policy can be analyzed in terms of strategies for how equality should be reached. Squires uses the terms inclusion, reversal and displacement to describe gender equality strategies (Rees, 1998, 2006; Squires, 2008). A first *strategy of inclusion* aims to include women in areas from which they previously have been excluded. This strategy is based on the idea of sameness, indicating that rules and actions must apply to both women and men. According to this perspective, the lack of gender equality exists because women historically have been excluded from the labor market, politics and other social contexts (Verloo & Lombardo, 2007). The strategy therefore seeks to remove any direct form of gender discrimination which leads to the unequal treatment of men and women. Each individual should have the same access to rights and opportunities and be treated according to the same principles and standards.

The strategy of inclusion has been important in EU policy. The origin of the principle of equal treatment goes back to article 119 in the European Economic Community Treaty of 1957 (later 141, now 157) on women's and men's rights to equal pay, originally introduced into the Treaty in reference to distortion of market competition. Here, gender equality was not a goal, but a means to reach fair competition in relation to principles of a free, competitive market and economic growth. Article 119 referred to women as paid *workers* and still provides a basis for the development of legislation for equal opportunities in the EU. Article 119 was nevertheless a principle without clear legal definition, nor did it come with any organizational capacity for action. In the 1970s, the Defrenne versus Sabena case (case nr 43/75) gave substance to the article, as the European Court of Justice held that the article was enforceable not merely between individuals and the government, but also between private parties (Hoskyns, 1996). The ruling set the principle of *direct effect*, and formed a basis for the Commission to establish a framework for supporting national harmonization of women in paid work. It also set a base of women as workers and the principle of equal treatment continued to be characterized as an economic issue. From this it follows that legislation on gender equality in relation to work is comprehensive, but with a strong focus on working life (Rees, 2006). Feminists have criticized this approach to gender equality, as it seeks to change society without really challenging the male norms or the existing patriarchal structures. The equal treatment approach stems from the basic principle of men and women as similar and the belief that if hindrances and distortions in society are removed and men and women are treated equally, then inequality will disappear accordingly.

If the strategy of inclusion focuses on men and women as similar, the *reversal strategy* instead addresses differences between men and women and focuses on equality of outcomes rather than equality of opportunities. The reversal strategy is based on a view of women as different from men and seeks recognition for the female identity by enhancing what is specific about women (Squires, 2008). Rees argues that the differences between men and women can be viewed as existing due to a complex range of social, historical and economic reasons that have led to unequal choices among, and access to, careers (Rees, 2006). Because men and women are different, it is necessary to overcome their unequal starting positions in the society with specific actions. The solution is therefore to address these differences by targeting women specifically in the form of positive discrimination, through which the share of women is increased by the use of positive actions or quotas (Rees, 2006). Reversal strategies promote policies that, through active processes, try to enhance equality as a response to the inequality and discrimination towards historically excluded groups – primarily women and minorities. Instead of equality of possibilities, as in the first strategy, the focus is on equality of outcomes. Problems with this strategy are that it risks overemphasizing gender differences and that it still operates under a male norm in society.

Reversal policies were played out in the 1980s and 1990s, as the EU gradually moved from inclusion strategies towards reversal approaches (Rees, 2006). A number of directives targeted, for example, structural discrimination against part-time workers (Directive 97/81/EC) and protection of health and safety for pregnant women and women breastfeeding (Directive 92/85/EEC). These measures aimed at facilitating the process for women to combine work with family life, clearly motivated by economic goals and the need to enlarge the workforce in a society experiencing the demographic changes of an aging population and decreasing birth rates (Calvo et al., 2009: 317). In addition to this, the European Court of Justice reaffirmed the rights of the member states to adopt positive actions. The inclusion of Justice and Home Affairs into the Maastricht Treaty also served to open up the possibility for the EU to act on violence against women. The agreement on social policy in the Maastricht Treaty confirmed the EU's orientation towards workers by including the wording of article 119. Together, all these initiatives made it possible for the EU to act beyond the narrow equal treatment approach of an inclusion strategy.

Both the strategy of inclusion and the strategy of reversal are grounded in liberal feminist philosophy (Lombardo, 2003). The third strategy of *displacement* is, however, different, as it problematizes the gendered world itself (Squires, 2008). This approach seeks to deconstruct the regimes that engender by deconstructing the category of being a woman (there is not one woman perspective but many) and by problematizing the gendered world itself. Existing structures and institutions are not viewed as gender-neutral, but as favoring one gender over another (usually men) in a variety of subtle and often invisible ways. Displacement strategies can be transformative, as they also address representation, decision making and private spheres of life, and they seek to tackle deeply rooted organizational cultures and practices within which inequalities are embedded (Rees, 2006). For displacement strategies, gender *mainstreaming* is put forward as a means for change (Squires, 2008), defined as "the (re)organisation, improvement, development, and evaluation of policy processes so that a gender equality perspective is incorporated in all policies and at all stages by the actors normally involved in policy-making" (Council of Europe, 1998).

Mainstreaming was adopted by the European Commission in 1996 as a way to reach gender equality (Pollack & Hafner-Burton, 2011). This is, however, a rather vague definition where gender mainstreaming can be many different things and it is unclear what type of strategy it supports (Squires, 2005). Rees (1998) describes gender strategies as development of gender equality taking place through stages. Many scholars agree that "adding women in" is a necessary first step towards gender equality (Squires, 2008: 17). In terms of practical application, Stratigaki (2005) has warned that the strategy of mainstreaming risks leading to a dilution of effort towards positive action. Rees (2005), on the other hand, argues that equal treatment and positive action measures need to continue to be developed alongside mainstream approaches and view the three approaches as "approaches to gender equality in their own right, but also as tools in the delivery of gender mainstreaming" (Rees, 2005: 560). In line with this, the approaches should be seen as complementary rather than exclusive (Booth & Bennet, 2002).

Equal treatment for workers has a strong legal base in the EU. However, other areas related to gender equality (for example, social policy, educational policy and research and development) have a weak legal basis in EU legislation wherein their roles are limited to the promotion of cooperation between member states and, when necessary, to support and supplement their efforts. In these areas, policy shaping takes place through the framework of the Open Method of Co-ordination (OMC). Mainstreaming of gender equality has given the EU the possibility to take action in a number of areas where they have no provisions in the treaties, such as in the area of *Domestic violence* and *Women in science* (Calvo et al., 2009). Here, mainstreaming has made it possible for the EU to move outside areas covered in the treaty. The EU had a leading role in promoting mainstreaming in the Beijing Platform in 1995 (Calvo et al., 2009: 319) where mainstreaming was defined and where all participating nations agreed to work to incorporate the gender perspective into all policy-making areas (Pollack & Hafner-Burton, 2011; Calvo et al., 2009).

IMPLEMENTING THE SUSTAINABLE DEVELOPMENT GOALS

Goal Setting and Global Governance

The SDGs hold an idea of global governance through goal setting. The non-binding nature of the goals, the reliance on weak institutional arrangements and the extensive leeway that states enjoy is a method that is new and innovative to the UN (Biermann et al., 2017). Goal setting seeks to steer behavior through establishing priorities, identifying targets and providing ways to measure fulfilment. Biermann et al. (2017) argue that the SDGs are different from previous attempts to achieve global change in four ways: 1) Global governance by goal setting is detached from the international legal system. They are not legally binding and there is no obligation for governments to transfer the goals into their own legal systems. 2) The goals are combined with weak institutional arrangements at the intergovernmental level. 3) The SDGs address both the industrialized world and developing countries and conceptually no country can be defined as developed in terms of sustainability. 4) Global governance through goal setting grants leeway for national preferences and many of the targets set are qualitative with room for governments to decide on the basis of their own ambition and freedom of interpretation.

As the goal-setting strategy does not rest on legal grounds, other ways are needed in order to bring about change. One such strategy is through *policy learning,* which refers to a structured process of exchange of experiences and ways of thinking about specific policy issues (Kemp & Weehuizen, 2005). The idea is to bring about changes in power structures by empowering key change agents and influencing how problems are conceptualized (Lehtonen, 2008). Important mechanisms in focus are *Peer Review* and *Network of Peers.* Peer reviews aim for mutual learning and improvement towards a best practice (Groenendijk, 2009) and take place through a systematic examination and assessment of performance with the aim of helping reviewed states to improve policymaking, adopt best practices and comply with established standards and principles (Pagani, 2002). Participation is voluntary and the result generally takes the form of a report where progress and shortfalls of the reviewed country are described, and recommendations are made (Pagani, 2002: 4). The effectiveness relies on a mechanism of peer pressure (OECD, 2019), not in the form of legally binding acts, but rather as a mechanism of soft persuasion that can encourage states to change, achieve goals and meet certain standards.

The Implementation Process

The SDGs hold the potential for a transformative agenda, but the implementation depends on the institutional arrangement to follow up and to hold authorities to account. In this way, the success of a goal-setting model will depend on the extent to which states formalize their implementation (Biermann et al., 2017). How this will take place is less clear. As stated by the UN Committee of Experts on Public Administration:

> There is no universal blueprint for implementing the Goals. Policy making and policy implementation will have to reflect specific national and local conditions, including the political environment. Ensuring participatory decision-making and consulting people is the way to arrive at the kind of policies that will succeed in implementing the Goals in a given society. (United Nations, 2017b: 3)

National ownership is viewed as key to development. The Agenda document (United Nations, 2015) describes how the follow-up and review processes are planned and the principles that will guide these processes. These include that the implementation process should be voluntary and country-led, taking into account different national realities, capacities and levels of development. Regular and inclusive reviews of progress at the subnational, national, regional and global levels will be conducted. These should use already existing networks of follow-up and reviews. UN member states are encouraged to develop national responses in order to implement the Agenda, building on already existing planning instruments (§78). They are also encouraged to "conduct regular and inclusive reviews of progress at the national and subnational levels which are country-led and country-driven" (§79). This also means that global review will be primarily based on national official data sources.

On the regional level, the importance is placed on peer learning as a way of implementing the goals, where follow-up and reviews can "provide useful opportunities for peer learning, including through voluntary reviews, sharing of best practices and discussion on shared targets" (§80).

Support will be provided by the UN regional commissions. An important role for follow-up and review is assigned to the *High Level Political Forum* (HLPF) under the General Assembly and the Economic and Social Council. HLPF is the main UN platform on sustainable development, whose role is to conduct regular reviews of the SDGs at the global level. The HLPF should be state-led and involve ministers and other high-level participants, providing a platform for partnership. A global indicator framework has been developed by the *Inter-Agency and Expert Group on Sustainable Development Goal Indicators* and agreed by the *Statistical Commission* and adopted by the Economic and Social Council and the General Assembly in 2016 (United Nations, 2016). The *Annual SDG Progress Report* (see §83) will inform the HLPF, based on the global indicator framework and data produced by national statistical systems and information collected at the regional level. The global indicators will be used to monitor the SDGs and the related targets and they will be complemented by indicators at the regional and national levels, developed by member states. National reviews are expected to serve as a basis for the regular reviews by the HLPF. In 2018, 46 countries presented voluntary national reviews, and since 2016, 111 reviews have been presented by 102 countries. In their reviews, countries describe, with varying degrees of formality, steps taken to incorporate the 2030 Agenda into national policies and plans. The reports are then synthesized by HLPF into an overall report examining the efforts, challenges and lessons learned of the reporting countries (HLPF, 2018).

In the area of gender equality, there are also a number of UN agencies with responsibilities to monitor and follow up the SDG process. UN-Women form a single UN body with the task of achieving gender equality and women's empowerment, including setting global standards for achieving gender equality, working with governments and civil society to design laws and policies and working to achieve the SDGs (UN-Women, 2017). Also involved is the Commission on the Status of Women, the principal global intergovernmental body exclusively dedicated to the promotion of gender equality and the empowerment of women. The Commission promotes women's rights by documenting women's lives throughout the world and shaping global standards on gender equality. In addition to this, the Commission also contributes to the follow-up of the SDGs to support gender equality and the empowerment of women.

EU IMPLEMENTATION OF SDGS

The role of the EU gender equality policy's relation to the SDG on gender equality can be analyzed by using theories of Europeanization which seek to understand the process in which supranational organization (e.g. the EU) institutions can influence member states or the other way around. The concept of Europeanization offers a framework for understanding how and why member states are affected by the EU or the UN. A *top-down approach* to Europeanization refers to how the EU shapes institutions, processes and political outcomes in member states or other countries by downloading EU policies to give rise to domestic change. A *bottom-up approach* analyzes how member states and other domestic actors shape EU policies, politics and polity by uploading their preferences to the EU institutions. A horizontal approach to Europeanization views member states' change as the result of a bi-directional process where member states also shape EU policies and institutions by "uploading" their own policies and institutions to the European level and then adapt to outcomes made at the EU level by "downloading" EU policies and institutions into the domestic arena. Radaelli et al. (2006: 62) argue that states can export their domestic policies via "uploading" them to the EU in order to have them "downloaded" elsewhere. In this way, member states are not passive followers of EU demands on domestic change; instead, they act to shape EU policies, institutions and processes which they later have to adapt.

In the EU, the overall responsibility for the implementation of the 2030 Agenda and its SDGs is at the national level. From this it follows that the impact of the 2030 Agenda depends on the extent to which states successfully formulate national measures to translate the SDGs and their targets into concrete action. In many of the policy areas related to Agenda 2030, the EU can only support, coordinate and complement member states' policies or it has a shared responsibility with the member states. The treaties lack provisions in most of the areas that relate to gender targets in the agenda. An exception is equal treatment related to working life. Hence, gender equality has been explicitly pointed out as an area for which the use of soft tools is needed in order to push for the development of gender equality and work against discrimination (European Commission, 2010a: 15).

In EU policy, learning forms an important part of the OMC process, where "Mutual learning processes" are a central part. In this process, the domestic politicians and civil servants are central actors. Traditional policymaking patterns have since 2000 increasingly been complemented by the use of "soft" governance tools allowing for member states to coordinate policy without removing formal power, as member states are responsible for their compliancy to the measures they have agreed to on the EU level. This model of OMC has developed as a compromise, as it retains member state responsibility for an area while giving the EU a coordinating and policy-shaping role (Warleigh-Lack & Drachenberg, 2011: 207). The process was launched as part of the package from the Lisbon meeting of 2000 together with the European Employment Strategy (European Council, 2000). The OMC represents a voluntary and intergovernmental mode of cooperation. The Commission plays a monitoring and agenda-setting role. The Council of Ministers then sets the policy goals and guidelines by unanimity and member states submit annual reports on their progress and these reports are commented on and evaluated by the Commission. The OMC is applied in areas where the national situation differs substantially or where only limited competences exist on the EU level, which is the case in the area of gender equality, but also in areas such as employment policy, social policy, education policy and research and development. The Commission draws up a report on progress made towards the objectives that are set both at the EU level and within the member states. The progress and fulfilment of the targets set up are evaluated in national reports. These reports also form bases for mutual learning processes, during which officials and stakeholder representatives meet during conferences and workshops in order to represent and discuss important issues and progress.

The lack of a strategy for implementation of the SDGs has been criticized by the European Parliament and other non-governmental actors (European Parliament, 2019b; Deshayes, 2019). A report from the European Parliament recommended that the Commission develop a comprehensive post-2020 SDG implementation strategy, integrate the SDGs in the EU's economic monitoring (European Semester) and budgeting processes and scale up the use of peer-learning mechanisms at all levels of governance. The SDG Watch Europe, a civil society alliance of 90 European non-governmental organizations, has criticized the EU strategy for not engaging with the individual SDGs and targets. Thus, there is so far no coherent European framework for the implementation of the 2030 Agenda. Although there is a lack of strategy on the EU level, an overview done by the European Parliament showed that a majority of countries have or are about to update their National Development Plan with the SDGs, and that in around half of the countries these strategies are actually operational (European Parliament, 2019b: 8).

The EU has, however, stated its ambition to coordinate and support the national implementation processes in the European countries. In November 2016, the European Commission presented its strategy for a sustainable European future, which set out key European actions supporting the 2030 Agenda goals (European Commission, 2016b). The document is mainly an overview of existing policy and its linkage to the SDGs, but points out no new actions. The strategy summarizes the main action being undertaken by the EU for each of the goals. In the section on gender equality, it is stated that the most important priorities contributing to the goal on gender equality are justice and fundamental rights, a stronger global actor and a union of democratic change (European Commission, 2016b: 21).

The key actions mentioned in the document that further address gender equality internally are more limited. Focus is on female participation in working life and the need "to better utilise female talent and improve the participation of women in the labour market" (European Commission, 2016a: 21). The EU will continue its work based on equal treatment legislation and gender mainstreaming (integration of the gender perspective into all other policies). The document focuses more on achieved improvements and less on new developments. One new measure presented was an initiative to address the challenges of work–life balance, resulting in a new directive in June 2019 which introduced a set of legislative actions in order to modernize the existing EU legal and policy frameworks, with the aims of better supporting a work–life balance for parents and carers and encouraging a more equal sharing of parental leave between men and women (Directive 2019/1158).

Since 2017, the SDGs have been monitored by Eurostat. Reports are based on a set of indicators considered relevant for an EU context. In the area of gender equality, the EU focuses on four topics: gender-based violence, education, employment and leadership positions (Eurostat, 2019).

The current EU policy on gender equality has been detailed in a number of documents, the most important being the *Strategy for Equality between Women and Men* (2010–15) (European Commission, 2010b), which provided a framework for gender equality combining specific measures with an equality perspective into all EU policies, and the *European Pact for Gender Equality* (European Commission, 2011), which emphasized the importance of using women as a potential recruitment pool and the need to remove obstacles to women's participation in the labor market. Both the Strategy and the Pact emphasized the contribution made by equality to economic growth and sustainable development but lacked an accompanying earmarked budget (Crepaldi et al., 2015). After 2020, there is no existing strategic plan for gender equality. In 2015, the Commission was clearly reluctant to adopt a new strategy (Pimminger, 2015) and instead finally issued *Strategic Engagement for Gender Equality 2016–2019,* focusing on five prioritized key areas for action: equal economic independence for women and men; equal pay for work of equal value; equality in decision making; dignity, integrity and ending gender-based violence; and the promotion of gender equality beyond the EU (European Commission, 2015). Unlike the former strategy, this document is not a Communication to the European Parliament and the Council, but instead a low-status internal document without binding provisions or requests for member state commitments (Hubert and Stratigaki, 2016). The focus is primarily on gender equality as necessary for meeting the target set in Europe 2020 to reduce unemployment (§ 4–7). The first point set out to "close the gender gaps in employment and social protection, including the gender pay gap, with a view to meeting the objectives of the Europe 2020 Strategy, especially in three areas of great relevance to gender equality, namely employment, education and promoting social inclusion in particular through the reduction of poverty, thus contributing to the growth potential of the European labour force" (European Council, 2011).

The Commission seeks to improve gender equality by increasing female labor market participation, reducing the gender pay, earnings and pension gaps and thus fighting poverty among women, promoting equality between women and men in decision making and combating gender-based violence and protecting and supporting victims. It is further described how gender is addressed in country-specific recommendations that form a part of the European semester (the annual EU cycle of economic and budgetary coordination) and that gender equality on the EU level is monitored in the Annual Reports and included in the cohesion policy and funding programs.

Enhancing women's labor market participation was presented under the Europe 2020 strategy (European Commission, 2011) as a way to reach the target of lifting 20 million people out of poverty or social exclusion and achieving a 75 percent employment rate. Women's inactivity in the labor market is explained by a number of factors, such as the availability of jobs on offer, taxation systems based on a model of a single-earner family and the availability and affordability of care facilities. An important focus is placed on accessible and affordable childcare, which supports mothers' labor market participation (Plantega & Remery, 2015). Follow-ups show that gender equality in the EU has improved in terms of leadership positions and participation of women in the labor market. The share of women who are inactive due to caring responsibilities has, however, grown, and in terms of education, progress towards gender equality has been mixed. Men are more likely to leave education early and the increase in participation in higher education is stronger for women. Although more women than men have completed tertiary education, the employment rate of female graduates is lower and male graduates are more likely to have found employment than their female counterparts (Eurostat, 2019). The present decade has, however, also witnessed a visible drive against gender equality and the women's human rights agenda across continents (European Parliament, 2018). Looking at the EU, the Gender Equality Index shows persistent inequalities with only marginal progress from 2005 to 2015. The implementation of EU equality laws and policies, as well as the effectiveness of gender mainstreaming within EU institutions and within member states, remain very uneven in Europe (European Parliament, 2019b). Analysis of selected EU member states has revealed that a backlash against gender equality and women's rights has occurred in the last few years (European Parliament, 2018).

CRITIQUE AGAINST EU GENDER EQUALITY POLICY

In spite of the positive figures on the development of gender equality presented by the Commission (European Commission, 2015), the gender equality policy of the EU has been criticized by the European Parliament, by the European Women's Lobby and by a number of feminist scholars (European Parliament, 2019a). The European Women's Lobby has criticized the lack of commitment to equality between women and men in the negotiations of the future budget of Europe and called for the inclusion of equality between women and men as a horizontal key priority in the multiannual financial framework 2021–27, and the inclusion of a gender mainstreaming clause in the Common Provisions for the funds. They state that:

> equality between women and men is no longer a visible horizontal provision for the future EU budget and subsequently will not be a priority for the spending period post 2020. The dilution of gender equality into other priorities is an indication that equality between women and men has lost its importance on the EU agenda. Women represent half of the population and while some progress has been made to achieve equality between women and men, gender equality is still not a reality in the EU and beyond. (European Women's Lobby, 2018)

Joanna Maycock, secretary general of the European Women's Lobby, argued that the progress towards gender equality has stalled, leaving women facing significant and enduring barriers in many aspects of life including health, safety, education, employment, work–life balance, power and economics. The 2015 EIGE Gender Equality Index shows that the process of reducing inequality between women and men has stopped (European Women's Lobby, 2018). Jacquot (2017) argues that the European policy of gender equality has been gradually dismantled since the Europe 2020 strategy in 2010. From being forced by legal and financial instruments, the gradual change towards soft law and mainstreaming has meant a reduction of funding, and legislative initiatives, and a weakening of different institutional structures. As a paradox, the gradual dismantling of the gender equality policy has run parallel with an even stronger affirmation of the importance of gender equality as a fundamental value of the EU (Jacquot, 2017).

The "business case" for gender equality, which refers to the underlying arguments or rationales regarding why stakeholders should support gender equality, has been criticized by several scholars (Özbilgin & Ahu Tatli, 2011; Perriton, 2009; Bowles & McGinn, 2008). The strong focus in the EU on gender equality as employment policy has been criticized. The European Women's Lobby argues that the wording of the Pact, which states that gender equality policies are "vital to economic growth, prosperity and competitiveness", has led to a narrowed-down approach to women's rights and gender equality in the economic area, where the main focus has been on increasing women's employment in quantitative terms. Although the economic perspective is important, gender equality fails to be put in a framework of human rights, which is at the core of European values (European Women's Lobby, 2019). The European Women's Lobby's recommendation for the European Commission on how the gender perspective could be strengthened in future country reports on the SGDs states that gender equality needs to go beyond increasing female participation in the labor market. The European Women's Lobby calls for the use of gender mainstreaming and gender budgeting throughout the European semester and for it to take into account the multiple types of discrimination and inequalities that women face (European Women's Lobby, 2019).

CONCLUSION

The EU and UN have similar perspectives on gender equality, which are based on a rhetorically strong argument for a rights-based approach, but which in practice include a more functional approach where gender equality is viewed as a means for growth and prosperity. The preamble of the Agenda 2030 document is strongly framed in human rights terms, as the SDGs seek to "achieve gender equality and the empowerment of all women and girls" (United Nations, 2015). The signing of the Agenda by the member states brings the possibility of morally holding governments to account for development in this area. However, although the human rights framing is prominent in the preamble, the targets and associated monitoring indicators are not framed as rights and implementation is in practice voluntary for the member states. Also, the EU places a strong emphasis on gender equality as a human right (article 2 TEU) and the Commission stresses that gender equality is one of the fundamental values of the EU, firmly established in the acquis communautaire.

The EU has been an important uploader of gender equality policy to the global level. Compared to many other countries, EU policy in the area of gender equality is far-reaching and developed. The influence of the SDGs on the EU is less evident. SDG targets will be implemented in the EU as a part of the gender equality policy already pursued and the EU has a comparative advanced position on gender equality policy and is an uploader of gender equality policy rather than a downloader. The SDGs on gender equality create a possibility for the EU to act as a role model which emphasizes its far-reaching efforts in the area, while at the same time facing critique for lack of strategy and implementation in the form of budgeting.

EU and UN gender equality policies are both examples of a paradox wherein the strengthening of gender equality as a fundamental right rhetorically is followed by a weakening of the instruments that are supposed to carry through change. The rights-based approach and the focus on gender equality as a fundamental human right would traditionally be expected to be related to a policy instrument of authority such as regulation and legislation. The process of implementation for the SDGs suggested by the UN instead emphasizes policy instruments for soft policy: learning instruments in the form of peer networks and peer review. In this way, goal number 5 is an example of a rights-based approach without legal provisions.

The UN is clearly adopting the approach successfully used by the EU in soft policy areas, such as education and employment. But in the EU, gender equality policy rests on two legs: legislation and soft policy, and the most influential part consists of rules and regulations in the area of working life, with strong legal provisions. This is a primary reason for success and has led to a number of directives in the area of gender equality. The influence of the second part, consisting of soft policy, is less evident, which raises the question of how far gender equality can reach based only on soft policy instruments and without any legal base. Although gender equality is described as an important value that everyone agrees on, previous research shows that when colliding with other core values, gender equality is often forced to yield, as other beliefs are considered more important (Skjeie & Teigen, 2003). In the European context, scholars agree that inclusion policies with strong legal anti-discrimination legislation and regulation in the form of binding directives were a necessary base for advancing the area of gender equality. On the global level, this is in part lacking, and without such a base it is likely to be difficult to influence gender equality and mainstreaming.

The key to success might be found in the strategy of gender equality as an economic means. The strategy of gender equality pushed by the UN and the EU is a strategy of using the economic argument in order to convince stakeholders and member states that gender equality is related to economic benefits. Both the UN and the European Commission argue that gender equality contributes to economic growth and this is presented as an innovative way to promote gender equality. The global goals represent a comprehensive attempt to strive for global gender equality, but they do not suggest any far-reaching economic change; they are instead in line with a neoliberalist perspective. The innovative strategy of using economic arguments for supporting moral issues has been used successfully by political entrepreneurs before in history, such as the abolition of slavery in the United States (Woods, 2012) and the support of corporate social responsibility (European Commission, 2001). There is, however, a risk that the economic case will prevent criticism and limit the scope of gender equality, leading to a narrowed-down approach to women's rights and gender equality in the economic area, where the main focus is to increase women's employment in quantitative terms.

REFERENCES

Bidegain Ponte, N., & Enríquez, C. R. (2016). Agenda 2030: A Bold Enough Framework towards Sustainable, Gender-Just Development? *Gender and Development, 24*(1): 83–98.

Biermann, F., Kanie, N., & Kim, R. E. (2017). Global Governance by Goal-Setting: The Novel Approach of the UN Sustainable Development Goals. *Current Opinion in Environmental Sustainability, 26*: 26–31.

Booth, C., & Bennet, C. (2002). Towards a New Conception and Practice of Equal Opportunities? *European Journal of Women's Studies, 9*(4): 430–46.

Bowles, H.R., & McGinn, K.L. (2008). Untapped Potential in the Study of Negotiation and Gender Inequality in Organizations, *Academy of Management Annals,* 10.5465/ 19416520802211453, *2*(1): 99–132.

Calvo, D., Burns, T. R., & Carson, M. (2009). Toward a New Social Order? Mainstreaming Gender Equality in EU Policymaking. www.researchgate.net/ publication/272488200_Toward_a_new_social_order_mainstreaming_gender_equa lity_in_EU_policymaking

Council Directive 2019/1158 on Work–Life Balance for Parents and Carers.

Council Directive 92/85/EEC on the Introduction of Measures to Encourage Improvements in the Safety and Health at Work of Pregnant Workers and Workers Who Have Recently Given Birth or Are Breastfeeding.

Council Directive 97/81/EC of 15 December 1997 concerning the Framework Agreement on Part-Time Work.

Council of Europe (1998). Gender Mainstreaming, Conceptual Frameworks, Methodology and Presentation of Good Practices, Final Report of Activities of the Group of Specialists on Mainstreaming, Strasbourg, Council of Europe.

Crepaldi, C., Loi, D., Pesce, F., & Samek, M. (2015). Evaluation of the Strengths and Weaknesses of the Strategy for Equality between Women and Men 2010–2015, Research Paper, Brussels: European Commission.

Cuberes, D., & Teignier-Baqué, M. (2011). Gender Inequality and Economic Growth, Background Paper, World Bank.

Deshayes, M. (2019). Equality between Women and Men in the EU: Transforming European Political and Decision-Making Institutions. In SDG Watch Europe (ed.), *Falling through the Cracks, Exposing Inequalities in the EU and Beyond.* Luxembourg: SDG Watch Europe.

Esquivel, Valeria (2016). Power and the Sustainable Development Goals: A Feminist Analysis, *Gender and Development*, *24*(1): 9–23.

European Commission (2001). Promoting a European Framework for Corporate Social Reasonability, Green Paper, Luxembourg, Office for Official Publications of the European Communities.

European Commission (2010a). An Agenda for New Skills and Jobs: A European Contribution towards Full Employment, Strasbourg, November 23, COM (2010) 682 final.

European Commission (2010b). Strategy for Equality between Women and Men 2010–2015, Brussels, September 21, COM(2010) 491 final.

European Commission (2011). *Gender Equality between Women and Men 2010–2015.* Luxembourg: Publications Office of the European Union.

European Commission (2015). *Strategic Engagement for Gender Equality 2016–2019.* Luxembourg: Publications Office of the European Union.

European Commission (2016a). Next Steps for a Sustainable European Future. European Action for Sustainability, Strasbourg, November 22, COM(2016) 739 final.

European Commission (2016b). Key European Action Supporting the 2030 Agenda and the Sustainable Development Goals. COM(2016) 739 final.

European Council (2000). European Council Meeting in Lisbon, 23 and 24 March 2000: Conclusions.

European Council (2011). The European Pact for Gender Equality 2011–2020 (2011/C 155/02).

European Court of Justice (1976). Case 43/75, Defrenne v Sabena [1976] ECR 455.

European Parliament (2018). Backlash in Gender Equality and Women's and Girls' Rights. Policy Department for Citizens' Rights and Constitutional Affairs Directorate General for Internal Policies of the Union. PE 604.955.

European Parliament (2019a). Promoting Equality between Women and Men. Briefing, EU policies – Delivering for Citizens. PE 628.272 – June.

European Parliament (2019b). Europe's Approach to Implementing the Sustainable Development Goals: Good Practices and the Way Forward. Directorate General for External Policies.

European Union (1992). *Treaty on European Union (Consolidated Version), Treaty of Maastricht* , February 7, Official Journal of the European Communities C 325/5; December 24, 2002.

European Women's Lobby (2018). Press Statement Call to Put Gender Equality at the Heart of the Future Budget of the EU. Brussels, December 12.

European Women's Lobby (2019). Women for Europe, Europe for Women: A New Kind of Leadership for the 21st Century. European Women's Lobby Manifesto for the 2019 European Elections.

Eurostat (2019). Sustainable Development in the European Union, Monitoring Report on Progress towards the SDGs in an EU Context.

Fukuda-Parr, S. (2016). From the Millennium Development Goals to the Sustainable Development Goals: Shifts in Purpose, Concept, and Politics of Global Goal Setting for Development. *Gender and Development*, *24*(1): 43–52.

Fukuda-Parr, S., & Hulme, D. (2011). International Norm Dynamics and the "End of Poverty": Understanding the Millennium Development Goals, *Global Governance*, *17*(1): 17–36.

Groenendijk, N. (2009). EU and OECD Benchmarking and Peer Review Compared. Paper presented at Third EUCE Annual Conference: The EU in a Comparative Perspective. Union Centre of Excellence, Dalhousie University, Halifax, NS, Canada, April 26–28.

Gupta, J., & Vegelin, C. (2016). Sustainable Development Goals and Inclusive Development. *International Environmental Agreements: Politics, Law and Economics, 16*(3): 433–48.

Harcourt, W. (2005). The Millennium Development Goals: A Missed Opportunity? *Development, 48*(1), 1–4.

High Level Political Forum on Sustainable Development (HLPF) (2018). Voluntary National Reviews Synthesis Report 2018. Department of Economic and Social Affairs United Nations.

Hix, S. (2005). *The Political System of the European Union.* London: Palgrave Macmillan.

Hoskyns, C. (1996). *Integrating Gender: Women, Law and Politics in the European Union.* London: Verso.

Hubert, A., & Stratigaki, M. (2016). Twenty Years of EU Gender Mainstreaming: Rebirth out of the Ashes? *Femina Politica, 2*: 21–36.

Hyman, R. (2008). Britain and the European Social Model: Capitalism against Capitalism. London School of Economics: Institute for Employment Studies. IES Working Paper: WP19.

Jacquot, S. (2017). European Union Gender Equality Policies since 1957, Encyclopédie pour une histoire nouvelle de l'Europe. https://ehne.fr/en/article/gender-and-europe/gender-citizenship-europe/european-union-gender-equality-policies-1957

Kabeer, N., & Natali, L. (2013). Gender Equality and Economic Growth: Is There a Win-Win? *IDS Working Papers, 417*: 1–58.

Kemp, R., & Weehuizen, R. (2005). Policy Learning, What Does It Mean and How Can We Study It? Oslo: NIFU STEP.

Lehtonen, M. (2008). Mainstreaming Sustainable Development in the OECD through Indicators and Peer Reviews. *Sustainable Development, 16*(4): 241–50.

Lombardo, E. (2003). EU Gender Policy: Trapped in the Wollstonecraft Dilemma? *European Journal of Women's Studies, 10*(2): 159–80.

Maceira, H.M. (2017). Economic Benefits of Gender Equality in the EU. *Intereconomics, 52*(3): 178–83.

OECD (2012). World Development Report 2012: Closing the Gender Gap: Act Now. Paris: OECD Publishing.

OECD (2019). Peer Pressure: A Related Concept. www.oecd.org/site/peerreview/peerpressurearelatedconcept.htm

Office of the High Commissioner for Human Rights (OHCHR) (2008). *Claiming the Millennium Development Goals,* Geneva: OHCHR.

Özbilgin, M., & Tatli, A. (2011). Mapping Out the Field of Equality and Diversity: Rise of Individualism and Voluntarism, *Human Relations, 64*(9): 1229–53.

Pagani, F. (2002). Peer Review: A Tool for Co-operation and Change. An Analysis of an OECD Working Method. OECD, SG/LEG(2002)1.

Perriton, L. (2009). We Don't Want Complaining Women! A Critical Analysis of the Business Case for Diversity, *Management Communication Quarterly, 10*(1177).

Pimminger, I. (2015). *A Quiet Farewell? Current Developments in EU Gender Equality Policy, Perspective,* Berlin: Friedrich-Ebert-Stiftung.

Plantega J., & Remery C. (2015). The Provision of Childcare Facilities: A Comparative Review of 30 European Countries, 2009; Ylenia Brilli, Daniela Del Boca, and

Chiara Daniela Pronzato, Does Child Care Availability Play a Role in Maternal Employment and Children's Development? *Evidence from Italy, Families and Society*, working paper series, *31*.

Pollack, M.A., & Hafner-Burton, E. (2011). Mainstreaming Gender in the European Union, *Journal of European Public Policy*, 7(3): 432–56.

Radaelli, C.M. (2006). Europeanization: Solution or Problem?. In *Palgrave Advances in European Union Studies* (pp. 56–76). London: Palgrave Macmillan.

Razavi, S. (2016). The 2030 Agenda: Challenges of Implementation to Attain Gender Equality and Women's Rights. *Gender and Development, 24*(1): 25–41.

Rees, T. (1998). *Mainstreaming Equality in the European Union, Education, Training and Labour Market Policies.* London: Routledge.

Rees, T. (2005). Reflections on the Uneven Development of Gender Mainstreaming in Europe. *International Journal of Feminist Politics*, 7(4): 555–74.

Rees, T. (2006). *Mainstreaming Equality in the European Union.* London: Routledge.

Rossilli, M.G. (1999). The European Union's Policy on the Equality of Women. *Feminist Studies, 25*(1): 171–81.

Skjeie, H., & Teigen, M. (2003). *Menn imellom.* Oslo: Gyldendal.

Squires, J. (2005). Is Mainstreaming Transformative? Theorizing Mainstreaming in the Context of Diversity and Deliberation. *Social Politics: International Studies in Gender, State and Society, 12*(3): 366–88.

Squires, J. (2008). *Gender in Political Theory.* Cambridge: Polity Press.

Stratigaki, M. (2005). Gender Mainstreaming vs Positive Action: An Ongoing Conflict in EU Gender Equality Policy. *European Journal of Women's Studies, 12*(2): 165–86.

Stuart, E., & Woodroffe, J. (2016). Leaving No-One Behind: Can the Sustainable Development Goals Succeed Where the Millennium Development Goals Lacked? *Gender and Development, 24*(1): 69–81.

United Nations (2015). United Nations General Assembly: Transforming Our World: The 2030 Agenda for Sustainable Development. UN Doc. A/70/L.1 of September 18.

United Nations (2016). Final List of Proposed Sustainable Development Goal Indicators, Report of the Inter-Agency and Expert Group on Sustainable Development Goal Indicators (E/CN.3/2016/2/Rev.1).

United Nations (2017a). Report of the Committee of Experts on Public Administration on Its Sixteenth Session 2017/23 [on the Recommendation of Committee of Experts on Public Administration (E/2017/44)].

United Nations (2017b). Report on the Sixteenth Session (24–28 April 2017) of the United Nations Committee of Experts on Public Administration (CEPA). New York: United Nations.

United Nations (2018). Why Equality Matters. www.un.org/sustainabledevelopment

UN-Women (2017). United Nations Entity for Gender Equality and the Empowerment of Women. Strategic Plan 2018–2021. UNW/2017/6/Rev.1.

Utting, P. (2013). Pathways to Sustainability in a Crisis-Ridden World, in Rémi Genevey, R.K. Pachauri, and Laurence Tubiana (eds), *Reducing Inequalities: A Sustainable Development Challenge*, New Delhi: Energy and Resources Institute, pp. 175–90.

Verloo, M.M.T., & Lombardo, E. (2007). *Contested Gender Equality and Policy Variety in Europe: Introducing a Critical Frame Analysis Approach.* Budapest: CEU Press.

Walby, S. (1999). The European Union and Equal Opportunities Policies. *European Societies*, *1*(1): 59–80.

Warleigh-Lack, A., & Drachenberg, R. (2011). Spillover in a Soft Policy Area? Evidence from the Open Method of Co-ordination in Education and Training. *Journal of European Public Policy*, *18*(7): 999–1015.

Woods, M. (2012). What Twenty-First-Century Historians Have Said about the Causes of Disunion: A Civil War Sesquicentennial Review of the Recent Literature. *Journal of American History*, *99*(2): 415–39. www.un.org/en/sections/issues-depth/gender-equality/

Young, B. (2000). Disciplinary Neoliberalism in the European Union and Gender Politics, *New Political Economy*, *5*(1): 77–98.

5.   Agenda 2030 and the EU on migration and integration

Anna Parkhouse

Migration is a global phenomenon that recently has developed into becoming high politics and a political priority for international organisations and member states alike. The increasing migration inflows, having become the "new normal" in the new global disorder (Parkes, 2016), in parallel to a looming demographic crisis[1] in the states at the receiving end, has contributed to strengthen the interdependence between migration and integration. Indeed, with an ageing population in parallel to a declining working population, the importance of how to more effectively use the skills and competences of migrants and refugees in labour markets, increasingly characterised by labour shortages, has become key, both for inclusive growth but also for the sake of social cohesion. At the same time, the migration exodus has brought up the problem of *brain drain* in the countries of origin which has led developed countries to formulate more effective policies on return with the aim of mitigating the loss of competence in the developing countries. Migration is politically sensitive to the extent that it is strongly associated with issues pertaining to national sovereignty involving questions about asylum, citizenship and human rights, i.e. who is entitled to live, work and use the states' welfare systems. In the political arenas (globally, nationally and on the subnational levels), migration has become one of the most decisive and divisive issues. This, in turn, has contributed to a polarisation in the migration debate, centred on the issue whether the migratory influx should be seen as a threat[2] to the survival of the European welfare state, or rather, based on the demographic crisis argument, as a prerequisite for its survival.

Migration as part of the Sustainable Development Goals (SDGs) was first acknowledged in the United Nations (UN) in 2013. Migration and integration-related targets were integrated in the 2030 Agenda on SDGs, adopted by the UN General Assembly in September 2015 (UNGA, 2015). Apart from UN agencies, the European Union (EU) has been a forerunner in the 2030 Agenda in general, both concerning reflections on the shaping and the implementation of the SDGs. In the following, we investigate the potential role of EU political entrepreneurship in facilitating the orderly and safe migration and mobility of people as well as promoting more effective socio-economic inclusion of migrants, specifically focusing on labour market integration. By adhering to the definition used in the book, a political entrepreneur is someone who "operates beyond traditional and routinized procedures and is innovative and creative in using formal and informal institutions and networks to improve the public sector's activities towards entrepreneurs and entrepreneurship by developing and promoting new norms that have not been embedded in traditional day-to-day public activities" (see Chapter 4). After an overview of the UN Agenda 2030 and the SDGs pertaining to migration and integration, we move on to analyse the role of the EU as a political entrepreneur in implementing more sustainable migration and integration in the EU. The chapter concludes with discussing the results and providing some policy advice for the future.

AGENDA 2030 ON MIGRATION AND INTEGRATION

Although the sustainability perspective is currently at centre stage of the international migration nexus, this was not the case previously, as attested by the fact that international migration did not figure in the Millennium Development Goals. In 2006, however, and with the establishment of the High-Level Dialogue on International Migration and Development, convened by the UN General Assembly, this platform paved the way for a more systematic take on international migration. This meant the establishment of an inter-agency group whose task it was to promote the application of international norms and instruments, "for increasing system-wide coherence, and for strengthening the response of the UN system and the international community to the opportunities and challenges presented by international migration" (UNGA, 2015). Since 2007, and the establishment of the Global Forum on Migration and Development, the annual meetings of the high-level platform have served as a platform for informal dialogue and cooperation on matters related to international migration, such as rights of migrants, climate change and its impact on migration and forced migration. It was only in 2013 that migration was acknowledged as part of the SDGs. At the second High-Level Dialogue on Migration and Development, the General Assembly of the UN adopted a declaration acknowledging that the role of migration is a key factor for sustainable development. In September 2015, the 2030 Agenda on SDGs was adopted by the UN General Assembly (UNGA, 2015).

In 2017, approximately 258 million people, representing 3.4 per cent of the world's population, were international migrants (UN DESA, 2017). During 1990–2017,[3] the number of international migrants increased by 105 million (69 per cent). Even though the migration routes are still predominantly moving from the developing regions of the South to the developed regions of the

North,[4] especially since 2010,[5] international migrants are increasingly moving in the direction of the developing regions of the South. At the same time it should be underlined that the increase of international migrants in the countries of the Northern Hemisphere has been considerable since their share currently makes up 11.6 per cent of the total population in these countries (UN DESA, 2017). This increase has contributed to diminish the unequal distribution of resources and opportunities between the developed and the developing worlds. Indeed, in 2017, the flow of remittances, i.e. migrants sending money home to their countries of origin, amounted to approximately 450 billion US dollars. Even though the remittances are private and constitute a major part of families' total income in the countries of origin, at the same time they help societies develop by generating jobs and transforming economies, notably in the rural areas. The remittances account for more than three times the amount of official development assistance and foreign direct investment combined (IOM, 2019).

There is no universally agreed-upon definition of a migrant but the International Organization for Migration (IOM) defines a migrant as "any person who is moving or has moved across an international border or within a State away from his/her habitual place of residence regardless of a) the person's legal status; b) whether the movement is voluntary or involuntary; c) what the causes for the movement are; and d) what the length of the stay is" (IOM, 2018: 13). For statistical purposes, the IOM defines an international migrant as "a person who changes his or her country of usual residence" (IOM, 2018: 13). In terms of legal status, whereas refugees enjoy legal protection,[6] international migrants and asylum seekers are unprotected and arrive in the host country as illegal immigrants or as displaced persons who seek asylum upon entry to the host country. When an asylum seeker is approved asylum, the status of the asylum seeker changes into that of a refugee (Constant & Zimmermann, 2016: 3). However, with increasing and more complex migratory movements in parallel to demands for more effective integration, the distinction between the categories is becoming less relevant, paving the way for the term "mixed migration" (Lulle & King, 2016: 23). Although the scale and pace of international migration is difficult to predict, the triggers of migration, i.e. conflict, human rights violations, climate change and demographic developments, in parallel with the technological advancements facilitating migration, indicate that the number of international migrants is likely to continue to increase (IOM, 2019: 2). Thus, whereas migration is a global process and a global challenge that would necessitate global governance, at the same time it is blatant that the decision making within the realm of migration, and particularly integration, falls under the competence of member state authorities.

Of the 17 SDGs and their accompanying 169 targets,[7] the migration-related goals are integrated into the Agenda 2030 in three different ways. First, there is the *migration-specific* target (10.7), which emphasises that countries should "facilitate orderly, safe, regular and responsible migration and mobility of people, including through the implementation of planned and well-managed migration policies" (UNGA, 2015). Second, there are a number of *migration-related* targets, which deal with measures to mitigate the brain drain of the countries of origin (3c); to increase the number of scholarships for study abroad (4b); to eradicate human trafficking (5.2, 8.7, 16.2); to protect the labour rights for migrant workers, and especially for migrant women (8.8); to reduce the transaction costs of remittances (10c) and, last, to strengthen the provision for legal identity, including through birth registrations (16.9). Third, the *disaggregation by migratory status* aims to strengthen and facilitate the comparative assessment and analysis of the outcomes of the migratory goals for the foreign-born population, compared to the native-born population (17.18). In contrast to other international regimes, the international framework of the 2030 Agenda is not legally binding to the signatory states. The lack of rules and compliance mechanisms subsequently leave considerable leeway for implementation on the part of the signatory states. To address this apparent weakness, the Addis Ababa Action Agenda was adopted on 15 July 2015. The Action Agenda is broader than the 2030 Agenda at the same time as it is an action programme, zooming in on the actions necessary to implement the SDGs. The Action Agenda calls on the member states to ensure that "migration is governed with full respect for human rights, to combat xenophobia, and to facilitate migrant integration through education of migrant and refugee children and through social communication strategies" (UNGA, 2015). Even though there is still no specific UN agency that is responsible for migration issues, the IOM[8] has been recognised as the global lead agency on migration. A number of other international organisations and agencies as well as member states and their subnational levels are however crucial for effective implementation. Furthermore, the importance of reaching policy coherence and more effective interlinkages between different policy areas, such as development policy, trade policy, foreign and security policy and asylum policy, are a precondition for the successful implementation of the SDGs. In fact, the 2030 Agenda has been named a "declaration of interdependence" which is specifically emphasised in target 17.14, which calls for pursuing "policy coherence and an enabling environment for sustainable development at all levels and by all actors" (IOM, 2018). Indeed, effective implementation is challenged by the fact that although migration is a global process, migration governance and integration involve multilevel governance, where decisions are made not only within the realm of member state authority but where achievement of the SDGs will depend on how effectively the goals are implemented at subnational levels, such as the regional and local levels (EC, 2019a). In the following, we investigate the potential role of EU political entrepreneurship in facilitating the orderly and safe migration and mobility of people as well as promoting more effective socio-economic inclusion of migrants, specifically focusing on labour market integration.

EU POLITICAL ENTREPRENEURSHIP ON MIGRATION AND INTEGRATION IN EUROPE

The migration crisis of 2015, in parallel to an escalating demographic crisis, would contribute to strengthening the link between migration and integration in the EU. Already in 2010 inclusive growth as "fostering a high employment economy delivering social and territorial cohesion" (EC 2010: 3) was one of the mutually reinforcing priorities of the Europe 2020 strategy. During the mandate period of the Juncker Commission (2014–19), sustainability, including inclusiveness, have been cornerstones of the Agenda and the EU and its member states have been instrumental in the shaping of the 2030 Agenda for Sustainable Development (EC 2019a).

The overarching goal of SDG 10 is the reduction of inequalities. In the EU context, this goal addresses the reduction of inequalities within the EU member states, between countries, and focuses on the area of migration and social inclusion. The more migration-specific target centres on the inequalities between countries and calls for "the facilitation of orderly and safe migration and mobility of people" (SDSN & IEEP, 2019: 199). Since global inequality is expected to lead to increased migration, the Commission is careful to point out the need for more sustainable migration management. This would in turn necessitate the convergence and coherence in-between different policy areas, such as trade and investment policy, foreign and security policy, development policy and the enlargement policy, where all perspectives would "contribute to tackling the causes of inequality outside Europe" (EC, 2019a: 95). SDG 10 also addresses the reduction of inequalities within countries and here the EU is emphasising the necessity to promote the "social inclusion of migrants" (SDSN & IEEP, 2019: 201). The inadequate inclusion of migrants and refugees into the host societies of the EU is a challenge and with increased migration into the EU, the risk of increased socio-economic exclusion has risen substantially since 2005 (SDSN & IEEP, 2019: 201). Indeed, since inadequacy of socio-economic inclusion would seriously "hamper economic growth, macroeconomic stability, and can potentially undermine social cohesion" (EC, 2019a: 95), the linkage between migration flows, integration and the policies to handle them is at centre stage of the migration–integration nexus. This also indicates that for sustainable migration (the facilitation of orderly and safe migration and mobility) and integration (social and labour market inclusion), this would necessitate more effective policies for legal migration (including asylum policy) as well as labour market integration policies. As research on political entrepreneurship has shown, crises can be regarded as potential windows of opportunities in which political entrepreneurs have room for manoeuvre to promote innovative measures and policy changes in view of responding to societal challenges. However, since most of the decision-making authority in the area of migration and particularly within the area of integration is within the area of member state competence (Art. 79 (4), TFEU, Lisbon Treaty), how likely is it that innovative measures are not only effectively promoted but also implemented? In the following, we investigate the potential role of EU political entrepreneurship in facilitating the orderly and safe migration and mobility of people as well as promoting more effective socio-economic inclusion of migrants, specifically focusing on labour market integration.

POLICIES TO FACILITATE THE ORDERLY AND SAFE MIGRATION AND MOBILITY OF PEOPLE

Asylum and migration policies have been on the EU agenda for nearly 30 years. Within the framework of justice and home affairs (including nine policy areas), asylum and migration was established as a new policy area in the Treaty of Maastricht in 1993 (Ucarer, 2013). The development of the policy area should be seen as a spillover from the completion of the Single Market and therefore as a logical consequence of the passport-free union (Nugent, 2010). Consequently, a strengthened Schengen cooperation was also integrated into the EU institutional framework. In the context of the EU migration policy area, third-country nationals, or migrants, are defined as persons "born in a country outside the EU and persons born in the EU but not holding the citizenship of a Member State".[9]

The five-year Tampere programme (2000–2005) was to be the first of a number of strategic action programmes in the launch of the policy area. In parallel with increasing the rights and free movement of those legally staying in the EU, the fight against illegal migration was strengthened. The Tampere programme was also the starting point for the Common European Asylum System, designed to harmonise national asylum systems. Minimum levels of legislation combined with poor compliance with the regulations did however result in the Tampere programme's goals also becoming priority objectives in the subsequent policy programmes in The Hague (2005–10) and in Stockholm (2010–14) (Collett, 2014). In 2009, the Common European Asylum System was institutionalised as a common policy in the Treaty of Lisbon (Art. 78 (1), TFEU, Lisbon Treaty). At the same time, the solidarity clause and the principle of fair division of responsibility between EU member states was institutionalised (Art. 222, TFEU, Lisbon Treaty). The right to asylum is based on the Geneva Convention and the principle of non-refoulement[10] and is also governed by the EU Charter of Human Rights (Art. 18 of the EU Charter). Up until the ratification of the Treaty of Lisbon in 2009, the division of competences in the policy area was divided according to the pillar structure introduced by the Treaty of Maastricht in 1993. Even though the whole policy area was "communitarised" in the Treaty of Amsterdam, unanimity in the Council of Ministers was guaranteed over a transitional period of five years (Ucarer, 2013). This meant that the legislative powers of the European Parliament remained severely limited.[11] From 2004, the decision-making powers of the European Parliament were, however equalled to those of the Council of Ministers. The European Court of Justice would also receive a mandate to interpret and judge in litigation. However, although a considerable part of the decision making was transferred to the supranational level, the rules and regulations of the Treaty of Amsterdam were anything but clear and were in fact another example of complex "legal engineering"[12] for the purpose of meeting political ends (Ucarer, 2013: 285). The Treaty of Lisbon involved significant reforms also in this policy area and in decision making. With the disappearance of the pillar structure, shared authority was introduced as a legislative principle (Art. 4, TFEU, Lisbon Treaty). The challenges identified by the EU pertaining to SDG 10 and the need to facilitate the "orderly and safe migration and mobility of people" are principally based on the European Agenda on Migration, adopted in May 2015, and the lessons drawn from the migration crisis of 2015. In line with the pillars of the European Agenda on Migration three goals were identified, namely to reduce the incentives of illegal migration and to save lives; to secure external borders; and to implement a strong common asylum policy (EC, 2015).

When it comes to reducing the incentives of irregular migration and saving lives, the Commission has put in place a number of policy changes and action programmes since 2016. Swift and direct action to respond to the human tragedies in the Mediterranean Sea were set in motion by increased funding to EU agencies and member states, most in need of support. Hotspots with staff deployed from EU agencies were set up with the aim of supporting the identification, registration and fingerprinting of arriving migrants in member states, such as Greece and Italy. Another direct action was to strengthen the work on targeting the criminal networks and their smuggling activities in order to work more effectively to prevent the exploitation of vulnerable migrants. In view of tackling the structural causes of irregular migration and taking a more holistic approach, including development cooperation and humanitarian assistance, the more long-term priority of the Commission has been to strengthen existing partnerships and to set up new ones with partners outside of Europe. Central to these partnerships[13] has been to enable the more effective implementation on return and readmission arrangements[14] and more generally to help public authorities in countries of origin and transit with migration management but also with the strengthening of socio-economic development. An unprecedented funding of 9.7 billion euro has been invested to this effect, especially via the Syria Trust Fund, the EU Trust Fund for Africa and the Facility for Refugees in Turkey (EC, 2019c). In particular, the EU–Turkey Statement, adopted in March 2016, has been indispensable to the EU strategy of reducing irregular migration flows from the eastern Mediterranean. The agreement also regulates returns from Greece and the resettlement[15] of Syrian refugees to EU member states (EC, 2019b: 4).

In the area of securing the external borders, the Commission strategy since 2016 has been to strengthen the operational capability and scope of the European Border and Coast Guard Agency (Frontex) in view of establishing a European integrated border management as a shared responsibility between the Agency and member states' national authorities (EC, 2019b: 16). In November 2019, the Council adopted a new regulation on the European Border and Coast Guard, which significantly reinforces its role, both in terms of an extended mandate with increased powers as well as a strengthening in terms of staff and technical equipment (Council regulation, 2019/1896).[16] The extended mandate of the Agency has meant increased support to member state activities, especially in the area of return,[17] border controls and closer cooperation with third countries, "including those beyond the EU's immediate neighbourhood" (EC, 2019b: 17). To improve the functioning of the European Border Surveillance System, the regulation also provides for its incorporation into the European Border and Coast Guard Framework (EC, 2019b: 17–18). The extended mandate has also meant a significant increase in the number of border control tools and "the interoperability of information systems and key new information systems" (EC, 2019b: 18).[18]

In the area of implementing a more robust common asylum policy, already in June 2015, the European Council had agreed on a temporary relocation scheme[19] of over 40,000 asylum seekers over a period of two years. This decision was later adopted by the Council of Ministers in September 2015 (Council decision, 2015/0209). In 2016, the Commission initiated the establishment of the resettlement efforts as a way of constructing safe and legal pathways for the refugees, most in need of international protection, to reach Europe legally. The same year, the Commission proposed a reformed asylum policy package to revise the current regulations such as the Dublin Regulation (determining which member state is responsible for the asylum seeker), the Eurodac Regulation (extending the scope of the fingerprint database of asylum seekers), the Asylum Procedure Regulation (streamlining the rules for fair and efficient rules), the Qualification Regulation (setting the criteria for protection standards and rights for asylum seekers) and last the Reception Conditions Directive (ensuring that asylum seekers benefit from harmonised and dignified reception standards). Two new regulations are also part of the package, namely the EU Asylum Agency Regulation (agency delivering operational support to member states) and the Resettlement Framework Regulation (new instrument establishing a legal pathway for vulnerable persons in need of international protection) (EC, 2019b: 18).

Taking into consideration that the unprecedented migratory inflows of 2015 had created political turmoil and a humanitarian crisis for many of the 2.5 million first-time asylum applicants,[20] EU actions on reducing irregular migration and saving lives have certainly been successful, at least in the short term. Indeed, in September 2019, the number of irregular border crossings had dropped by 90 per cent, compared to September 2015. Of the 23 partnerships, it is particularly the EU–Turkey Deal which led to the swift closing down of the eastern Mediterranean route, which already in 2017 had prevented 1 million to migrate via Turkey to Greece (EC, 2018). Apart from drastically decreasing the number of migrants to the EU, the more holistic approach of the partnerships signals a more long-term commitment. This has also largely contributed to incorporate and link the asylum and migration policy area to other policy areas, such as the Common Security and Defence Policy, development policy as well as into the EU's global strategy (Ceccorulli & Lucarelli, 2017). With the aim of saving lives and securing the external borders, the other prioritised strategy of the EU has been the strengthening of EU border management. This has in turn meant the establishment of the European Border and Coast Guard Agency (an upgrade of Frontex) and the launch of migration-related Common Security and Defence Policy operations, especially carried out in Mali and Niger, on the main migration routes towards Libya. Indeed, by 2019, EU rescue operations had saved over 23,000 migrants in the Nigerian desert and as many as 760,000 migrants at sea (EC, 2019b: 1). The development of EU border policy with an extended mandate and budget has meant that the common European Border and Coast Guard Agency has developed into becoming the EU's largest agency.

When it comes to implementing a strong common asylum policy, the Commission proposal for a reformed asylum policy package has to date been relegated to a political moratorium. Since the EU member states have decided to opt for a package approach, it is particularly the persisting blockade of the revision of the Dublin Regulation and the revision of the Asylum Procedures Regulation that remain the main obstacles to legislative reform. Considering that a more robust asylum policy is one of the central building blocks of the Commission strategy to establish a sustainable migration management, the failure of reform is alarming. One challenge is the division of competences, meaning that many decisions still remain within the realm of member state authority. Furthermore, despite the inclusion of the solidarity clause (Art. 80, TFEU, Lisbon Treaty), another challenge is that the Commission has no means of enforcing any supranational power. Indeed, the lack of solidarity and burden sharing, especially voiced and acted upon from the four Visegrad states, member states that coined the concept of "flexible solidarity" (Scücs, 2017: 145), has been a recurrent problem since the 2015 crisis.

The traditionally entrepreneurial role of the Commission in promoting new legislation and action programmes has however been more successful in the other areas, facilitating the orderly and safe migration and mobility of people. In fact, when it comes to the reduction of irregular migration, the saving of lives and the securing of external borders, it is unquestionable that the innovative measures promoted by the Commission have been vital for the speedy and significant decrease in the number of irregular border crossings. It is particularly the innovative approach of the 90 projects, set up within the Facility for Refugees in Turkey, where member states and Turkey have jointly been fully involved in the targeting of the projects, including the launch of the "fast-track procedures to accelerate delivery" (EC, 2019b: 5). Also, and as pointed out by the Court of Auditors, the rapidity with which the considerable funds, amounting to approximately 6 billion euro, were mobilised for the Facility was made five times faster than traditional assistance (EC, 2019b: 5). However, although the fast-track procedures, along with the relocation and hotspot systems, have been both innovative and efficient insofar as they have contributed to rapidly preventing migrants from accessing EU territory, there are serious shortcomings. Indeed, since all systems are based on a principle of selection dynamics, where migrants are "sorted out" on the basis of nationality, distinguishing between those genuinely eligible for international protection and those who are not, there is cause for alarm. Indeed, here it is clear that the logic of the supporting order is potentially a threat to every individual's right to seek asylum, a fundamental principle of international law and EU law (Geneva Convention; EU Charter of Human Rights). The system is however not only questionable from a legal and moral perspective. Considering the strengthened geopolitical position of the Turkish regime in the Syrian war, along with the unprecedented refugee crisis[21] in the northern Idlib region of Syria, it is unlikely that the Turkish regime will continue holding the EU under its arms, all funding considered. Indeed, the recent closed border policy of Turkish President Erdogan and the significant increase in migrant arrivals to the Greek Islands, Malta and to Cyprus are clear signals as to the vulnerability of the Deal (EC, 2019b: 1–3).

POLICIES TO FACILITATE LABOUR MARKET INTEGRATION FOR THIRD-COUNTRY NATIONALS

Already in 2005, an action programme for the more effective integration of third-country nationals was emphasised against the *looming* demographic crisis (EC, 2005). However, progress has been rather slow and although inclusive growth as "fostering a high employment economy delivering social and territorial cohesion" (EC, 2010: 3) was already at the core of the Europe 2020 Strategy, there was little reference to the integration of migrants. It was in the Stockholm programme (2010–14), with the aim of making the EU more competitive, that an action programme for more effective integration policy measures was formulated (Collett, 2014). The necessity to strengthen the link between migration and integration was further intensified in the wake of the unprecedented migration inflows in 2015. Broadly defined, integration refers to "the process of becoming an accepted part of society" (Penninx & Garcés-Mascarenas, 2015). The Commission refers to the integration process as a dynamic two-way process between the third-country nationals and EU citizens (EC, 2005, 2016b). The challenges identified by the EU as regards SDG 10 linked to integration and the need to facilitate socio-economic inclusion of third-country nationals are primarily targeted on implementing policies for more active labour market integration (SDSN & IEEP, 2019: 95). This is also in line with the fourth pillar of the European Agenda on Migration, which is centred on strengthening effective policies for legal migration, specifically zooming in on the necessity to attract both students and "other talented and highly-skilled persons" (EC, 2015; Lulle & King, 2016: 22). Labour market integration here refers to the right to work, the right to be self-employed and the right to study.

In order to facilitate more active labour market inclusion at the same time as strengthening the competitiveness of the EU, the Commission launched *A New Skills Agenda for Europe* in 2016 (EC, 2016c). Since skills, defined as to "what a person knows, understands and can do", is at the very essence of competitiveness, innovation, growth but also vital for social cohesion, the focus on how to use migrants' skills in a more efficient and sustainable way has become key (EC, 2016c). The focus has been to attract and to more effectively integrate the highly skilled third-country nationals on the EU labour markets. Consequently, in 2016, the Commission proposed the revision of the Blue Card Directive.[22] In view of meeting the large influx of asylum seekers in 2015–16 and to strengthen their right to work, the scope of future Blue Card holders has been proposed to be extended also to encompass "beneficiaries of international protection and non-EU family members of EU citizens" (EC, 2016e). Admittance of the category of asylum seekers is, however, conditional upon having the right to work according to EU asylum rules and the qualification recast directive (2011/95/EU). In line with supporting entrepreneurship "as a vital channel to foster third-country nationals' contribution to economy and society as a whole" (EC, 2016a), the Commission has also proposed that future Blue Card holders should be able to hold employment at the same time as having the right to be self-employed. Last, a reformed Blue Card Directive would replace any national schemes running in parallel (2016e).

Another directive to attract talent and to facilitate for third-country nationals to study, do research and train or volunteer in the EU is the recast Students and Researchers EU Directive (2016/801/EU). In the recast directive, the focus is not only to attract third-country students and researchers but also to facilitate to retain them. Indeed, by increasing employment opportunities for students during their study period as well as facilitating access to the labour market for graduates, the aim is to strengthen the competitiveness of the European higher education landscape at the same time as meeting the priorities of the EU labour markets. The recast directive is also introducing swifter application procedures, from a maximum of 90 days to 60 days (2016/801/EU). In addition, with the aim of strengthening both the coherence of the EU legal framework at the same time as supporting the member states in improving a more comparable and consistent system for the recognition of qualifications, a revision of the European Qualifications Framework has been proposed by the Commission (EC, 2016c: 9). Additionally, in view of strengthening the coherence and consistency of EU internal policies on legal migration by "simplifying and streamlining the current EU framework" (EC, 2016f: 5), the Commission launched the *Legal Migration Fitness Check*.[23] The Commission is also supporting member states to implement legal migration projects with key partners (origin and transit countries) with the aim of better matching the skills of these third-country young graduates and workers with EU labour market needs. The five mobility programmes already implemented have so far been limited to Egypt, Morocco, Tunisia and Nigeria but the Commission is encouraging member states to initiate projects beyond North Africa (EC, 2019b: 19). The Commission has also developed a skills profiling tool to facilitate the better matching of competences and skills of third-country nationals. In 2017, the Commission launched the European Partnership for Integration where both public and private actors in several member states work together to specifically strengthen labour market integration of refugees. One such project is "Employers Together for Integration" (EC, 2019b: 19). Additionally, the Commission has increased its support to the subnational levels, currently supporting eight networks of cities' and regions' work on integration. Strengthened cooperation has recently been initiated with the Committee of Regions and the initiative "Cities and Regions for Integration of Migrants", a platform for European regional leaders and mayors to exchange ideas and best practice (EC, 2019b: 19–20).

Taking into consideration that by 2025 nearly half of the jobs on the EU labour market will require highly skilled competences (EC, 2016c) and that labour market integration of third-country nationals remains worryingly inadequate (SDSN & IEEP, 2019: 95), it is certain that a reformed Blue Card Directive would strengthen the legal rights of migrants, including refugees, to take up highly skilled employment and to be self-employed in the EU.

Whether these changes would facilitate for the 22 per cent of asylum seekers and refugees whose "return on higher education in terms of better employment prospects is lower for refugees than for the rest of the population" (Tanay & Peschner, 2017: 1) is however less certain. Indeed, even though a reformed directive would provide Blue Card holders with the same rights as a member state national in terms of "working conditions, education, recognition of qualifications, social security" (2009/50/EC), there are intrinsic shortcomings. Intrinsic insofar as there is not one integrated labour market in the EU but 27 different national systems with widely differing practices on, for instance, the recognition of qualifications from outside of the EU (Parkhouse & Stroemblad, 2018). In this context, even though the reforming of the European Qualifications Framework would mean a more comparable and consistent system for the recognition of qualifications, the impact of this Commission proposal is highly uncertain. Uncertain in the sense that the in-built conservatism of national educational institutions, as shown by the failure of implementing the Bologna Process within the higher education institutions, is sure to be hampering the development of a more efficient common European system for the recognition of qualifications and skills, which eventually slows down macroeconomic stability and inclusive growth.

In view of more effectively meeting the priorities of an EU labour market in need of increased highly skilled labour, the recast Students and Researchers EU Directive is promising. Indeed, by taking a more holistic approach of not only attracting but also retaining third-country students and researchers (2016/801/EU), it is clear that the perspective of the recast directive is to link measures to promote educational programmes more closely to labour market programmes and career possibilities. By increasing employment opportunities for students during their study period as well as facilitating access to the labour market for graduates, the directive would strengthen the competitiveness of the European higher education landscape at the same time as meeting the priorities of the EU labour markets. At the same time, it is clear that access to the labour market is conditional upon the level of unemployment rates of the member state, which remains member state competence (2016/801/EU).

The mismatch, and the misuse, of competences and skills of third-country nationals is equally challenging. Indeed, even though 25 per cent of third-country nationals are highly skilled, as many as 75 per cent of this group are "inactive, unemployed or overqualified for their jobs" (EC, 2016a: 10). It is therefore positive that the tackling of future skills mismatches forms one of the four key goals in the renewed agenda for higher education, adopted by the Commission in May 2017 (EC, 2017).[24] It is clear that the role of higher education institutions, as arenas of knowledge production and dissemination, are central building blocks of innovation systems in ensuring inclusive and sustainable growth. As asylum seekers are the most vulnerable in terms of labour market integration, the lack of including this category in the recast directive for more competitive higher education institutions in the EU is surprising.

Although it is certain that the Commission has taken its traditionally entrepreneurial role far to implement more active labour market integration policies and action programmes to facilitate for highly skilled migrants and refugees to have access to highly skilled employment, self-employment and to higher education, it is less clear whether these innovative reforms will actually lead to more effective labour market integration. Indeed, due to the fact that much of the decision-making power is member state competence, as institutionalised by the Treaty of Lisbon (Art. 4, TFEU, Lisbon Treaty), the leeway of the Commission is undercut and limited to promoting and supporting member states in the area of integration (EC, 2016c). Consequently, even though the EU can legislate and adopt binding legal acts in significant parts of the policy area, decisions regulating "who enters, on what basis, for how long and in what number" (Geddes, 2015: 78) are still essentially member state competence. In this context, it is important to remember that even though the demographic and the migration crises are European phenomena, the differences in national interests and varying economic, judicial and political prerequisites are preventing a common European solution. Indeed, ever since the Eastern enlargement in 2004, the EU 15 has attracted a labour force particularly from the Central and Eastern European member states. This has created large discrepancies and a fragmentation of labour markets, creating an unbalanced labour mobility inside the EU, paradoxically contributing to intra-EU competition and a brain drain *problematique* (EC, 2016a). This fragmentation, fuelled also by the migration crisis and the considerable differences in member states' willingness to the reception of asylum seekers in 2015, is clearly hampering the efforts of the Commission to strengthen both coordination and coherence of the policy areas. Consequently, this is also opening up enhanced flexibility where many member states have national schemes running in parallel[25] to the Blue Card and which in many cases have proven more successful (EC, 2017). This has created a situation where member state governments as well as regional and local actors are pressurised into finding innovative ways for more effective labour market integration, such as promoting and implementing their own national schemes of attracting "highly skilled workers as part of the global competition for talent" (EC, 2018: 11). Even though the Commission emphasises that the "full participation and early integration of all third-country nationals, including refugees" (EC, 2016b: 3) is vital for the sake of both inclusive growth and social cohesion, it is clear that possibilities for asylum seekers to access the labour market are limited and temporally conditioned by national legislation.

CONCLUSION

It is certain that the entrepreneurial role of the Commission has been key in promoting and supporting member states in implementing effective policies to facilitate the orderly and safe migration to the EU, at least in the short term. The sustainability of the new securitised EU migration management is however less certain and poses problems, which would need to be addressed by the EU member states. Indeed, since the policy shift is contributing to undermining the right to seek asylum, which is an individual right, guaranteed by international and EU law, by extension this is violating the human rights of asylum seekers at the same time as undermining the EU's legitimacy. Additionally, due to a lack of solidarity and burden sharing in the EU, the outsourcing of EU migration management or the "externalisation of the burden" to third countries is equally problematic. This puts the headlights on a broader dilemma that not only questions the sustainability of the EU's migration management but also the very legitimacy of the EU as a global actor. Indeed, since EU member states traditionally have been the most fervent advocates of the responsibility to protect the concept,[26] at least in theory, the lack of taking responsibility for its own migration management is undermining its legitimacy, both internally as well as externally. To create a sustainable migration management would however necessitate a more robust asylum policy system. Since discussions on a reformed asylum policy have been relegated to a political moratorium since 2015 the likelihood of any robust changes in the area is slim.

Just like the shared governance *problematique* is blatant in the area of asylum and migration, so is the case in the area of implementing more effective policies for labour market integration. However, even though the political leverage of the Commission is minor, its political entrepreneurial role has nevertheless been important in the promotion of more effectively integrating migrants and asylum seekers in EU labour markets. It is understandable that the focus of the Commission has been on attracting and retaining highly skilled competences in order to both meet the priorities of the EU labour market needs at the same time as alleviating the effects of the ageing population. The better use of competences does however require that national institutions, particularly higher education institutions, would devise more effective systems for the validation of qualifications and skills. This would necessitate reform and a change of mindset, both on the individual as well as on the organisational level. Additionally, even though the focus of the Commission has been on facilitating integration for highly skilled migrants and asylum seekers, the large majority of the latter group belongs to the category of those having the lowest levels of education. The lack of initiatives from the Commission pertaining to the category, which is the most vulnerable, is surprising. In order to meet the inadequate socio-economic inclusion of this category, there is a real need for policymakers on the member state level, as well as on subnational levels, such as local and regional authorities, to devise policies and systems which would facilitate access to low-skilled employment. One recommendation would be to launch an EU-wide discussion on the matter, preferably within the framework of the already existing EU initiative on "Cities and Regions for Integration of Migrants", the platform for exchanging ideas and best practice.

NOTES

1. The demographic crisis refers to an ageing population, longer life expectancies and a declining working age population (EC, 2011: 2).
2. The threat concerns both who should have the right to the welfare system but also who should have the right to access the national labour market, potentially in competition with the domestic labour force.
3. Most of the increase occurred from 2005 (UN DESA, 2017).
4. In 2017, 57 per cent of international migrants were living in the high-income states of the Northern regions, compared to 43 per cent in the developing regions of the South (UN DESA, 2017).
5. According to recent statistics, the annual growth rate of the countries in the North has been declining to 1.6 per cent between 2010 and 2017, down from 2.3 per cent between 1990 and 2010 (UN DESA, 2017).
6. The Geneva Convention of 1951 and its 1967 Protocol are the international legal documents, regulating the rights of displaced people and the obligations of the sovereign states having signed and ratified the documents (Zimmermann, 2017).
7. The accompanying targets involve concrete measures for the realisation of the goals (UNGA, 2015).
8. The mandate of the IOM is to help facilitate the orderly and humane management of migration, to promote international cooperation, to assist in finding practical solutions to migration problems and finally to provide migrants, including refugees and internally displaced persons, with humanitarian assistance (IOM, 2019).
9. In EU vocabulary, the definition of a migrant can also refer to second- and third-generation migrants who are legally residing on EU territory (EC, 2011).
10. The principle of non-refoulement means that refugees have the right not to be returned to a country in which their lives are threatened (Art. 33, Geneva Convention).
11. By using the consultation procedure, in which the European Parliament only had an advisory role, in parallel to using the unanimity principle in decision making in the Council of Ministers, the legislative powers of the European Parliament were limited (Ucarer, 2013).
12. The maze of rules and regulations in the area created a system that was difficult to comprehend even for legal experts (Ucarer, 2013).
13. To date the cooperation on active policies on return and readmission encompass arrangements with 23 partner countries. Negotiation of a 24th agreement with Belarus is in process (EC, 2019b: 15).
14. The aim of readmission arrangements is to facilitate the return of third-country nationals (EC, 2019b: 10).

15. Resettlement means the transfer of displaced persons, who have been identified by the EU as in need of international protection, to another state that can provide protection and other rights (EC, 2015).

16. The standing forces of border and coast guards and return experts are planned to consist of up to 10,000 operational staff (of Frontex and member states) by 2027, also including a rapid reaction force which would be operational until 2024 (Council regulation 2019/1896).

17. The mandate gives Frontex the right to support member states at all stages of the return process, including the right to control third-country nationals without a legal right to remain on EU territory, the right to acquire travel documents from third countries, to provide support for voluntary departure and to oversee reintegration in the country of origin (EC, 2019b: 16).

18. Regulation (EU) 2019/817 (20 May 2019) and Regulation (EU) 2019/818 (20 May 2019). Key new systems are the EU Entry/Exit System and European Travel Information and Authorisation System. Also essential are the measures to reinforce the Schengen Information System and to extend the European Criminal Records Information System to third-country nationals (EC, 2019b: 18).

19. In February 2016, the Council adopted a decision to temporarily suspend Sweden's obligations regarding relocation (EU) 2015/1523 and (EU) 2015/1601. In March 2016, the Council adopted a decision of temporary suspension to relocate 30 per cent of applicants located in Austria (EU) 2015/1601.

20. A first-time asylum applicant is a person who applied for asylum for the first time in a given member state (SDSN & IEEP, 2019: 212).

21. The escalated fighting in the Syrian region of Idlib, neighbouring Turkey, has led to a massive inflow of almost 1 million refugees to the region.

22. The requirements of the Blue Card Directive, adopted in May 2009, is a higher education qualification of at least three years and work experience amounting to at least three years. The United Kingdom, Ireland and Denmark do not apply the Blue Card Directive (2009/50/EC).

23. The Legal Migration Fitness Check is based on five indicators of comparison (relevance, coherence, effectiveness, efficiency and added value) and covers the following directives: Family Reunifications Directive (2003/86/EC), Recast Long-Term Residents Directive (2011/51/EU), EU Blue Card Directive (2009/50/EC), Single Permit Directive (2011/98/EU), Seasonal Workers Directive (2014/36/EU), Intra-Corporate Transfer Directive (2014/66/EU) and the Recast Students and Researchers EU Directive (2016/801/EU) (EC, 2016f).

24. The renewed EU Agenda for higher education identifies four key goals for strengthened cooperation in higher education. Apart from the tackling of skills mismatches and the promotion of excellence in the development of skills, the other key goals are the building of inclusive and connected higher education systems; the focus on higher education institutions as contributors to innovation; and the support of more effective higher education systems (EC, 2017).

25. For instance, Austria, Germany and the Netherlands had national schemes to attract highly skilled third-country nationals (EC, 2017, 2018).

26. In 2005, the Responsibility to Protect concept was formalised and endorsed in the World Summit Outcome by the UN General Assembly when they declared that states have a responsibility to protect their populations against genocide, war crimes, ethnic cleansing and crimes against humanity. Cf. GA Resolution 60/1, 2005 World Summit Outcome, 24 October 2005, paragraphs 138–9. See European

Union Priorities for the 63rd General Assembly of the United Nations, 16 June 2008, paragraph 18.

REFERENCES

Ceccorulli, M. & S. Lucarelli. 2017. "Migration and the EU global strategy: Narratives and dilemmas". *International Spectator*, 52 (3).

Collett, E. 2014. "Future policy development on immigration and asylum: Understanding the Challenge". Migration Policy Institute Europe, Policy Brief Series, No. 4.

Constant, A.F. & K.F. Zimmermann. 2016. "Towards a new European refugee policy that works". CESifo Dice Report, 4/2016.

Council Decision (EU) 2015/0209, Temporary emergency relocation scheme, 22 September 2015.

Council Decision (EU) 2015/1523, Temporary suspension of Sweden's obligations regarding relocation, 24 February 2016.

Council Decision (EU) 2015/1601, Temporary suspension of relocation for applicants to Austria, 8 March 2016.

Council Directive 2009/50/EC, Blue card directive, 25 May 2009.

Council Directive 2011/95/EU, Qualification recast directive, 13 December 2011.

Council Directive 2016/801/EU, Recast students and researchers directive, 11 May 2016.

European Commission (EC). 2005. A common agenda for integration framework for the integration of third-country nationals in the European Union. Brussels: COM(2005) 389 final.

European Commission (EC). 2010. Europe 2020. A strategy for smart, sustainable and inclusive growth. Brussels: COM(2010) 2020.

European Commission (EC). 2011. European agenda for the integration of third-country nationals. Brussels: COM(2011) 455 final.

European Commission (EC). 2015. A European agenda on migration. Brussels: COM(2015) 240 final.

European Commission (EC). 2016a. Evaluation and analysis of good practices in promoting and supporting migrant entrepreneurship. Guide book. Brussels, 15 September 2016.

European Commission (EC). 2016b. Action plan on the integration of third country nationals. Brussels: COM(2016) 377 final.

European Commission (EC). 2016c. A new skills agenda for Europe. Working together to strengthen human capital, employability and competitiveness. Brussels: COM(2016) 381 final.

European Commission (EC). 2016d. Press release on reforming the Blue Card directive, Strasbourg, 7 June.

European Commission (EC). 2016e. Commission proposal on reforming the Blue Card directive. Brussels: COM(2016) 378.

European Commission (EC). 2016f. Annual report on migration and asylum. European Migration Network. Brussels, 25 April.

European Commission (EC). 2017. Commission communication on a renewed agenda for higher education. Brussels: COM(2017) 247 final.

European Commission (EC). 2018. Annual report on migration and asylum 2017. European Migration Network. Brussels, 15 May.

European Commission (EC). 2019a. Reflection paper. Towards a sustainable Europe by 2030. Brussels: COM(2019)22, 30 January.

European Commission (EC). 2019b. Progress report on the implementation of the European agenda on migration. Brussels: COM(2019) 481 final, 16 October.

European Commission (EC). 2019c. Press release on European agenda on migration, four years on, Brussels, 16 October 2019.

Geddes, A. 2015. Migration: Differential institutionalization and its effects, in F. Trauner & A. Ripoll Servent (eds), *Policy Change in the Area of Freedom, Security and Justice: How EU Institutions Matter*. London: Routledge.

Geneva Convention on the Status of Refugees, 28 July 1951.

International Organization for Migration (IOM). 2018. *Migration and the 2030 Agenda: A Guide for Practitioners*. Geneva: IOM Publishing.

International Organization for Migration (IOM). 2019. *World Migration Report 2020*. Geneva: IOM Publishing.

Lulle, A. & R. King. 2016. *Research on Migration: Facing Realities and Maximising Opportunities: A Policy Review*. Luxembourg: Publications Office of the European Union.

Nugent, N. 2010. *The Government and Politics of the European Union*. Basingstoke: Palgrave Macmillan.

Parkes, R. 2016. People on the move: The new global (dis)order, Chaillot Papers, No. 138, Paris.

Parkhouse, A. & P. Stroemblad. 2018. Exploring preconditions for political entrepreneurship and integration in European societies, in C. Karlsson, C. Silander & D. Silander (eds), *Governance and Political Entrepreneurship in Europe: Promoting Growth and Welfare in Times of Crisis*, Cheltenham, UK and Northampton, MA, USA: Edward Elgar Publishing.

Penninx, R. & B. Garcés-Mascarenas. 2015. The concept of integration: Towards an analytical and policy framework, in R. Penninx & B. Garcés-Mascarenas (eds), *Integration of Migrants into What? Integration Processes and Policies in Europe*. Cham: Springer.

Scücs, T. 2017. The cultural integration of immigrants and refugees: Shifting narratives and policies in the European Union, in R. Bauböck and M. Tripkovic (eds), *The Integration of Migrants and Refugees: An EUI Forum on Migration, Citizenship and Demography*. Florence: Robert Schumann Centre for Advanced Studies.

SDSN & IEEP. 2019. *The 2019 Europe Sustainable Development Report*. Paris: Sustainable Development Solutions Network and Institute for European Environmental Policy.

Tanay, F. & J. Peschner. 2017. Labour market integration of refugees in the EU. LFS workshop, Copenhagen, 4–5 April.

Ucarer, E.M. 2013. The area of freedom, security and justice, in M. Cini & N. Pérez-Solórzano Borragán (eds), *European Union Politics*. Oxford: Oxford University Press.

United Nations Department of Economic and Social Affairs (UN DESA). 2017. International Migration Report 2017. Available from www.un.org/en/development/ desa/population/migration/publications/migrationreport/docs/MigrationReport2017 .pdf

United Nations General Assembly (UNGA). 2015. *Transforming Our World: The 2030 Agenda for Sustainable Development*. A/RES/70/1. United Nations General Assembly.

Zimmermann, K.F. 2017. Refugee and migrant labour market integration: Europe in need of a new policy agenda, in R. Bauböck and M. Tripkovic (eds), *The Integration of Migrants and Refugees: An EUI Forum on Migration, Citizenship and Demography*. Florence: Robert Schumann Centre for Advanced Studies.

6. Agenda 2030 and the EU on industry, innovation and infrastructure

Akis Kalaitzidis

In 2015 the United Nations (UN) adopted what has come to be known as the Agenda 2030. The agenda is an ambitious step towards meeting 17 Sustainable Development Goals (SDGs) for the planet. These goals set by the UN are set to eradicate poverty and promote global peace as a continuation of the previously set Millennium Development Goals and note:

> We commit ourselves to working tirelessly for the full implementation of this Agenda by 2030. We recognize that eradicating poverty in all its forms and dimensions, including extreme poverty, is the greatest global challenge and an indispensable requirement for sustainable development. We are committed to achieving sustainable development in its three dimensions – economic, social and environmental – in a balanced and integrated manner. We will also build upon the achievements of the Millennium Development Goals and seek to address their unfinished business.[1]

This report is a result of many painstakingly worked conferences around the world, most notably the Rio +20 summit and the Paris Climate Agreement (Chasek et al., 2016). As noted in the report *Transforming Our World*, the aims are inclusive of people, the planet, prosperity and peace. The agenda sets 17 SDGs with 169 associated targets which aim to support collective development in our world today. Vulnerable people must be empowered and significant attention should be paid to gender inequality and gender differences, poverty must be eradicated in all its forms by seeking to enhance sustainable economic growth that would dynamically affect the way people live, especially in the less developed world.

Clearly an ambitious project, Agenda 2030 would not be without its detractors and they come from both the right and left of the political spectrum. On the right typically the criticism is anti-globalist and refers to Agenda 2030 as "A recipe for global socialism" (New American, 2016). Criticism tends to focus on the loss of sovereignty due to the complicated nature of global problems and, as such, some academics have called it *The Sovereignty Fetish* (Fourie & O'Manique, 2016: 275). Sovereignty is detrimental to solving global problems and yet it is the fallback position on most governments delegating most global problems to be dealt with as the lowest common denominator and not as the emergencies they truly are. Fourie and O'Manique argue that "States rights trump human rights. Sceptics of Agenda 2030 point out that in words of one respondent, this dilutes the promise of the development project as a truly transformative global compact – a 'new special contract' between governments and citizens" (Fourie & O'Manique, 2016: 275). "Through a close analysis of the SDGs, I draw the conclusion that there are substantial provisions (in this framework) which privileged the up-holding of commercial interests over commitments to universally ensure entitlements to address fundamental life sustaining needs," argues another critic (Weber, 2017: 400).

Yet, one region of the world is reaffirming its commitment to the Agenda 2030 and that is Europe. In this chapter I will be discussing, firstly, the efforts the European Union (EU) is making towards the Agenda 2030 and especially towards the energy sector, and secondly, I will be discussing industry innovation and infrastructure in the EU, their challenges and reforms as well as the reforms implemented, if any. Finally, the chapter discusses the EU's commitment to promoting the SDGs across the world with a focus on supporting the increasing capacities of the world states to promote these goals.

SDG 7 AFFORDABLE AND CLEAN ENERGY

The implementation of SDG 7 aims to ensure access to affordable, reliable, sustainable and modern energy for all and is closely related as shown in previous chapters with climate change as well as economic growth. The UN states how "Advancement in SDG-7 has the potential to spur progress across SDGs on poverty eradication, gender equality, mitigation of and adaptation to climate change, food security, health, education, sustainable cities and communities, clean water and sanitation, jobs, innovation, transport and refugees and other situations of displacement" (UN SDG 7, 2018). Energy is central to the well-being of modern communities as access to modern electricity has increased globally by 9 percent between the years 2000 and 2016 (UN SDG 7, 2018). Despite this progress, more than 3 billion people live without access to clean fuel technologies, using mostly wood and coal for their cooking. The region with the biggest deficit in energy needs is Sub-Saharan Africa where approximately half a billion people are living without electricity (UN SDG 7, 2018).

According to the UN's facts and figures:

- 13 percent of the global population still lacks access to modern electricity.
- 3 billion people rely on wood, coal, charcoal or animal waste for cooking and heating.

- Energy is the dominant contributor to climate change, accounting for around 60 percent of total global greenhouse gas emissions.
- Indoor air pollution from using combustible fuels for household energy caused 4.3 million deaths in 2012, with women and girls accounting for six out of every ten of these.
- The share of renewable energy in final energy consumption reached 17.5 percent in 2015. (UN SDG 7, 2018)

The goals set by SDG 7 are:

7.1   By 2030, ensure universal access to affordable, reliable and modern energy services.

7.2   By 2030, increase substantially the share of renewable energy in the global energy mix.

7.3   By 2030, double the global rate of improvement in energy efficiency.

7.A   By 2030, enhance international cooperation to facilitate access to clean energy research and technology, including renewable energy, energy efficiency and advanced and cleaner fossil fuel technology, and promote investment in energy infrastructure and clean energy technology.

7.B   By 2030, expand infrastructure and upgrade technology for supplying modern and sustainable energy services for all in developing countries, in particular least developed countries, small island developing states, and land-locked developing countries, in accordance with their respec tive programs of support. (UN SDG 7, 2018)

THE EU ON SDG 7

The EU has set its sights on revamping its energy policy through innovation and by replacing major sources of energy with renewables. The EU has there-fore set a target for 2030 to reduce greenhouse emissions about 40 percent. In addition to that target they are raising their share of renewables to 32 percent and improving energy efficiency by 32 percent (European Commission, 2020a). In its long-term strategy, the EU was even more ambitious and called for a climate-neutral Europe by 2050 (COM (2018) 773 final). In order to achieve such a target energy will be the most important component. Energy is responsible for 75 percent of greenhouse gas emissions (COM (2018) 773 final). From transport to industry first but also to agriculture and buildings the entire sectors will require "scaling up" (COM (2018) 773 final). According to the European Commission the road to a net-zero greenhouse gas economy passes through seven main strategic blocks:

1. Maximization of the benefits from energy efficiency including zero-emission buildings.

2. Maximization of the deployment of renewables and the use of electricity to fully decarbonize Europe's energy supply.
3. Embrace clean, safe and connected mobility.
4. A competitive EU industry and the circular economy as a key enabler to reduce greenhouse emissions.
5. Development of a smart network infrastructure and interconnections.
6. Reap the full benefits of the bio-economy and create essential carbon sinks.
7. Tackle the remaining CO_2 emissions with carbon capture and storage. (COM (2018) 773 final)

Ultimately, energy is about industry and industry is about steady and smart growth for countries who want to achieve continuous development, not to mention those who need to build the infrastructure in its entirety. One example could be upgrading the electricity grids to promote the sustainable goals the EU has set. Other examples would include nuclear power plants, the carbon capture and storage industry, in addition to renewables which are becoming an intricate part of the EU plan, such as solar and photovoltaic energy and wind turbines. Haragugi and Kitaoka argue that "smart industrialization, linked to a structural understanding of the evolution of manufacturing productive capacities, is essential for reducing income, productivity, technology and skill gaps and has crucial impact on the creation of decent work" (Haraguch & Kitaoka, 2015: 459).

The EU industrial capacities must first adopt and then keep innovating if they are to meet these standards and those set by Agenda 2030. The EU aims to reach its sustainability goals by focusing on the following four areas: (a) moving from linear to circular economy, (b) building sustainability from farm to fork, (c) future proofing energy, buildings and its mobility and (d) ensuring a socially fair transition (European Commission 2020b). Because of the possibility of creating new jobs in a circular economy which is sustainable and biodiverse the EU is the potential world leader in the attempt to create a more sustainable future for our planet.

EU POLITICAL ENTREPRENEURSHIP ON INDUSTRY INNOVATION AND INFRASTRUCTURE IN EUROPE

Sustainable development has become the heart of the European economy and naturally the EU is a leader in promoting and implementing the UN SDGs. There has been evident progress in most goals with some such as infrastructure, industry and innovation lagging somewhat. Industry is at the heart of the matter considering it is the main employer and an engine of growth for the continent. The Commission's vision of 2030 states: "In 2030 European Industry will be a global player that will responsibly deliver value for society the environment and the economy" (European Commission, 2019a). The Commission encourages the European industry to transform by embracing the automation and digitization of manufacturing products and data services. There are five drivers of such success: (a) leadership in technology, innovation and sustainability, (b) anticipating and developing skills, (c) strategic value creation networks, (d) a fair, competitive and agile business environment and (e) social fairness and well-being (European Commission, 2019a).

In order to implement this type of vision the EU must take the following strategic steps:

> Manage a fast and inclusive transformation: design an appropriate ecosystem, stimulating innovation and technology uptake; accelerate the transformation towards climate neutral circular and resource-efficient industry; ensure reliable access to sufficient and affordable low carbon energy and raw materials supply, while respecting planetary boundaries; boost the EU digital economy; finance the transition. Champion global competitiveness: ensure a greater role for the single market to benefit from a continent-wide market; strengthen strategic value chains; lead in an open, fair, multilateral trading system; take global action for EU industrial; leadership. Address social inclusiveness and values: ensure social fairness of industrial transition; spread benefits of the transformation in the European regions; build a learning society anticipating and developing skills; ensue co-ownership and inclusive governance for the transformation; build an enabling environment for more sustainable business activities. (European Commission, 2019a)

Much is still left to be done in transforming the industrial base, for example the decarbonization of the industrial manufacturing sectors, which should be evenly affected so as to not cause disruption to the economy and life of people. In fact, the EU already has identified some strategic actions that can bring about the quick transformation of industry such as the Green Deal with industry, standardization of carbon emissions and setting targets so that the EU would become an industrial champion in the circular economy (European Commission, 2019a). In addition to this transformation a parallel transformation to digitization and 3D printing could provide a much needed boost towards transforming the economy and employing millions. Towards that eventuality the EU has created programs such as INVESTEU and Horizon Europe in order to promote scientific excellence and the development of innovative technologies and to promote successful young market businesses.

Industry is also related to mobility and as such mobility in the EU is a big contributor to greenhouse gases. For that reason the EU is thinking about its strategies for the future. In its effort to promote SDGs in the EU in that area the EU has produced a report called *Europe on the Move* which reflects its attention to the subject matter. According to the report *Europe on the Move* is a wide-ranging set of initiatives that will make traffic safer; encourage smart road charging; reduce CO_2 emissions, air pollution and congestion; cut red tape for businesses; fight illicit employment and ensure proper conditions and rest times for workers. The long-term benefits of these measures will extend far beyond the transport sector by promoting growth and job creation, strengthening social fairness, widening consumers' choices and firmly putting Europe on the path towards zero emissions.

Vice-president for jobs, growth, investment and competitiveness, Jyrki Katainen, said: "Our approach to mobility is much broader than just the transport sector. We see new developments in transport also in the context of newly emerging economic trends like collaborative or circular economy. Hence, it is as an opportunity to modernise the entire European economy and push it in a more sustainable direction." The commissioner for transport, Violeta Bulc, also noted:

> The EU has a unique opportunity to not only lead the modernisation of road transport at home, but also globally. Our reforms will set the foundation for standardised, digital road solutions, fairer social conditions and enforceable market rules. They will help decrease the socio-economic costs of transport, like time lost in traffic, road fatalities and serious injuries, health risks from pollution and noise, whilst serving the needs of citizens, businesses and nature. Common standards and cross-border services will also help make multimodal travel a reality across Europe. (European Commission, 2017)

Furthermore, the numbers are indisputable that mobility is the largest part of the economic activity of the world and the one that needs most improvement if the Agenda 2030 targets are to be met. In *Europe on the Move* the European Commission cites:

> In the EU, the transportation and storage sector employs more than 11 million people, accounting for more than 5 per cent of total employment and almost 5 per cent of EU Gross Domestic Product. It accounts for about 20 per cent of EU exports to the EU's main trade partners. Road transport is the main transport mode used in the EU, accounting for almost half of the total freight transport activity (almost three-quarters on land) and dominating citizens' personal transportation. It is estimated that EU road transport companies directly employ around 5 million people working in around 915,000 companies, mostly small and medium-sized. (COM(2017) 283 final)

Thus, the demands on the transportation and mobility of the EU's networks are expected to rise and the EU needs to address the changes by changing consumer behavior and the accompanied road safety, as well as employment and competitiveness in the whole of the EU. "EU citizens spend an average of almost 10 hours per week using transport, travel an average distance of 34.7 km per day, and spend 13 per cent of their total consumption on transport-related items" (COM (2017) 283 final). Since the transportation sector alone is one fifth of the EU greenhouse gas emissions (COM (2017) 283 final), it makes sense to start from addressing mobility first. In addition to transportation alone mobility would have to include employment as a vast amount of investment exists in the transportation employment sectors and affects the lives of Europeans in every country. For example, the European automotive industry would have to adapt to the new regulations that will be born out of the Agenda 2030 adaptations in the EU framework. People who work in these sectors will also have to adapt their skills to the changing technologies and rules. Just as in the United States where a full 25 percent of jobs are at risk of being lost to automation (CNBC, 2019), similarly the EU's automotive industries which provide millions of jobs will have to adjust.

Further challenges to the mobility of Europeans include road safety, increased infrastructural needs, as well as digitization. The EU's physical infrastructure counts over 217 000 km of railways, 77 000 km of motorways, 42 000 km of inland waterways, 329 key seaports and 329 airports (European Commission, 2020b). Road safety continues to be problematic as noted:

> While great progress has been achieved in the past decades making the EU the world's safest road transport region, the high number of fatalities and serious injuries still cause great human suffering and unacceptable economic costs, estimated at EUR 100 billion annually. In 2016, 25,500 people lost their lives on EU roads and a further 135,000 people were seriously injured. (COM(2017) 283 final)

Serious investment in infrastructure and automation is needed if these fatalities are to be reduced. The infrastructure system has suffered in the past decade due to the economic downturn in the continent which was hit by the severe economic crisis. For this reason the Juncker Commission has created the InvestEU program, which makes available a further 650 billion euros for investment in infrastructure. This type of infusion will have a multiplier effect and will produce far more than 650 billion euros of investment in the European road networks. Yet more money is needed as the estimate for upkeep for such a network is to the tune of 130 billion euros a year (COM(2017) 283 final). Finally, digitization brings a whole new set of challenges for industry, infrastructure and development in the EU. Connectivity and social networks are changing the landscape and are promoting vehicles with additional features which could be a positive development but need to be supported by a European network that will allow all apps, ride-sharing schemes and modern vehicles to operate on. Experts in the field are concluding that in the short term the EU may have some solutions such as (a) "Investing in more efficient vehicles with existing technologies, making smaller, lighter vehicles, and advanced internal combustion engines", (b) "Reducing overall road transport demand" and (c) fostering CO_2 emission legislation (Lue et al., 2016: 243).

Considering the size of the car market in the EU as well as the pace of innovation on vehicles, the most important reform to be taken would be related to emission standards. Clearly the EU was rocked by what is now known as the diesel emissions scandal which plagued German-manufactured Volkswagen in recent years. The scandal involved the intentional programming of diesel engines on Volkswagen cars to defeat emission control systems in laboratory settings. "Volkswagen became the world's top-selling carmaker trumpeting the environmental friendliness, fuel efficiency and high performance of diesel-powered vehicles that met America's tough Clean Air laws" (CBS, 2015). Unfortunately for everyone the car maker was cheating the emission standards and got caught. The EU took notice and:

> A proposal for a new robust EU framework for type approval has been put forward and is among a series of EU measures designed to restore consumer confidence in the automotive industry and rebuild trust in the regulatory system. We now need swift agreement by the European Parliament and Council to put this ambitious and much-needed legislation in place. In addition, new test procedures have been introduced to test emissions from cars in real driving conditions as well as in the laboratory, and will apply to new types of vehicles from September 2017. (COM(2017) 283 final)

The Commission believes that the new standards will contribute to further innovation in the area of emissions and will promote cleaner, more efficient vehicles on the roads of the EU. Clearly the emissions battle is not won and everyone should be aware of what their vehicle is responsible for. Better-informed consumers make better buyers and promote the battle towards zero emissions. In this context, the Commission is hoping to promote all available options towards achieving a goal close to zero emissions. The best option available is public transportation and so the EU "are committed to investment in clean public transport and are also promoting active and sustainable modes of transport, supported by multimodal travel information services, which offer users a range of mobility options, including bicycle and car-sharing schemes" (COM(2017) 283 final). In that sense, the Commission is proposing several schemes from smart road charging, to public procurement as a market driver for cleaner transport, to ensuring a fair and competitive market for transport in its internal market through (a) creating a fair market for road haulage, (b) enhancing its social framework and employment conditions, (c) better compliance, (d) enforcement through smart digital technologies with better road safety and (e) supporting a change in skills (COM (2017) 283 final).

No implementation of reform would be complete without an emphasis on research and innovation. Only a massively coordinated effort in research and development of sustainable technologies would be able to move Europe to the forefront of the global climate change battle:

> The European Commission proposes to invest 35% of the 100 billion euro budget in climate objectives, through the development of innovative and cost effective zero carbon solutions … EU Research should focus on transformational carbon-neutral solutions in areas such as electrification (renewables, smart networks and batteries), hydrogen and fuel cells, energy storage, carbon-neutral transformation of energy intensive industries, the circular economy, the bio-economy and sustainable intensification of agriculture and forestry. (COM (2017) 283 final)

The innovation sector could be its own spur of economic growth and could add to the transformation of employment in the EU. This new money source would lead to new jobs in the sustainable sector which already is growing in the EU. Of course decarbonization of the EU economy will not be easy to achieve and several sectors would be affected adversely and would have to be compensated and retrained.

EU POLITICAL ENTREPRENEURSHIP ON INDUSTRY, INNOVATION AND INFRASTRUCTURE GLOBALLY

The EU as a large, wealthy international organization aims to help less developed countries with their SDGs but in order to do that in the less developed world it has to focus on poverty eradication in order to then promote sustainable growth. According to the European Commission the EU

> consistently and strongly supported the multilateral, rules based global order, with the United Nations at its core; A life of dignity for all that reconciles economic prosperity and efficiency, peaceful societies, social inclusion and environmental responsibility; and the rule of law, democracy and the principles of equality and solidarity. (European Commission, 2019b)

The EU, just as any other large political organization, is promoting its own version of world peace and, along with that, it is willing to help the states that accept the helping hand make progress towards the Agenda 2030 targets. In order to help make progress towards poverty eradication the European Commission has proposed the 4Ps scheme (people, planet, prosperity and peace) (European Commission, 2019b). The EU in general has supported more than 100 million people gain better access to food health and education by supporting "[l]ifelong learning and equitable education, including in crisis situations, and stepped up efforts to ensure that everyone has the knowledge, skills, capabilities and rights to enjoy life in dignity, engaged in society and contributing to their communities" (European Commission, 2019b).

Clearly the EU is a leader in those who care about planetary issues such as climate change and its impact worldwide. Climate change will impact rural areas and thus the world poor disproportionately and for that reason better world management of the global economy is needed. Although the EU has made an effort to protect ecosystems and promote greener practices in developing countries the problems continue.

> The EU has worked to promote the wider take-up of its own sustainable energy practices, while taking into account specific circumstances in developing countries... The EU allocated 3.7 billion of funding to sustainable energy from 2014–2020 and is on course to achieve: a) energy access for about 40 million people; b) additional renewable energy capacity of 6.5 gigawatts; and c) annual CO_2 emissions savings of around 15 million tones through energy efficiency measures. (European Commission, 2019b)

The third element of the EU scheme is prosperity and is intricately weaved with promoting inclusive sustainable growth and social protections in developing countries, the priority being building the capacities and social political entrepreneurship in those countries. The EU has attempted to achieve these goals by first providing budgetary support, second providing budgetary guarantees and, third, providing aid for trade and access to markets (European Commission, 2019b). The European External Investment Plan is such a vehicle for development with billions invested towards economic improvement in Africa, for example.

The fourth P stands for peace and the EU has attempted to improve its capacity, as well as that of other regional organizations, by supporting early warning studies, humanitarian responses to crises, conflict mediation and conflict resolution services and promoting the role of women in these processes. As the EU has been one of the strongest advocates of democracy internally, it helps to provide the tools necessary for developing countries.

Clearly, as the world's largest single market, EU policies affect countries across the globe. As noted above in this section the EU promotes open liberalized markets and the rule of law and as such it promotes these values with its trading partners. In order to do just that the EU must review its trading policies with the developing world. According to Kettunen et al., the "EU policy can interact with the Union's consumption patterns increasing or decreasing likely global spillovers. This can result in promoting positive cycles of change (i.e. increased resource efficiency), driving increasing demand for certain commodities and materials, or changing rules governing the nature or scale of supply and demand" (Kettunen et al., 2018). Besides arranging its internal market to focus on implementing the SDGs the EU will also have to manage external relations. "Overall, the EU trade policy has been assessed to have significantly increased exports from developing countries and contributed to their economic diversification, particularly in the Least Developed Countries (LDCs)" (Kettunen et al., 2018). Along with imports from the less developed world the EU has the ability to intervene and promote its aims through development cooperation. From humanitarian aid to micro-financial assistance to more robust funding for sustainable development in the less developed world the EU can be an engine of growth, stability and democracy.

CONCLUSION

The EU is a leader in the fight for climate change. The Intergovernmental Panel on Climate Change has issued its findings and sustainability is at the top of the agenda. The EU and its member states are responding with a drive towards a climate neutral economy. In 2017 the EU reaffirmed the Paris Agreement and in 2018 it issued a call for a cleaner planet (COM2018 (773) final). In the area of energy the EU recognizes that without energy initiatives there will be very little progress towards a climate-neutral economy as long as the energy sector is run on fossil fuels. The EU has therefore looked to reduce greenhouse gas emissions by about 40 percent. In addition to that target, it is raising its share of renewables to 32 percent and is improving energy efficiency by 32 percent overall driving very fast towards its goal.

Beyond energy the EU has promoted innovative policies regarding a climate-neutral economy through industry, innovation and infrastructure. The EU's physical infrastructure counts over 217 000 km of railways, 77 000 km of motorways, 42 000 km of inland waterways, 329 key seaports and 329 airports. With such an extensive network there is much to do and the economic downturn of the 2010s did not help the infrastructural projects along. For this reason the Juncker Commission infused money in the infrastructural area attempting to create a multiplier effect of not only creating additional employment but employment that is located in sustainable sectors. In its vision, the EU economy would be circular and its effect would only reinforce economically and socially sustainable development.

The EU is not only an economic and political union, it is also a global power, and for that reason it aims to influence other regions to follow democratic norms, the rule of law and trade for development. In this respect the EU has come up with a developmental scheme based on the 4Ps (people, planet, prosperity, and peace) (European Commission, 2019b). Overall the EU has aimed at creating conditions in which local capacities can grow sustainably providing an economy of dignity and growth.

NOTE

1.   https://sustainabledevelopment.un.org/post2015/transformingourworld

REFERENCES

CBS (2015). Volkswagen Thwarted Pollution Regulations for 7 Years, September 21.

Chasek, P. L., F. Wagner, A. Leone, A. Lebada & N. Risse (2016). Getting to 2030: Negotiating the Post-2015 Sustainable Development Agenda. *Review of European Community and International Environmental Law*, 25(1).

CNBC (2019). Automation Threatening 25% of Jobs in the US, Especially the "boring and repetitive" ones: Brookings, January 25.

European Commission (2017). Europe on the Move. https://ec.europa.eu/docsroom/documents/36468

European Commission (2018). A Clean Planet for All: A European Strategic Long Term Vision for a Prosperous, Modern, Competitive and Climate Neutral Economy. COM (2018) 773 final, November.

European Commission (2019a). A Vision for the European Industry until 2030. Accessed February 12, 2020 at https://ec.europa.eu/docsroom/documents/36468

European Commission (2019b). Supporting Sustainable Development Goals across the World: The 209 Joint Synthesis Report of the European Union and Its Members. COM (2019) 232 final, October.

European Commission (2020a). 2030 Climate and Energy Framework. Accessed on February 12, 2020 at https://ec.europa.eu/clima/policies/strategies/2030_en

European Commission (2020b). Fact Sheet, EU Delivering on the UN 2030 Agenda. Accessed February 12, 2020 at https://ec.europa.eu/info/sites/info/files/factsheet-eu-delivering-2030-agenda-sustainable-development_en.pdf

Fourie, P. & C. O'Manique (2016). "It Sells, But It Does Not Fly": An Early Assessment of the 2030 Agenda for Sustainable Development. *Development*, 59: 274–9.

Haraguchi N. & K. Kitaoka (2015). Industrialization in the 2030 Agenda for Sustainable Development. *Development*, 58(4): 542–62.

Kettunen, M., C. Boywer, L. Vaculova & C. Charveriat (2018). Sustainable Development Goals and the EU: Uncovering the Nexus between External and Internal Policies. Institute of European Environmental Policy.

Lue A., C. Bresciani, A. Colorni, F. Lia, V. Maras, Z. Radmilovic, L Whitmarsh, D. Xenias & E. Anoyrkati (2016). Future Priorities for a Climate Friendly Transportation: A European Strategic Research Agenda Towards 2030. *International Journal of Sustainable Transportation*, 10(3): 236–46.

New American (2016). UN Agenda 2030: A Recipe for Global Socialism. January 4.

United Nations (2015). Transforming Our World: The 2030 Agenda for Sustainable Development.

United Nations (2018). Sustainable Development Goal 7.

Weber, H. (2017). Politics of "Leaving No One Behind": Contesting the 2030 Sustainable Development Goals Agenda. *Globalization*, 14(3): 399–414.

7. Agenda 2030 and the EU on climate change

Darlene Budd

For nearly a half-century, the European Union (EU) has recognized the dangers associated with environmental neglect. Policy entrepreneurship on environmental issues has led to ambitious commitments to reduce emissions from greenhouse gases and fairly distribute the cost of climate policy measures among developed and developing nations. The EU follows a "leadership by example" approach to prioritize global climate change that includes adaptation strategies, emissions tracking systems, education initiatives and policy coordination mechanisms (Oberthür & Roche Kelly, 2008). Focused on the Sustainable Development Goals (SDGs) and facilitating progress of all nations, the EU remains uniquely positioned to play a key leadership role in addressing global climate change and facilitating country progress toward the SDGs.

The first EU environmental policies to protect citizens from air and water pollution were created during the 1970s. Legislative measures to regulate waste management practices of corporations and maintain safe living conditions for citizens were discussed at the Paris Summit of the European Economic Community in October 1972 and included in the First Action Plan put forward by the European Commission in 1973 (Damro & Hardie, 2008). The plan addressed the environmental conditions associated with the expansion of urban areas and changes in consumption patterns (Sekercioglu, 2018: 35–6). Subsequent action plans embraced a "deepening" strategy that increased cohesion among EU member states and enhanced the group's policymaking abilities by addressing a wide range of environmental issues. By the time of the first United Nations (UN) Intergovernmental Panel on Climate Change (IPCC) in 1988, the EU was viewed as a world leader on environmental policy (Sekercioglu, 2018: 35–6).

It was not until the first UN IPCC assessment report, issued in 1990, declared "emissions resulting from human activities are substantially increasing the atmospheric concentrations of greenhouse gases" that countries began to consider the dangers associated with emissions from greenhouse gases (Harvey, 2018). To address human-caused climate change, the UN

Framework for Climate Change (UNFCC) was created in 1992. However, it was not until 2014, when a UNFCC "reality check" report revealed the fact that CO_2 concentration levels increased 40 percent since pre-industrial times and human activity is the cause of most of the earth's 0.85°C warming since 1880 (Meinshausen, 2016). The report notes specific effects such as heatwaves and heavy rains, arctic ice decreasing at an average of 3.8 percent each decade since 1979, and the likelihood that global sea levels would rise 26 to 82 cm by 2100. The concluding remarks of this report state that "only an aggressive mitigation scenario can keep temperature increases below 2°" (Meinshausen, 2016) and set the context for political entrepreneurship on the part of EU actors.

The ambitious emissions goals included in the EU 2030 Climate and Energy framework highlight the EU's desire to lead the fight against global climate change by cutting emissions, increasing energy efficiency and increasing the use of renewable energy sources. The 2030 climate and energy goals are closely aligned with UN SDG 13 on climate action that emphasizes mitigation plans to improve country resilience to climate changes, comprehensive global climate change adaptation policies, and education programs to increase climate change literacy and awareness among citizens of all ages. This chapter discusses: (1) UN SDG 13 targets, UN agreements that address global climate change and EU 2030 climate and energy goals that align with SDG 13 targets; (2) several challenges associated with managing and coordinating the climate action efforts of 28 members states, the reforms needed, and efforts to implement reforms; (3) EU political entrepreneurship and leadership to leverage such actions globally; and (4) future possibilities for developed and developing country coordination efforts.

UN SDG 13, THE EU AND CLIMATE AND ENERGY FRAMEWORK

The UN SDG 13 to "take urgent action to combat climate change and its impacts" acknowledges that "the global nature of climate change calls for the widest possible international cooperation aimed at accelerating the reduction of global greenhouse gas emissions and addressing adaptation to the adverse impacts of climate change" (A/RES/70/1/Art.31). SDG 13 targets focus on preparedness to address climate-related hazards and disasters, integration of climate change policy across government offices and agencies, and climate change education, adaptation, and capacity-building measures. The specific targets and indicators for SDG 13 are summarized in Table 7.1.

Member countries have agreed to follow the eight indicators that accompany SDG 13 target goals developed by the Inter-Agency and Expert Group on Sustainable Development Goals to meet the target goals included in

Table 7.1   *SDG 13: targets and indicators*

Targets	Indicators
Target 13.1: *Strengthen resilience and adaptive capacity* to climate-related hazards and natural disasters in all countries	13.1.3: Proportion of local governments that adopt and implement local disaster risk reduction strategies in line with national disaster risk reduction strategies 13.1.1: Number of deaths, missing persons and persons affected by disaster per 100,000 people 13.1.2: Number of countries with national and local disaster risk reduction strategies
Target 13.2: *Integrate climate change measures* into national policies, strategies and planning	13.2.1: Number of countries that have communicated the establishment or operationalization of an integrated policy/strategy/plan which increases their ability to adapt to the adverse impacts of climate change, and foster climate resilience and low greenhouse gas emissions development in a manner that does not threaten food production (including a national adaptation plan, nationally determined contribution, national communication, biennial update report or other)
Target 13.3: *Improve education, awareness raising and human and institutional capacity* on climate change mitigation, adaptation, impact reduction and early warning	13.3.1: Number of countries that have integrated mitigation, adaptation, impact reduction and early warning into primary, secondary and tertiary curricula 13.3.2: Number of countries that have communicated the strengthening of institutional, systemic and individual capacity building to implement adaptation, mitigation and technology transfer, and development actions
Target 13.A: Implement the commitment undertaken by developed country parties to the United Nations Framework Convention on Climate Change to a goal of mobilizing jointly $100 billion annually by 2020 from all sources to address the needs of developing countries in the context of meaningful mitigation actions and transparency on implementation and fully operationalize the *Green Climate Fund* through its capitalization as soon as possible	13.A.1: Mobilized amount of United States dollars per year starting in 2020 accountable towards the $100 billion commitment
Target 13.B: Promote mechanisms for raising capacity for effective climate change-related planning and management in *least developed countries and small island developing states*, including focusing on women, youth and local and marginalized communities	13.B.1: Number of least developed countries and small island developing states that are receiving specialized support, and amount of support, including finance, technology and capacity building, for mechanisms for raising capacities for effective climate change-related planning and management, including focusing on women, youth and local and marginalized communities (SDG 13)

SDG 13 (A/RES/71/313 3). These indicators track local and national government risk reduction strategies and plans to adapt to the adverse effects of climate change. Education programs and plans that improve human and institutional "readiness" to respond to climate change conditions and events are reported and recorded. Recognizing the fact that less developed countries and some small islands are especially vulnerable to the effects of climate change and often the least able to fund climate change mitigation, adaptation and education programs, developed countries are tasked with contributing to the Green Climate Fund.

Two indicators included in SDG 13 track developed countries' contributions as well as projects funded with Green Climate contributions. The Green Climate Fund was created at the 2010 Conference of Parties (COP) meeting in Cancun, Mexico and is a key institution for global climate finance. At the 2015 G7 Summit meeting in Germany, countries formally agreed to collectively raise $100 billion per year by 2020 for the Green Climate Fund (G7 Summit, 2015). To measure SDG 13 progress, country contributions to the fund are recorded as investments supported by the Green Climate Fund (SDG13). To guide and facilitate intergovernmental actions that address climate change, the 2030 Agenda for Sustainable Development designates the UNFCC as the primary forum for negotiating and initiating the global responses to climate change. The primary stated goal of the UNFCC is to "stabilize atmospheric concentrations of greenhouse gases (GHGs) to avoid dangerous anthropogenic interference with the climate system" (UNFCC). In the final clause of the convention, member states pledge their "determin[ation] to protect the climate system for present and future generations" (UNFCC). To meet the goals and targets outlined in SDG 13, members of the UNFCC formed the COP that serves as the governing body of annually held UN Climate Change Conferences to assess progress in dealing with climate change (Karybekova, 2018).

The history of EU leadership in the UNFCC and at COP meetings is noteworthy. For example, during negotiations at the third COP (COP3) conference held in Kyoto, Japan, EU members proposed ambitious caps on emissions of global greenhouse gases for the largest emissions producers and challenged other industrialized countries to acknowledge and accept the responsibility of providing assistance and support to developing countries and emerging economies. Representatives at the 1997 meeting signed the Kyoto Protocol and committed to meeting the objective of the UNFCC to reduce the onset of global warming by reducing greenhouse gas concentrations in the atmosphere to "a level that would prevent dangerous anthropogenic interference with the climate system" (UNFCC Article 2). The EU took the lead in ratifying the Kyoto Protocol in 2002 even after President George W. Bush announced in 2001 that the United States (US) would withdraw from the agreement

(Schreurs & Tiberghien, 2007). The decision to honor its commitment to reduce CO_2 emissions meant that the EU would have to convince numerous other industrialized countries to also ratify the agreement. In order for the agreement to go into effect, signatures of 55 percent of industrialized states were required (Schreurs & Tiberghien, 2007). EU climate diplomacy and persuasion were successful and the agreement went into effect in 2005.

The first major UN agreement signed by countries following the introduction of the SDG Agenda 2030 is the Sendai Framework for Disaster Risk Reduction (2015–30). This voluntary, non-binding agreement "recognizes that the State has the primary role to reduce disaster risk but that responsibility should be shared with other stakeholders including local government, the private sector and other stakeholders" (Sendai Framework, 2015). The framework emphasizes cooperation among nations to strengthen resilience and adaptive capacity to climate-related hazards and natural disasters in all countries (UNDRR, 2019). The EU played a key role in the negotiations of the Sendai Framework, adopted its own action plan to guide the implementation of the Sendai Framework in EU policies, and committed to reducing disaster risks inside and outside the EU (Obradovich & Fowler, 2017). The action plan includes the EU Civil Protection Mechanism to facilitate disaster preparedness and prevention, and also provides services following man-made and natural disasters. Resources include firefighting planes and helicopters, medical evacuation capacities and a medical team trained for setting up a field hospital (EU, 2020). Mechanism assistance was critical to recent devasting disasters and complex emergencies around the world. Examples include the Ebola outbreak in the Democratic Republic of the Congo (2018), the aftermath of tropical cyclone Idai in Mozambique (2019), the earthquake in Albania (2019), and forest fires in Sweden (2018), Bolivia (2019), and Greece (2019) (EU, 2020).

Preparation and coordination among EU members began many months prior to the 2015 COP21 meeting in Paris, France. Prioritizing input from policymakers, private and public stakeholders, the European Council developed and introduced its 2015–30 climate goals prior to the 2015 COP21 meeting. EU Agenda 2030 Climate and Energy Framework goals include:

- At least 40 percent cuts in greenhouse gas emissions (from 1990 levels).
- At least 32 percent share for renewable energy.
- At least 32 percent improvement in energy efficiency. (EUCO 169/14, 2014)

These goals formed the basis of the EU's contribution to the new global climate change agreement. At the meeting, EU leaders were able to successfully convince the major emitting countries to support an ambitious set of goals and dynamic review process (Parker et al., 2017). The Paris Agreement on

Climate Change "is the first universal, legally binding global deal to combat climate change and adapt to its effects" (UNFCC, 2015), in order to keep global temperatures from rising 2 degrees Celsius. The EU contributed content to the final agreement and helped persuade other industrial countries to sign.

EU POLITICAL ENTREPRENEURSHIP ON CLIMATE CHANGE IN EUROPE

The EU made the commitment to reduce greenhouse gas emissions beginning in the early 1990s by "climate proofing" and "mainstreaming" climate policy (CAN, 2018). The EU member country practice of including many policy sectors in planning and program development, encouraging coordination at various levels of government, and seeking input from stakeholders is increasingly becoming a "new norm" not previously considered in the traditional way of developing public policies (Silander & Silander, 2016). This relatively new approach to policymaking is an example of EU political entrepreneurship that provides government officials with the "big picture" needed to balance climate change policy goals with overall development goals.

Strategies to meet the SDG 13 must consider both the trade-offs as well as potential synergies among people, planet, prosperity, peace and partnership (Fader & Cranmer, 2018). For example, SDG 1 (End poverty in all its forms everywhere) is a "people" goal that produces the highest level of synergy with other goals (Pradhan et al., 2017). Understandably, addressing SDG people goals associated with eradicating poverty, promoting heathy lives, and eliminating hunger (SDGs 1, 2, and 3), providing inclusive and equitable education (SDG 4), and achieving gender equality (SDG 5) are the most compatible to achieving the remaining 12 SDGs in the planet and prosperity categories. The number and magnitude of trade-offs between goals increases with efforts to address "planet" and "prosperity" goals. For example, establishing sustainable consumption and production patterns (SDG 12) is associated with the most trade-offs and, not surprisingly, also has the highest synergy level of combating climate change (SDG 13) (Pradhan et al., 2017). The challenge of aligning climate change mitigation and adaptation responses with economic growth and prosperity influences the coordination and success of climate change policies in the EU. For example, EU member states most reliant on coal are Poland, Germany, Bulgaria, the Czech Republic, and Romania. Germany and Poland together are responsible for 54 percent of EU emissions from coal (Carrington, 2014). While phasing out coal will be difficult for all of these countries, Germany is better equipped financially to achieve this goal and provide for displaced workers.

Emissions must be reduced for environmental and humanitarian reasons, but there are challenges to achieving this goal in the EU. Three of these challenges

Table 7.2   *Climate action goals, challenges, reform, and implementation*

EU responses to challenges to achieve climate action goals		
Challenges	**Reforms needed**	**Implementation**
Harm to human and economic security	Emission cuts Resilience and adaptation measures	2013 Adaptation Strategy Sendai Resilience Framework
Misconceptions about climate change science	Awareness programs Climate curriculum Teacher training	Action for Climate Empowerment Burgenland Declaration (Austria) Climate Change Education (Italy)
EU enlargement Climate policy coordination	Flexibility and funding to support emissions cuts and transition to renewable energy sources	Just Transition Mechanism Carbon leakage protections

are summarized in Table 7.2. First, ensuring the human and economic security of citizens requires balanced policies that provide policy planning, assistance, and resources. Second, misconceptions about climate change science are many, and climate education programs are needed. Third, EU enlargement requires policy coordination among EU member states. Each of these challenges is addressed in various reforms that have been implemented in EU member states to varying levels. These reforms and the examples of policy implementation actions are discussed below.

To address the challenges associated with reducing emissions and slowing the effects of climate change, EU members agree that reforms are needed. Countries must become more resilient and develop adaptability strategies while also working to cut emissions from greenhouse gases. A climate change curriculum is needed as is teacher training on the subject. Integrating climate action priorities to reduce the use of fossil fuels, increase the availability and use of renewable energy sources, and improve energy efficiency are the goals.

Challenge 1: Harm to Human and Economic Security

In 2003 and 2010 fatalities from heatwaves in Europe totaled 70,000 and 56,000, respectively (Kron et al., 2019). In 2019, summer temperatures in Germany reached a record-breaking 42.6 C (108 F), and France broke its heat record twice, with the highest temperature measuring 46 C (114.8 F) (Kron et al., 2019). The same heatwave that brought record temperatures to France sparked the worst wildfires to hit Spain in 20 years (Henley & Jones, 2019). Later the same year, Venice in Italy experienced multiple flooding events and the high-water mark of 1.5 meters was reached three times in one week for the first time in recorded history (Henley & Giuffrida, 2019).

Similar events and statistics may become the new norm as the percentage of the European population affected by weather-related disasters is predicted to increase from 5 percent in 1981–2010 to 67 percent by 2100 and the record number of heat-related fatalities in 2003 may become the new norm by 2050 (Kron et al., 2019). Resilience and adaptation measures (SDG 13.1) can mitigate the human and economic insecurity caused by such events. In the near term, countries that experience a climate disaster need to receive human services and financial support when national response capacities to fight forest fires are exhausted (EU ECHO, 2020). In the long run, CO_2 levels must be significantly reduced.

Reform 1: Emission cuts, resilience, and adaptation measures
Ultimately, renewable energy sources need to replace fossil fuels. In an effort to make this transition, the EU introduced an Emissions Trading System (ETS) in 2005. In keeping with the EU's political entrepreneurial efforts, the EU ETS became the world's first international ETS and has served as a model for countries around the world to follow to reduce emissions from greenhouse gases (Venmans, 2012). The ETS facilitated a 21 percent reduction in emissions from EU manufacturers included in the system since 2005, exceeding the original 20 percent cut in emissions included in the 2020 Climate and Energy Framework. Based on the "polluter pays" concept, EU manufacturers are allotted a certain emissions level (Borghesi & Montini, 2016). Once a manufacturer reaches the limit or exceeds the allotted tonnage, additional credits must be acquired from other manufacturers that have limited emissions by restricting output, improving efficiency, or switching to renewable energy sources (Conniff, 2009). The cap is gradually reduced over time to mitigate the pollution problem and decrease total emissions.

With a history of documented economic benefits and environmental effectiveness (see Borghesi & Montini, 2016), the European Commission introduced the 2050 Roadmap that includes the ETS to transform the EU into a "competitive, low-carbon economy by 2050" (EC 2050, 2011: 3). The plan establishes clear goals to cut domestic greenhouse gas emissions by at least 80 percent by 2050 compared to 1990 and includes the EU Climate and Energy 2030 goal to achieve a minimum 40 percent cut in domestic greenhouse gas emissions (from 1990 levels). However, updated statistics and scientific analyses have led EU officials to agree that meeting the Paris Agreement goal of keeping climate change well below 2°C – and aiming for no more than 1.5°C – requires more aggressive policies that include a zero-carbon emissions plan to achieve climate neutrality this century (Roberts, 2019).

Incremental reforms and adaptation measures are due in part to activist pressure and public demands on government to prioritize climate change policies. Examples of citizen involvement in EU climate change policies are many. Following heatwaves and wildfires during Sweden's hottest summer on record in 2018, 15-year-old Greta Thunberg went on a school strike outside the Swedish Parliament (Crouch, 2018). The strike inspired students across Europe to organize climate change rallies and share posts and photos using the #FridaysForFuture hashtag. Climate protesters of all ages outside the European Parliament in Brussels declared a climate emergency prior to the COP25 UN Climate Conference in Madrid, Spain (Rankin, 2019). Dissatisfied with the outcome of the Parliament's climate talks, Climate Action Network International issued a press release warning that, "Governments cannot ignore the groundswell of public opinion demanding an urgent response to the climate crisis. We have seen the will of the people, especially the youth, and it will continue to assert itself" (CAN, 2019). Civil society in many EU member states plays a critical role in galvanizing citizen support for climate action policies.

Implementation 1: 2013 Adaptation Strategy and Sendai Resilience Framework

Recognizing that climate change has had and will continue to have detrimental impacts on the environment, human health, and the economy, the EU introduced the 2013 EU Strategy on Adaptation to Climate Change (EU Adaptation Strategy, 2013). The plan encourages all member states to adopt comprehensive adaptation strategies, provides participating countries access to an information platform, and includes funding sources to increase the resilience and adaptation capacities of member countries. An evaluation of the strategy included input from citizens, organizations, and professionals involved in climate change adaptation. As of 2018, 25 EU member states had adopted a national adaptation strategy and 15 had developed a national adaptation plan (EEA, 2018). Including stakeholder input in the evaluation process gives entities outside government a sense of agency that helps to ensure continued support of the policies included in the strategies and plans.

At the local government level, the EU plays an important role providing the organizational structure for climate change policy coordination. The Covenant of Mayors was developed in 2008 as an initiative to support local government efforts to reduce emissions through specific action plans that promote energy-saving strategies and increase the use of renewable energy sources (Pablo-Romero, 2018). The organization is based on the premise that cities and surrounding towns have a critical role to play in mitigating climate change due to the fact that Europeans living in urban areas consume three quarters of the energy produced in the EU and are responsible for a similar share of CO_2 emissions. Considering public and private interests, local governments are able to mainstream sustainable energy issues into local planning and development strategies that ultimately may shift citizens' behavior and perceptions of the climate change issue.

Challenge 2: Misconceptions about Climate Change Science

Climate change literacy plays a significant role in determining whether a young person possesses the knowledge, attitude, and concern that translate into a climate-friendly behavior pattern. For example, researchers find that the more knowledgeable students are about the socio-scientific aspects of climate change, the "more likely they are to have the opinion that humans are causing climate change and that both individuals and governments are responsible for addressing climate change" (Harker-Schuch & Bugge-Henriksen, 2013). Students with low levels of knowledge about climate change have little concern about the environment and report little to no interest in joining a collective effort to address the issue (Kuthe et al., 2019). In many instances, students do not possess the basic climate science concepts necessary to fully comprehend the issues of global warming and climate change (Shepardson et al., 2009). Misconceptions about the causes of climate change are a major challenge to accomplishing climate change goals (Choi et al., 2010), thus, increasing awareness about the impact of climate change (UN SDG Target 13.3) is an important policy action.

Climate change education addresses the causes and consequences of climate change and provides students with the knowledge necessary to develop effective responses to climate change (UNESCO, 2015). Currently, there is no EU-wide climate change education program. For this reason, at least in part, many teachers report feeling ill-equipped to fill the gaps in knowledge that exist among their students (Plutzer et al., 2016). In the United Kingdom, two thirds of teachers surveyed in 2019 believed more time should be spent teaching students about climate change, and three fourths of these teachers "do not feel they have received adequate training to educate students about climate change" (Taylor, 2019). The need for more teacher training and classroom lessons on sustainability and the environment is evident. Understanding the science of global climate change is critical to increasing climate change literacy and awareness among citizens of all ages. Such changes will influence individuals' perceptions and concern about the environment. Recognizing the significance of global climate change will increase the receptivity of citizens to the idea of policy changes to reduce CO_2 emissions and support policymaker efforts to "integrate climate change measures into national policies, strategies and planning" (SDG 13.2).

Reform 2: Awareness programs, climate curriculum, and teacher training

Nearly unanimous support exists among individuals and government leaders for climate education, which is a consistent theme in UN agreements addressing global climate change. Article 6 of the UNFCC (1992) emphasizes the "importance of education, training and public awareness on climate change". Article 10e of the Kyoto Protocol (1998) states that "all Parties shall facilitate at the national level public awareness of, and public access to information on, climate change". The Paris Agreement combines the message of UNFCC Article 6 and the urgency of Kyoto Protocol Article 10e "Article 12: Parties shall cooperate in taking measures, as appropriate, to enhance climate change education, training, public awareness, public participation and public access to information, recognizing the importance of these steps with respect to enhancing actions under this Agreement" (FCCC/CP/2015/10/Add.1).

Currently, lessons on global climate change are interspersed in science classes for students at various grade levels. A consistent, mandated curriculum on climate education does not exist in any EU member country. Organizations recognized by the EU as important stakeholders of education, social, economic and culture issues have asked the European Council to increase funding for education on the environment. In a resolution signed by the European Students' Union organization, student leaders representing 45 universities urge administrators of higher education institutions "to allocate economic resources to develop educational programs with sustainability on the agenda". Referencing the six priority areas outlined in the UNFCCC Action for Climate Empowerment (ACE) agenda, the European Students' Union urges European institutions and governments to work with universities to develop climate change education programs that may serve as models for other institutions and companies working to preserve the planet (ESU BM75, 2018).

Speaking at the UN Conference on Climate Change in Madrid, Spain, Education International (EI), an international teachers' union organization representative, reiterated the organization's resolve to contribute to solving the climate crisis by tackling the climate emergency from the classroom. The EI representative called on governments to ensure that climate change education became a core element of the curriculum, beginning from early childhood. The EI pledge also emphasized the importance of climate change education as part of teacher education and continuous professional development. "Supportive education systems are vital for teachers and educators to be able to help their students to acquire the knowledge, skills, attitudes and values needed to take action for a sustainable future" (Magnard, 2020).

Recognizing the importance of citizen and stakeholder input, government representatives attending the Climate Change Conference held in Bonn, Germany (SB50) agreed "to significantly strengthen climate education, awareness and public engagement (ACE)" (UN, 2019). Participants agreed to scale up climate change education and training programs in their countries and host public awareness events to inform citizens of the environmental dangers and health implications associated with global climate change. Better access to information on ACE issues will not only promote a more informed citizenry but should also encourage public participation and action on climate change issues.

Implementation 2: Action for Climate Empowerment, Burgenland Declaration and climate change education

While no sweeping changes to climate education in the EU have been implemented, Austria introduced the Burgenland Declaration of the ACE. Described as the "kick-off" of a global initiative to catalyze wider engagement and support for the implementation of Article 12 of the Paris Agreement and the ACE Agenda, country leaders signed the declaration calling for the need to close the "education, training, and knowledge gap on climate change" (UNFCC, 2019). Further support for raising ambition and mobilizing commitments for the ACE agenda emerged among countries, non-state actors, and youth attendees of the UN Climate Conference (COP25) in Madrid, Spain. At the conference, Italy's minister of education, Lorenzo Fioramonti, reaffirmed the urgency of implementing climate change education stating that a key part of Italy's response is to "go all-out on making sustainable development an integral part of education". Pledging that Italy will lead efforts to gain support for ACE, Fioramonti announced plans to make Italy the first country to make climate change lessons compulsory in schools (Horowitz, 2019). Italy's pledge and the Burgenland "kick-off" Declaration for ACE are examples of the entrepreneurial role that EU member states consistently play to promote progressive climate change policies among nations in Europe and around the world.

Challenge 3: EU Enlargement Climate Policy Coordination

In addition to mainstreaming climate change into national policies, coordination among countries will allow the EU to reach the SDG 13 climate action targets while pursuing Agenda 2030 emissions reduction goals. Variation in country size, geography, and resources have always existed among EU members. EU enlargement has increased the variations among countries and created what some policymakers believe is an "increasingly problematic dimension for European climate policy" (Marcinkiewicz & Tosun, 2015). Another identified difference among members is the perception citizens possess regarding the threat of climate change.

Social movements in the late 1980s and the growth of green technology industries in western and northern EU countries forced policymakers to prioritize climate change (Wurzel & Connelly, 2011). The history, governance, and transition experiences of the eight formerly communist countries of central and eastern Europe that joined the EU in 2004 have not produced the same attitudes and values regarding the importance of climate protection. Due to such differences, the EU's policy ambition has at times been limited, particularly by increasingly assertive opposition from the so-called Visegrád Four: Poland, Hungary, the Czech Republic, and Slovakia (Bauerova, 2018). Policymaking is also constrained at times by an overriding concern with minimizing the burden of regulation, in the interests of industrial competitiveness and jobs (Jordan et al., 2012). The persistent problem of funding the implementation of climate action policies has become even more acute since the 2008 financial crisis (UNESCO, 2015). Attitudes among citizens and political parties must change but so must the funding mechanism for implementing changes in economically strapped countries dependent on fossil fuels.

Reforms 3: Flexibility and funding
Citizens increasingly perceive climate change as a threat and cite it as a top priority for government (Fagan & Huang, 2019). A shift in public opinion and increased participation in climate action organizations have mobilized citizens in many European member states to vote for members of parliament and political parties that also view global climate change as a priority. However, agreement on targets and timelines to meet the emissions reduction goals included in the 2030 Climate and Energy Framework has not been unanimous among EU members. Challenges exist as does resistance from countries that have reservations about the feasibility of achieving significant reductions in emissions. For example, Poland relies on coal for more than 90 percent of its electricity, and blocked early proposals to increase the EU's CO_2 emissions targets ultimately included in the 2030 Climate and Energy Framework (Nelsen, 2017). Job losses, increased costs for businesses, and the possibility of stalled economic growth take priority over the environment in the minds of many Polish citizens and lawmakers. In general, less support for climate change policies exists among citizens in post-communist countries. Fewer activist groups, a weak civil society, and scant mention of climate change action by political parties in post-communist countries are likely contributing factors (Chaisty & Whitefield, 2015).

Opposition from Poland has not deterred members of parliament from pursuing the goals outlined in the 2050 Roadmap. For example, the official vote on a proposed 2050 EU Decarbonization Plan to achieve a low-carbon economy outlined in the 2050 roadmap took place in 2019 at the EU Summit meeting in Brussels. A unanimous vote was required to implement the plan. Voicing objections to the specific timeline, Poland vetoed the plan with support from Hungary, Estonia, and the Czech Republic (Keating, 2019).

Countries such as Poland are not willing to commit to increased cuts in emissions without additional funding. Despite the no vote, European Commission president Ursula von der Leyen announced the European Green Deal that outlines the European Commission's commitment to achieve carbon neutrality by 2050 (Barrett, 2019). The EU continues to reform emission reduction targets and these reforms include additional funding to facilitate policy coordination among EU member states.

Implementation 3: Just Transition Mechanism and carbon leakage protections

In 2018, a new set of ambitious EU ETS goals for the Phase 4 (2021–30) period were introduced. The goals include fewer allowances (or credits) available for businesses to trade or purchase along with an accelerated timeline for credit cuts over time. As regulations on the fossil fuel industry and coal-powered manufacturing continue to tighten, EU officials anticipate increased investment in energy efficiency technologies and businesses. In the near term, Phase 4 of the ETS will continue to protect certain industries from carbon leakage (EU ETS, 2019).

The ETS cap and trade program necessarily makes carbon-intensive products manufactured in EU countries "more expensive and therefore disadvantaged on the global market" (Palakcová, 2019). As a result, European companies may choose to curb production or shift their investments (and thus their emissions) to other countries outside the EU. "Whole industries could theoretically be outsourced, and the EU would end up re-importing the emissions it is striving to reduce" (Palakcová, 2019). This would damage both the environment and the European economy. To prevent this scenario, protections that provide free emissions allowances for certain industries included on an ETS approved list will remain in place. While some environmental activists object to the concessions, countries such as Poland will be protected from sudden economic disruption.

The recently proposed European Green Deal considers the resource needs of reluctant eastern European EU members. The Just Transition Mechanism included in the Green Deal will provide financial assistance to coal-dependent regions (Keating, 1/14/2020) while at the same time encouraging public and private investment to stimulate "transition to a climate-neutral, green, competitive and inclusive economy" (EC, 2020). An estimated €100 billion in grants, private investment and support from the European Investment Bank is expected by European Commission officials (Morgan, 15/01/2020). This figure has been described by one German member of the European Parliament as "too little to match the scale of transformation needed to confront the planetary emergency" and a trade union group stated that "the funding proposed for

10 years is what would be needed every year to achieve climate neutrality by 2050 in a fair way" (Morgan, 15/01/2020).

While more money is always needed and criticisms are inevitable, the European Green Deal has also been described as a viable plan to prove the feasibility of decarbonization. "No longer the hazy aspiration of a few climate action enthusiasts; it is a detailed mainstream policy document affecting every sector in one of the richest, most sophisticated economies in the world" (Valatsas, 2019). In addition to funding assistance, technological spillovers for renewable energy and complementary technologies such as energy storage will lower the cost of energy for all countries including emerging markets (Valatsas, 2019). A successful European Green Deal will prove that prosperity is not incompatible with climate sustainability.

EU POLITICAL ENTREPRENEURSHIP ON CLIMATE CHANGE GLOBALLY

Leadership and entrepreneurial efforts to drive the EU climate agenda have contributed to a more aggressive and coordinated set of actions taken by governments around the world. With a proven track record of engaging mayors and other local government officials to voluntarily commit to developing climate change action strategies and plans (Gesing, 2017), the Covenant of Mayors initiative went global in 2016. A UN-supported Global Covenant of Mayors quickly received commitments from over 10,000 cities in 138 countries across six continents that represent more than 80 million people (GCoM, 2020). The fact that the Covenant of Mayors organization originated in the EU and with the support of the UN became a global organization highlights the close working relationship between the EU and the UN as well as EU leadership and entrepreneurship.

EU-inspired ETS have been implemented in countries and regions around the world including Switzerland, the Regional Greenhouse Gas Initiative comprised of ten northeast states in the US, California in the US, Québec in Canada, New Zealand, the Republic of Korea and pilot schemes in China (Narassimhan et al., 2018). The lessons learned from practical experiences of tradable permit schemes and continuous analytical efforts identify ETS not as a goal by itself, but as a tool to achieve environmental goals most cost effectively (Schmalensee & Stavins, 2017). Emissions trading reduces compliance costs which allows countries or regions to achieve ambitious environmental objectives that otherwise may not be possible with "command-and-control" regulations (Philibert & Reinand, 2004). The EU ETS has facilitated international efforts to build a global and comprehensive greenhouse gas mitigation regime.

Another way EU political entrepreneurship has influenced the world is by setting the example of what is possible. The efforts of one teen, Greta Thunberg, led to a youth movement that has the potential to shift public opinion and policy. For example, during the weeks leading up to the 2019 UN Climate Action Summit in New York City, over 6 million students around the world joined the Global Climate Strike (Taylor, 2019). The Fridays For Future organizers believe the youth protests have helped to "put the climate crisis high on the political agenda" (Welle, 2019), force politicians around the world to review the scientific fact that the Earth is "clearly and unequivocally" facing a climate emergency (Calma, 2019), and accept the challenge of reversing the climate change trend.

While the outcome of the EU's proposed Green Deal remains a question mark, its content and tone embody the entrepreneurial spirit needed to motivate citizens and governments around the world to take climate change action. Based on the need for collective action, the plan stresses "cooperation with partner countries" that include the largest emitters in Asia as well as the potential big emitters in Africa. Pledging support to ensure a sustainable economic transition, European Commission high representative Joseph Borrell Fontelles stated: "we will use all the means at our disposal – from trade policy and technical assistance, to capacity building and development cooperation, as well as our crisis management tools when needed. If we deliver a Green Deal for Europe, making the EU the leading example for a just and sustainable transition, we will have the credibility to press and help others to do the same. Then we can really make a difference to the future of our planet" (EEAS, 2019).

Providing over 40 percent of the world's public climate finance, the EU is the world's biggest climate finance donor (EEAS, 2019). EU experience and dedicated resources will help countries around the world meet the climate action targets included in SDG 13 and live healthier and longer lives.

CONCLUSION

The ultimate goal of a political entrepreneur is to "develop and promot[e] new norms that have not been embedded in traditional day to day public activities" (Silander & Silander, 2016: 10). The urgency with which so many individuals and governments around the world view the issue of climate change is due in large part to aggressive policies and the entrepreneurial spirit of the EU. Innovative trading systems to reduce emissions, climate strikes, and "green diplomacy" have helped produce "new norms" in family homes, businesses and local government offices. National parliamentary debates increasingly reflect the demands of citizens to make global climate change a priority.

Much work still needs to be done within the EU. The challenges to ensure the safety of citizens and reduce damages from climate events, increase awareness and climate change literacy, and facilitate a coordinated policy on global climate change will continue to push the boundaries of science, test corporations, and demand creative policy solutions from government. Schools, citizen groups, and individuals play an important role that requires more education for students and better training for teachers. Flexibility and additional financial support for post-communist countries' efforts to move away from fossil fuels is necessary. Energy sources and energy use must change. In the current "take-make-use-waste" lifestyle, products are used once and thrown away (Valášek, 2019). Future trends may include products that are built to last using clean energy sources.

The Green Deal's carrot-and-stick approach to trade may eventually create citizen demand for green household goods and ecofriendly products. The deal requires EU members to only agree to new comprehensive trade agreements that include parties that have signed up to and are implementing the Paris Agreement (Valatsas, 2019). This requirement would exclude the US under the current Trump administration. Due to the size and importance of the EU market, as well as popular support for the climate agenda in western Europe, the EU may commit to this rule and initiate a dramatic shift in world trade policy.

REFERENCES

A/RES/70/1/Art. 31. Transforming Our World: The 2030 Agenda for Sustainable Development. United Nations. Accessed February 3, 2020 at www.un.org/ga/search/view_doc.asp?symbol=A/RES/70/1&Lang=E

A/RES/71/313 3. Work of the Statistical Commission Pertaining to the 2030 Agenda for Sustainable Development. United Nations. Accessed February 5, 2020 at http://ggim.un.org/documents/A_RES_71_313.pdf

Barrett, E., 2019. "The European Commission President Announced a European Green Deal, Targeting a Carbon Neutral EU by 2050". *Fortune*, December 12. Accessed February 3, 2020 at_https://fortune.com/2019/12/12/european-green-deal-man-on-the-moon/

Bauerova, H., 2018. "The V4 and European Integration". *Politics in Central Europe*, 14(2): 121–39.

Borghesi, S. & M. Montini, 2016. "The Best (and Worst) of GHG Emission Trading Systems: Comparing the EU ETS with Its Followers". *Frontiers in Energy Research*, 4, July 29.

Calma, J., 2019. 2019 "Was the Year of 'Climate Emergency' Declarations". *The Verge*, December 27. Accessed February 3, 2020 at www.theverge.com/2019/12/27/21038949/climate-change-2019-emergency-declaration

CAN, 2018. "Climate Mainstreaming and Climate Proofing: The Horizontal Integration of Climate Action in the EU Budget: Assessment and Recommendation". *Climate Action Network*, August. Accessed February 5, 2020 at www.caneurope.org/docman/climate-finance-development/3373-assessment-eu-budget-climate-mainstreaming-can-europe-august-2018/file

CAN, 2019. Press Release. *Climate Action Network*, December 16. Accessed February 5, 2020 at
www.climatenetwork.org/press-release/people-promise-take-streets-world-leaders-leave-un-climate-talks-no-plan-climate

Carrington, D., 2014. "Germany, UK and Poland Top 'Dirty 30' List of EU Coal-Fired Power Stations". *The Guardian*, July 22. Accessed February 5, 2020 at: www.theguardian.com/environment/2014/jul/22/germany-uk-poland-top-dirty-30-list-eu-coal-fired-power-stations

Chaisty, P. & S. Whitefield, 2015. "Attitudes towards the Environment: Are Post-Communist Societies (Still) Different?" *Environmental Politics*, 24(4): 598–616.

Choi, S., D. Niyogi, D. Shepardson, & U. Charusombat, 2010. "Do Earth and Environmental Science Textbooks Promote Middle and High School Students' Conceptual Development about Climate Change? Textbooks' Consideration of Students' Misconceptions". *Bulletin of the American Meteorological Society*, 91(7): 889–98.

Conniff, R., 2009. "The Political History of Cap and Trade". *Smithsonian Magazine*, August. Accessed February 3, 2020 at www.smithsonianmag.com/science-nature/the-political-history-of-cap-and-trade-34711212/

Crouch, D., 2018. "The Swedish 15-Year-Old Who's Cutting Class to Fight the Climate Crisis". *The Guardian*, September 1. Accessed February 3, 2020 at www.theguardian.com/science/2018/sep/01/swedish-15-year-old-cutting-class-to-fight-the-climate-crisis

Damro, C. & L. Hardie, 2008. "The EU and Climate Change Policy: Law, Politics, and Prominence at Different Levels". *Journal of Contemporary European Research*, 4(3): 179–92.

EC 1/14/2020. "Financing the Green Transition: The European Green Deal Investment Plan and Just Transition Mechanism". *European Commission*. Accessed February 4, 2020 at https://ec.europa.eu/regional_policy/en/newsroom/news/2020/01/14-01-2020-financing-the-green-transition-the-european-green-deal-investment-plan-and-just-transition-mechanism

EC 2050, 2011. "The Roadmap for Transforming the EU into a Competitive, Low-Carbon Economy by 2050". *European Commission*. Accessed February 3, 2020 at https://ec.europa.eu/clima/sites/clima/files/2050_roadmap_en.pdf

EEA, 2018. "Number of Countries that Have Adopted a Climate Change Adaptation Strategy/Plan". *European Environmental Agency*, December 7. Accessed February 5, 2020 at www.eea.europa.eu/airs/2018/environment-and-health/climate-change-adaptation-strategies

EEAS, 2019. "The EU Green Deal: A Global Perspective". *European External Action Service*, December 12. Accessed February 3, 2020 at https://eeas.europa.eu/topics/climate-environment-energy/71928/eu-green-deal-%E2%80%93-global-perspective_en

ESU BM75, 2018. Resolution Regarding Climate Change. December 6. Accessed February 3, 2020 at www.esu-online.org/?policy=resolution-regarding-climate-change

EU, 2020. "EU Civil Protection Mechanism". *European Civil Protection and Humanitarian Aid Operations*, January 15. Accessed February 5, 2020 at: https://ec.europa.eu/echo/what/civil-protection/mechanism_en

EU Adaptation Strategy, 2013. "EU Adaptation Strategy". United Nations. Accessed February 5, 2020 at https://ec.europa.eu/clima/policies/adaptation/what_en#tab-0-1

EU ECHO, 2020. "Forest Fires". *European Civil Protection and Humanitarian Aid Operations*, January 15. Accessed February 5, 2020 at https://ec.europa.eu/echo/what-we-do/civil-protection/forest-fires_en

EU ETS, 2019. "The EU Emissions Trading System (EU ETS)". Accessed February 5, 2020 at https://ec.europa.eu/clima/sites/clima/files/factsheet_ets_en.pdf

EUCO 169/14, 2014. "Agenda 2030 Climate and Energy Goals Framework". *European Council*, October 24. Accessed February 3, 2020 at http://data.consilium.europa.eu/doc/document/ST-169-2014-INIT/en/pdf

Fader, M. & C. Cranmer, 2018. "Changes in Risk of Extreme Weather Events in Europe". *Environmental Science and Policy*, 100: 74–83. Accessed February 5, 2020 at https://e-tarjome.com/storage/panel/fileuploads/2019-08-27/1566897919_E13059-e-tarjome.pdf

Fagan, F. & C. Huang, 2019. "A Look at How People around the World View Climate Change". *Pew Research Center*. Accessed February 4, 2020 at www.pewresearch.org/fact-tank/2019/04/18/a-look-at-how-people-around-the-world-view-climate-change/

FCCC/CP/2015/10/Add.1. Paris Agreement. Accessed February 5, 2020 at www.un.org/en/development/desa/population/migration/generalassembly/docs/globalcompact/FCCC_CP_2015_10_Add.1.pdf

G7 Summit, 2015. Leaders' Declaration G7 Summit. Accessed February 5, 2020 at https://sustainabledevelopment.un.org/content/documents/7320LEADERS%20STATEMENT_FINAL_CLEAN.pdf

GCoM. Accessed February 4, 2020 at www.globalcovenantofmayors.org/

Gesing, F., 2017. "The New Global Covenant of Mayors for Climate and Energy and the Politics of Municipal Climate Data". *Zentra Working Papers in Transnational Studies No. 71/2017*. Accessed February 3, 2020 at www.researchgate.net/publication/326517650_The_new_Global_Covenant_of_Mayors_for_Climate_Energy_and_the_politics_of_municipal_climate_data

Harker-Schuch, I. & C. Bugge-Henriksen, 2013. "Opinions and Knowledge about Climate Change Science in High School Students". *AMBIO*. Accessed February 5, 2020 at www.ncbi.nlm.nih.gov/pmc/articles/PMC3758816/

Harvey, F., 2018. "How the UN Climate Panel Got To 1.5C Threshold". *The Guardian*, October 7. Accessed February 5, 2020 at www.theguardian.com/environment/2018/oct/08/how-the-un-climate-panel-ipcc-got-to-15c-threshold-timeline

Henley, J. & A. Giuffrida, 2019. "Two People Die as Venice Floods at Highest Level in 50 Years". *The Guardian*, November 13. Accessed February 3, 2020 at www.theguardian.com/environment/2019/nov/13/waves-in-st-marks-square-as-venice-flooded-highest-tide-in-50-years

Henley, J. & S. Jones, 2019. "Spain Battles Biggest Wildfires in 20 Years as Heatwave Grips Europe". *The Guardian*, June 27. Accessed February 3, 2020 at www.theguardian.com/world/2019/jun/27/hundreds-of-firefighters-tackle-blaze-in-north-east-spain

Horowitz, J. 2019. "Italy's Students Will Get a Lesson in Climate Change, Many Lessons". *New York Times*, November 5. Accessed February 5, 2020 at www.nytimes.com/2019/11/05/world/europe/italy-schools-climate-change.html

Jordan, A., H. van Asselt, F. Berkhout, & D. Huitema, 2012. "Understanding the Paradoxes of Multilevel Governing: Climate Change Policy in the European Union". *Global Environmental Politics*, 12(2): 43–66. Accessed February 5, 2020 at www.bu.edu/sph/files/2012/12/Jordan_2012_Understanding_the_Paradoxes_of_Multilevel_Governing_-_Climate_Change_Policy_in_the_EU.pdf

Karybekova, G., 2018. "International Instruments in the Field of Climate Change". *National Academy of Sciences of the Kyrgyz Republic.*

Keating, D., 2019. "EU Decarbonization Plan For 2050 Collapses after Polish Veto". *Forbes*, June 20. Accessed February 3, 2020 at www.forbes.com/sites/ davekeating/2019/06/20/eu-decarbonisation-plan-for-2050-collapses-after-polish -veto/#7f384b1a30b2

Keating, D., 2020. "EU Unveils Fund to Woo Poland on Climate". *Forbes*, January 14. Accessed May 20, 2020 at: www.forbes.com/sites/davekeating/2020/01/14/eu -unveils-fund-to-woo-poland-on-climate/#2d78b50142e2

Kron, W., P. Low, & Z. Kundzewicz, 2019. "Changes in Risk of Extreme Weather Events in Europe". *Environmental Science and Policy*, 100: 74–83. Accessed February 5, 2020 at www.climatechangepost.com/news/2019/8/26/damage-and -fatalities-extreme-weather-events-europ/

Kuthe, A., A. Korfgen, J. Stötter, & L. Keller, 2019. "Strengthening Their Climate Change Literacy: A Case Study Addressing the Weaknesses in Young People's Climate Change Awareness". *Applied Environmental Education and Communication*, DOI: 10.1080/1533015X.2019.1597661.

Kyoto Protocol, 1998. "Kyoto Protocol to the United Nations Framework Convention on Climate Change". *United Nations*. Accessed February 5, 2020 at https://unfccc .int/resource/docs/convkp/kpeng.pdf

Magnard, L., 2020. "COP 25: Educators Firmly Commit to Helping Address the Climate Emergency, Education and Solidarity Network", January 12. Accessed May 20, 2020 at www.educationsolidarite.org/en/actualite/cop-25-educators-firmly -commit-helping-address-climate-emergency

Marcinkiewicz, K. & J. Tosun, 2015. "Contesting Climate Change: Mapping the Political Debate in Poland". *East European Politics*, 31(2): 1–21.

Meinshausen, M., 2016. "Paris Climate Targets Aren't Enough, But We Can Close the Gap". *The Conversation*, June 29. Accessed February 3, 2020 at https:// theconversation.com/paris-climate-targets-arent-enough-but-we-can-close-the-gap -61798

Morgan, S., 2020. "EU Reveals Climate Fund Details as Critics Worry Cash Won't Be Enough", EURATIV, January 15. Accessed May 20, 2020 at www .climatechangenews.com/2020/01/15/eu-reveals-climate-fund-details-critics-worry -cash-wont-enough/

Narassimhan, E., K. Gallagher, S. Koester, & J. Rivera Alejo, 2018. "Carbon Pricing in Practice: A Review of Existing Emissions Trading Systems". *Climate Policy*, 18(8): 967–91.

Nelsen, F., 2017. "Think Tank: Coal Crisis, Not Climate Policy, Is Forcing Polish Energy Overhaul", EURACTIV. Accessed May 20, 2020 at www.euractiv.com/ section/electricity/interview/15-nov-think-tank-coal-crisis-not-climate-policy-is -forcing-polish-energy-overhaul/

Oberthür, S. & C. Roche Kelly, 2008. "EU Leadership in International Climate Policy: Achievements and Challenges". *International Spectator*, 43(3): 35–50.

Obradovich, N. & J. Fowler, 2017. "Climate Change May Alter Human Physical Activity Patterns". *Nature Human Behaviour*, 1. https://doi.org/10.1038/s41562-017 -0097

Pablo-Romero, M., 2018. "Analyzing the Effects of the Benchmark Local Initiatives of Covenant of Mayors Signatories". *Journal of Cleaner Production*, 176: 159–74.

Palacková, E., 2019. "Saving Face and Facing Climate Change: Are Border Adjustments a Viable Option to Stop Carbon Leakage?" *European View*, 18(2): 149–55.

Parker, C. F., C. Karlsson, & M. Hjerpe, 2017. "Assessing the European Union's Global Climate Change Leadership: From Copenhagen to the Paris Agreement". *Journal of European Integration*, 39(2): 239–52.

Philibert, C. & J. Reinand, 2004. "Emissions Trading: Taking Stock and Looking Forward OECD and IEA Information Paper", COM/ENV/EPOC/IEA/SLT(2004)3. Accessed February 4, 2020 at www.oecd.org/environment/cc/32140134.pdf

Plutzer, E., M. Mccaffrey, A. L. Hannah, J. Rosenau, M. Berbeco, and A. H. Reid, 2016. "Climate Confusion among US Teachers". *Science*, 351: 664–5. 10.1126/science. aab3907

Pradhan, P., L. Costa, D. Rybski, W. Lucht, & J. P. Kropp, 2017. "A Systematic Study of Sustainable Development Goal (SDG) Interactions". *Earth's Future*, 5(11).

Rankin, J., 2019. "'Our House Is on Fire': EU Parliament Declares Climate Emergency". *The Guardian*, November 28. Accessed February 3, 2020 at www.theguardian.com/ world/2019/nov/28/eu-parliament-declares-climate-emergency

Roberts, J., 2019. "'I would like people to panic': Top Scientist Unveils Equation Showing World in Climate Emergency". *EU Research and Innovation Magazine*. September 24. Accessed February 5, 2020 at https://horizon-magazine.eu/article/ i-would-people-panic-top-scientist-unveils-equation-showing-world-climate -emergency.html

Schmalensee, R. & R. N. Stavins, 2017. "Lessons Learned from Three Decades of Experience with Cap and Trade". *Review of Environmental Economics and Policy*, 11(1): 59–79.

Schreurs, M. A. & Y. Tiberghien, 2007. "Multi-Level Reinforcement: Explaining European Union Leadership in Climate Change Mitigation". *Global Environmental Politics*, 7(4): 19–46.

Sekercioglu, S., 2018. *Civil Society Impact on the European Union Climate Change Policy*. London: Transnational Press.

Sendai Framework, 2015. "Sendai Framework for Disaster Reduction 2015–2030". *European Civil Protection and Humanitarian Aid Operations*. Accessed February 5, 2020 at https://ec.europa.eu/echo/partnerships/relations/european-and-international -cooperation/sendai-framework-disaster-risk-reduction_en

Shepardson, D. P., D. Niyogi, S. Choi, U. Charusombat, 2009. "Seventh Grade Students' Conceptions of Global Warming and Climate Change". *Environmental Education Research*, 15(5): 549–70.

Silander D. & C. Silander, 2016. *Political Entrepreneurship: Regional Growth and Entrepreneurial Diversity in Sweden*. Cheltenham, UK and Northampton, MA, USA: Edgar Elgar Publishing.

Taylor, M., 2019. "Teachers Want Climate Crisis Training, Poll Shows". *The Guardian*, June 21. Accessed February 3, 2020 at www.theguardian.com/environment/2019/ jun/21/teachers-want-climate-crisis-training-poll-shows

UN Announcement, 2019. "Burgenland Declaration Champions Action for Climate Empowerment". United Nations, October 17. Accessed February 5, 2020 at https://unfccc.int/news/burgenland-declaration-champions-action-for-climate -empowerment

UN SDG13. Sustainable Development Goal 13. Accessed February 3, 2020 at https:// sustainabledevelopment.un.org/sdg13

UN SDG13.1. Sustainable Development Goal 13. Accessed February 3, 2020 at https:// sustainabledevelopment.un.org/sdg13

UN SDG13.2. Sustainable Development Goal 13. Accessed February 3, 2020 at https:// sustainabledevelopment.un.org/sdg13

UN SDG13.3. Sustainable Development Goal 13. Accessed February 3, 2020 at https://sustainabledevelopment.un.org/sdg13

UNDRR, 2019. United Nations Disaster Risk Reduction. Accessed February 5, 2020 at www.undrr.org/about-undrr

UNESCO, 2015. *Not Just Hot Air: Putting Climate Change Education into Practice.* Paris: United Nations Educational, Scientific and Cultural Organization. Accessed February 5, 2020 at: https://unesdoc.unesco.org/ark:/48223/pf0000233083

UNFCC, 1992. *United Nations Framework Convention on Climate Change.* New York: United Nations General Assembly. Accessed February 3, 2020 at https://unfccc.int/resource/docs/convkp/conveng.pdf

UNFCC, 2015. United Nations Framework Convention on Climate Change. Accessed May 20, 2020 at http://unfccc.int/paris_agreement/items/9485.php

UNFCC, 2019. "Governments Agree to Strengthen Climate Education, Awareness and Public Engagement". United Nations, July 8. Accessed February 5, 2020 at: https://unfccc.int/news/governments-agree-to-strengthen-climate-education-awareness-and-public-engagement

Valášek, T., 2019. "What Are Europe's Top Three Challenges? Not Brexit, Not Migration, Not Populism". *Carnegie Europe*, May 7. Accessed February 3, 2020 at https://carnegieeurope.eu/2019/05/07/what-are-europe-s-top-three-challenges-not-brexit-not-migration-not-populism-pub-79070

Valatsas, D., 2019. "Green Deal, Greener World". *Foreign Policy*, December 17. Accessed February 3, 2020 at https://foreignpolicy.com/2019/12/17/united-states-democrats-green-new-deal-eu-europe-technically-feasible-environment-progress/

Venmans, F., 2012. "A Literature-Based Multi-Criteria Evaluation of the EU ETS". *Renewable and Sustainable Energy Reviews*, 16(8): 5493–510.

Welle, D., 2019. "After a Year of Strikes Can Fridays for Future Maintain Momentum?" EcoWatch, August 21. Accessed February 3, 2020 at www.ecowatch.com/fridays-for-future-momentum-2639941330.html

Wurzel, R. K. & J. Connelly, 2011. The European Union as a Leader in International Climate Change Politics. New York: Routledge.

8. Agenda 2030 and the EU on affordable and clean energy

Henry Kiragu Wambuii

The city of Rio de Janeiro in Brazil is famous for many things. One of these is the historical 2012 United Nations Conference on Sustainable Development where the idea of Sustainable Development Goals (SDGs) was mooted. The main focus was to endow the world with workable and universally accepted goals to address the world's main challenges in the areas of environmental degradation and the need for enhanced conservation, political challenges and also economic hurdles. Adopted by United Nations state members in 2015, Agenda 2030 for Sustainable Development became the official agreed-upon roadmap for global action on several identified challenges that need to be addressed if the world has to attain a better, more sustainable future (United Nations, 2020).[1]

One of Agenda 2030's 17 stated SDGs to be followed by all countries of the world is sustainable goal number 7 on the need for affordable, clean energy. The goal's stated objective is to "ensure access to affordable, reliable, sustainable and modern energy for all" (United Nations, 2020). SDG 7 recognizes the importance of access to affordable, reliable and sustainable energy in unlocking unlimited potential for economic growth as well as enhancing essential improvements in global health and education, both seen as crucial ingredients in working to reduce glaring inequalities and persistent poverty across the world. Further, the envisioned sustainable and modern energy sources stand in contrast with traditional, unsustainable fossil fuels like coal and oil. Not only will the hoped-for modern forms of sustainable energy help in tackling urgent climate change challenges that have increasingly caused a threat to society, they are also necessary if we hope to protect and preserve the world's large forests, oceans and related water masses. Key sources of sought-after clean energy include energy harnessed directly from the sun (solar), electricity generated from running water sources (hydropower) and wind energy, derived directly from the wind's ability to turn wind turbines to produce energy. Also considered as part of the clean energy revolution are a host of biomass-derived fuels which have been used in among other places the public transportation sector.

European countries are by all accounts huge consumers of energy in every aspect of life. In order to sustain the regular home's cooking and washing needs along with heating and lighting purposes as well as the public sector's mass transportation and related industrial production, policy makers mindful of Europe's future wellbeing had to ensure the development of energy sources marked by reliability, sustainability and affordability. The European Commission explains the road ahead for the European Union (EU) in relation to SDG 7 and the quest for affordable, clean energy in its assertion that: "We have to move away from an economy driven by fossil fuels, an economy where energy is based on a centralized, supply-side approach and which relies on old technologies and outdated business models" (European Commission, 2015a). It is clear that the development of reliable, sustainable and affordable new sources of energy was considered to be a priority issue for the EU.

TOWARDS AN ENERGY UNION: EXAMINING THE EU'S ROLE IN ACHIEVING SDG 7

To realize the EU's dream for a progressive energy policy, it was necessary to come up with a dedicated energy strategy committed to the fulfillment of the EU's wish for sustainable, clean energy, as well as deliver on the EU's commitments to SDG 7. To be successful, such a strategy would have to pay full attention to the needs of individual European countries and especially to the divide between those gunning for a stricter climate change policy and those opposed to such accelerated efforts at climate change. Further, such a strategy would require harmonized coordination of policy and related legislation across the different member states of the EU.

Among the most influential forces in the formation of an encompassing energy strategy for the EU in 2015 was Donald Tusk, Poland's prime minister at the time. Poland is a traditional coal-driven economy and talk of reusable energy sources and related reduction in carbon emissions is a touchy topic. As Simon Evans explains, "Poland has resisted stronger EU climate policy in the past and has built its economy around coal, the most polluting source of electricity. So just who is Donald Tusk, what does he think about climate change – and does it matter?" (Evans, 2014).

As the new president of the European Council in 2015, Donald Tusk's presidency coincided with the EU's commitment to Agenda 2030. Coming from a background where fossil coal energy dominated, it was Donald Tusk's task now to help steer Europe to the harmonized attainment of "secure, sustainable, competitive, affordable energy for every European" (Raines and Tomlinson, 2016). Tusk's solution to the need for a workable goal was to advocate for a new approach that primarily favors continued economic growth but not at the cost of the environment. Such an approach would entail careful balancing between economic growth and the need to reduce carbon emissions along with other mechanisms for protecting the environment.

The resulting energy union strategy was made possible in February 2015 when the European Commission moved to commit to the "Framework Strategy for a Resilient Energy Union with a Forward-Looking Climate Change Policy". The new framework strategy not only echoed the United Nations' SDG 7 on the need to achieve secure, sustainable and affordable energy, but went a step further to proclaim the energy sector transformation goal for the EU in its stated quest to attain "secure, sustainable, competitive, affordable energy for every European" (Raines and Tomlinson, 2016). It was clear from the outset that such an undertaking would "require a fundamental transformation of Europe's energy system" (European Commission, 2015b). In the words of European Commission vice president Maroš Šefčovič, the adopted EU energy union was "undoubtedly the most ambitious European project since the formation of the coal and steel community which created the EU" (Renssen, 2015).[2] With both short-term and long-term goals envisioned, Europe clearly broadcast its determination to reduce reliance on fossil fuels and to reshape the economy to one driven by innovative energy and research-driven technology solutions.

The EU's new energy strategy was to be anchored on five different action pillars. To achieve sustainability, affordability and in order to create new renewable sources of energy, EU policy makers and technology experts had to pay full consideration to the issues of energy security, instituting a well-coordinated and fully integrated energy market for European countries, as well as the promotion of energy efficiency as a step towards demand moderation. Other envisioned key components of the five action pillars were the EU's commitment to lowering carbon emissions, as well as intensified research and innovation to keep the EU competitive (European Commission, 2015b).

Each of the five areas can be seen as intertwined and success in one area has positive implications for the other important areas. For instance, development of a fully integrated energy market for the EU could have resounding benefits in several areas. These include reaffirming Europe's energy security through readily available access to stable and reliable energy sources, lowering energy costs for consumers and even the much hoped-for expanded use of renewable sources of energy and associated reduced emissions benefits. Achieving efficiency in energy use on the other hand could directly result in reduced energy consumption, seen as a key factor in the EU's determination to break away from energy dependency.

Meanwhile, research and innovation is beneficial in several key areas, including reduction in carbon emissions, increase in energy efficiency due to modern innovations as well as better modes of energy consumption and storage, both essential elements in the building of a successful internal energy market. Further, through research and innovation on modern sources of renewable energy, the EU can stay competitive by attaining the leading position in energy production across the world, further freeing the EU from energy dependency. Besides, the EU can become a lead supplier of affordable and renewable sources of energy and, by so doing, the energy sector could contribute to many more jobs, an essential factor for improved living standards and related tackling of energy poverty issues.

DEFINING THE CHALLENGES FOR THE EU'S ENERGY UNION

Achieving Energy Security, Solidarity and Trust

For a region that is a huge importer of energy and that "consumes one fifth of the world's energy, but has relatively few reserves of its own" (European Commission, 2017),[3] access to stable, sustainable and affordable sources of energy is undoubtedly one of the most important considerations. The EU is a major importer of fossil fuels, mainly crude oil, coal and natural gas. The EU's energy dependency over the years is well documented in various analytical writings on sustainable, secure energy use. One such analysis describes the EU's prolonged and costly dependency over the years as follows: "In 2002, 47.5% of gross available energy within the EU was imported from outside. Between 2006 and 2016 import dependency remained more or less consistent, fluctuating around 53%. In 2017, however, the share increased to 55.1%, mainly due to increased import shares of natural gas and solid fuels" (European Commission, 2019).

The issue is made even more urgent given a tumultuous global arena and related geopolitics where prominent gas supplier states like Russia have sought to use their exports as a tool in a game of strategic application of hard power against perceived European enemies. With over 37 percent of EU natural gas coming from Russia (Kottasová, 2018), Russia's continued conflict with Ukraine, a country whose landmass forms a major pathway for natural gas flowing from Russia to continental Europe, continues to threaten the EU's power security with potentially huge economic losses due to the possibility of either an intermittent supply or even a complete shut off with a worsening political crisis. Thomas Raines and Shane Tomlinson aptly capture this European source of concern in their assertion that: "The war in Ukraine, following Russia's annexation of Crimea in early 2014, has ensured that the need to avoid potential gas shortages has taken center stage and has prompted efforts to coordinate the diversification of supplies" (Raines and Tomlinson, 2016).[4] Among others, such measures for energy dependency as investing in the development of renewable sources like wind, solar and battery-generated energy would have to be considered. Also necessary is the need for improvements in energy efficiency to help the EU take charge through upgrading and in some cases construction of new energy-generating and distribution-related infrastructure across the EU member states.

At a more analytical level, the issue of attaining energy security could be seen as involving other areas envisioned in the five pillars of the EU's energy union. These are the issue of developing integrated and economically viable European markets and the need to reduce carbon emissions across Europe. All these issues stand as big challenges for an EU committed to attaining the goals set by SDG 7 by the year 2030.

Building a Fully Integrated Internal Market

The EU Energy Union's intended goal is to harmonize the uninhibited flow of energy across the EU states by eliminating the many existing energy regulations as well as harmonizing the technical hurdles across the member states. Integration of the EU internal energy market will open the way for genuine competition among renewable energy providers. Further, integrating and opening up the EU's internal market is by all accounts a remarkable cost-effective strategy to bring about sustainable and affordable energy in line with SDG 7's stated goals. Appropriate legislation will ensure the setting of common internal energy market guidelines and linked infrastructures across the state members' borders. This will enhance competition among energy producers in the EU and in so doing keep the cost of energy low.

Such a venture is no doubt a far-reaching and deeply involved political, social and economic undertaking. Integrating internal markets entails well-concerted and meaningful environmental, economic and legislative procedures to be put in place across the member states. Further, a fully integrated internal EU energy market "requires a fundamental re-design to better integrate renewables and technological advances and to attract investment" (European Commission, 2015a). An EU assessment of the energy market at the time lays out the challenges ahead and calls out for action in its assertion that: "the current market design does not lead to sufficient investments, market concentration and weak competition remain an issue and the European energy landscape is still too fragmented. The EU has to give a new political boost to completing the internal energy market" (European Commission, 2015a).

This prevailing economic imperfection has led to continued high electricity prices for consumers in European states coupled with resulting energy poverty. According to the United Kingdom Department for Business, Energy and Industrial Strategy's *Fuel Poverty Methodology Handbook* (2020), "A household is said to be in fuel poverty if it needs to spend more than 10% of its income on fuel to maintain an adequate level of warmth (usually defined as 21 degrees for the main living area, and 18 degrees for other occupied rooms)" (2020). As Papada and Kaliampakos further point out, energy poverty continues to be a major issue of concern for European policy makers as it affects a huge amount of households. Energy poverty is not just a shortage issue but one that also has significant "social, economic, political, environmental and health implications" (Papada and Kaliampakos, 2018).

On another level, the issue of affordable energy could be seen as having social justice implications. Failure to afford adequate resources for heating one's home directly equates to suppressed ability to earn adequate income and calls for immediate political intervention. According to the European Commission, "In 2017, 18.4% of people with an income below 60% of the median *'equivalised income'*[5] (the 'poverty threshold') reported being unable to keep their homes adequately warm" (Eurostat, 2018). Undoubtedly, equity in energy affordability as such is one of the key considerations for European political entrepreneurship aimed at bringing about sustainable, affordable and renewable energy sources.

Although indications are that the number of energy poverty consumers is slightly decreasing over the years, the fact that a significant number of people remain in that category is of urgent concern. Among others, solutions to the issue of adequate heating would entail paying attention to the issues of insulation for buildings, adequate heating systems, consumers' income levels and even appropriate legislation among the member states that allows for financial rescue by the different member states.

Achieving Energy Efficiency

Along with the need for security and equitable distribution of energy is the urgency for more efficient sources of energy. At the onset of the Energy Union in 2015, the EU set as one of its major goals the need to increase energy efficiency among its member states by 20 percent by the year 2020 and to 27 percent by 2030. This would mean finding new renewable sources of energy to push back against the predominant fossil fuels in use at the time. Renewable energy can be generated from a range of sources, including bioenergy, hydropower, wind power, solar and geothermal sources.

By 2018, the EU's commitment to energy efficiency was starting to bear noticeable achievements. According to Eurostat, hydropower and wind energy provided the bulk of renewable electricity, with biomass taking care of renewable heating and liquid biofuels accounting for transport needs. The encouraging statistics reveal that: "The growth in electricity generated from renewable energy sources during the period 2008 to 2018 largely reflects an expansion in three renewable energy sources across the EU, principally wind power, but also solar power and solid biofuels (including renewable wastes) (Eurostat, 2020).

As earlier mentioned energy efficiency could be seen as directly resulting in quantifiable economic benefits in terms of reduced costs and to a large extent reduced general consumption, seen as key in weaning EU states off historical energy dependency. On the other hand, energy efficiency directly addresses the issue of climate change and the need for reduced carbon emissions. Developing efficient sources of energy entails careful assessment of sources that are renewable/sustainable, reliable and affordable and that are good for the environment in line with the stipulations of SDG 7. Such a task by all accounts involves the design of new, more energy-efficient systems as well as the harnessing of hitherto unused natural energy sources like biofuels, solar and wind energy that not only address very specific consumer needs but also help counter fossil fuels' harmful impact on the environment. It also involves a movement towards standardized infrastructure and new technologically-driven smart grids to afford the consumers a chance to practice positive energy-saving habits.

One target area for energy efficiency is the average household. Among the most prominent domestic uses of energy are lighting, cooking, heating and cooling as well as energy for necessary sanitation purposes and entertainment-related appliances. Another area is mass transportation at different levels, from automobiles to buses and trains. According to the European Environment Agency, "road transport accounts for the largest proportion of energy consumption in the transport sector, accounting for 73% of the total demand in 2017" (2019).

To both improve on gas efficiency and reduce accruing emissions, there is a need for legislation to further tighten existing standards on carbon emissions and enforce a more coordinated, technology-driven system of traffic management for all road-going vehicles. Such ventures as electrification of vehicles and use of energy-saving batteries are some of the ways that must be considered as the EU seeks to address the goals addressed in SDG 7.

Efforts to achieve energy efficiency in transportation could also entail a shift to more reliance on less polluting means of public transportation like rail and water-based modes of mass transportation. Given these defined energy consumption patterns, in order to achieve the goal of making the EU economy the "most energy efficient economy in the world" (Evans, 2015), the Energy Union had to clearly change the EU's focus from a fossil fuel-intensive, foreign energy-dependent economy into one fueled by innovative and affordable renewable sources that are widely used across the region and that are competitive across the world.

Cutting Carbon Emissions

Along with the practical goal for energy efficiency is yet another practical long-term goal for bringing positive changes to the environment. The issue of cutting carbon emissions predates the formation of the EU Energy Union and was indeed at the heart of the conflict in discussions on the way forward in transforming the EU's energy sector. In 2015, as the EU sought a fitting solution, Germany led the pack on the one hand gunning for accelerated reforms while Poland on the other led the cautious, fossil fuel-dependent economies opposed to restrictive quick and early reforms aimed at achieving lower carbon emissions.

As a compromise and along with the stipulations of Agenda 2030, the EU states committed to cutting greenhouse gas emissions by at least 40 percent by the year 2030. Along with this long-term goal was the short-term goal of increasing the use of renewable energy by 20 percent by 2020 accompanied by the cutting of carbon emissions by 20 percent by 2020 in comparison to 1990 levels. All these steps were clearly geared towards deemphasizing the use of fossil fuels, known to be a major source of harmful greenhouse gases, in order to combat persistent air pollution and undeniable climate change.

The coordinating agency for the fight against greenhouse gases was to be the EU's Emissions Trading System. The European Commission describes the agency set up in 2005, as the "cornerstone of the EU's policy to combat climate change and its key tool for reducing greenhouse gas emissions cost-effectively. It is the world's first major carbon market and remains the biggest one" (European Commission, 2020). Operating across all EU member states and beyond, including in non-member states like Norway, Iceland and Liechtenstein, the Emissions Trading System takes charge of regulating around 45 percent of the EU's total greenhouse gas emissions and presides over a system of emissions trading for over 11,000 industrial plants and power-generating stations in the covered area.

The agency places a price value on carbon emissions and heavy energy users must pay for allowances to produce emissions or pay a hefty fine for failure to comply.[6] Widely regarded as a fair system of regulating carbon emissions, the Emissions Trading System allows for the important function of coordinating heavy energy users and harmonizing the EU's carbon emissions across member states' borders. For a union making strides towards the building of its internal energy market, this role of the Emissions Trading System is illustrative of the way forward. Further, regulations on emissions encourage an increase in the use of renewable energies that do not have to pay for excessive carbon emissions. Indeed, encouraging the development of a host of renewable sources of energy is at the forefront of the EU cutting carbon emissions as a step towards achieving set goals by the year 2030 and beyond.

Instituting Research and Innovation

In order to transform energy generation and consumption patterns across the EU, it is important to come up with low carbon-emitting sources as well as the ability to store and regulate generated energy. Further, for effective research and innovation to happen, extensive cross-border coordination and legislation is necessary. In framing the energy strategy, research and increased innovation in modern energy-efficient technologies was considered to be of paramount urgency. Possible research areas include developing efficient products like clean electricity, smart grids and clean mass transportation solutions to benefit both domestic and business consumers, as well as transforming the public transportation sector.

Also important is the need to address energy storage solutions to ensure readily available and secure energy resources. Besides improving on energy security, this aspect of storage can also be seen as having very significant implications for the regulation of the EU's internal market. Effective energy storage allows for the key process of stabilization of energy by balancing power grids and, in so doing, regulating demand and supply. Whenever the system experiences excess electricity, it is put into storage whether for a short period of time or over an extended period. Energy storage is a key step towards maintaining a low carbon environment through improvements in efficiency and increases in readily available renewable energy.

Other considerations related to research and innovation are the need to transform Europe to being the world's leader in renewable energy as well as developing affordable sources of energy considered to be a "fair deal" for European consumers (European Parliament, 2019).[7] While effective industrial innovations mean a good deal for consumers, they also bring business profits, and equate to well-paying, reliable jobs, two factors that account for sought-after economic growth. Along with this is the need to train a new workforce as well as the retraining of existing personnel on new technologies and innovations, thereby sowing the seeds for a future marked by the production of renewable energy along with the associated benefits for EU consumers – both individuals and businesses.

ASSESSING THE EU'S GAINS IN ACHIEVING SUSTAINABLE CLEAN ENERGY

Any efforts to assess the EU's progress in delivering on affordable and clean energy, as well as efforts to monitor the EU's progress on its commitment to SDG 7 stipulations, must consider several key areas surrounding the issue of energy production and consumption. The indicators for progress include the amount of renewable energy produced, increase in the use of modern technology like smart grids, as well as the numbers of consumers switching to use renewable energy and related technologies. Other useful indicators are improvements in energy security measured by reductions in levels of imported energy and levels of reduction in energy-poor consumers. Based on data analysis between the years 2015 and 2019, the EU has made some headway in its quest for clean and affordable energy, though a significant amount of work remains to be done if the EU has to live up to its 2030 commitments on energy efficiency and carbon reductions.

A key area of progress for the EU has been a noticeable reduction in domestic consumers' use of fossil fuels, in particular petroleum and solid fuel products, for home purposes. As Eurostat notes, "data suggest that households have reduced direct consumption of fossil fuels for heating and used more renewable energy and electricity" (Eurostat, 2019a). As hoped for, this reduction in the use of fossil fuels has resulted in an increased consumption of renewable energy. The outstanding implications for this change in energy consumption has been an accruing benefit in a reduction of greenhouse gas emissions in the EU, though progress on the issue of energy efficiency is still elusive given the increased energy consumption.

On energy security, dependency on foreign energy is still an issue of concern. Russia continues to be a significant supplier of energy to the EU along with other European countries that are not part of the EU (mainly Norway) and the Middle East and Africa continue to supply oil and petroleum products to the EU. Yet despite this continued dependency on foreign energy sources, the EU's efforts to encourage the growth of an internal EU market is taking root with at least three member states leading the way in exporting energy to other EU states (Eurostat, 2019c). A take-away from this is the fact that fossil fuels continue to dominate the inter-EU energy trade with Denmark exporting both oil and natural gas, the Netherlands providing natural gas and Poland's comparative advantage being fossil fuels.

To further cushion member states from the risks of foreign dependency as well as bringing progress to other areas important to the achievement of SDG 7, in 2019, the EU displayed a remarkable act of political entrepreneurship when it adopted additional legislative acts to the *Clean Energy for all Europeans package*. The European Commission describes the package of legislative acts as an energy rule book with eight legislative acts geared to speed up the implementation of the EU's energy strategy (European Commission, 2017).[8] One of the acts seeks to bring about more preparedness in the EU's electricity sector and makes it a requirement for member states to have in place a ready plan of action in case of any crises in the sector. Further, member states are required to have a management plan to not only manage but more importantly to prevent such electricity crises.

Another key element of the legislation on risk preparedness is the requirement for cross-border coordination and cooperation, further cementing the case for solidarity and trust as well as clearing the path for the internal energy market to thrive. This existence of firm regulations governing the energy industry has been hailed as a key strength that militates against energy dependency. Tim Boersma and Michael E. O'Hanlon put the issue in better perspective in their assertion that: "The notion that Europe is weak and dependent on Russian natural gas is a relic from the past. Europe has a strong regulatory framework with which commercial entities, including Gazprom, have to abide. For those who doubt the impact of these regulations, just ask Google or Microsoft" (Boersma and O'Hanlon, 2016).

To help integrate the internal energy market and achieve affordable energy for consumers, the EU set as one of its goals the challenge to achieve at least a 10 percent electricity interconnection among all EU members by the year 2020. This would not only benefit consumers by lowering electricity prices, but would result in a more stable and reliable supply of energy. To enhance internal cooperation, the EU has also made strong political entrepreneurship decisions, including the formation of the Agency for the Cooperation of Energy Regulators to spearhead the process of coordinating various stakeholders involved in the field of energy across the EU. The Agency plays a watchdog role over the various stakeholders, setting guidelines and appropriate rules for interaction as well as fostering the formation of a common network among the energy players. These efforts to coordinate energy use have not been in vain as the EU continues to reduce the rate of energy poverty in the region. As Eurostat (2019a) proclaims, "In 2017, 7.8% of the EU population indicated a lack of access to affordable energy – 3.1 percentage points lower than in 2007".

Further, over the short life span of the energy union strategy, the EU has invested heavily in various infrastructural projects across member states. The go-to agency for the EU's infrastructure development is the Connecting Europe Facility. According to the European Commission (2016), the Facility is the "key EU funding instrument to promote growth, jobs and competitiveness through targeted infrastructure investment at European level" (European Commission, 2019).[9]

In 2018, the EU committed to investing a remarkable €873 million specifically earmarked for the development of clean energy infrastructure projects. These include the construction of an energy interconnection link between France and Spain. The Biscay Gulf France–Spain interconnection that includes both an off-shore and an underground component as it stretches to link the two countries will more than double the two countries' interconnection capacity and is a great step towards integrating the energy market. Another notable project is the construction of the SüdOstLink, an underground high-voltage cable facility offering a much needed transportation path for wind power produced in Saxony-Anhalt in the north to reach consumers in Bavaria in the southern part of Germany.

Other earlier projects that point to the EU's determination to integrate the energy market include the Balticconnector pipeline project (2016), a gas pipeline connecting Finland and Estonia. Developed with the express aim of integrating the eastern Baltic Sea region with the rest of the EU energy market, the Balticconnector project will also have major energy security implications by providing Finland with extra gas suppliers and allowing the country to use other gases like liquid natural gas and biogas.

To enhance efficiency, the EU has continued to work towards reduced consumption of energy. Two ways to approach this venture is to cut actual consumption, something that has been hard to do, and/or to come up with new, more power-efficient technologies to address every level of energy consumption. These include such household uses as heating, cooking, cleaning and even related entertainment, to industrial consumption, to even designing new energy-efficient vehicles and other mass transportation means. As a key indication of the EU's strong political leadership in the quest for affordable and clean energy, in 2016, the European Commission developed the *Clean Energy for All Europeans* package aimed at offering consumers a fair deal through increased clean energy innovations and improved delivery systems. In a November 30, 2016 memo, the European Commission explains that: "All consumers across the EU will be entitled to generate electricity for either their own consumption, store it, share it, consume it or to sell it back to the market. These changes will make it easier for households and businesses to become more involved in the energy system, to better control their energy consumption and respond to price signals".

The development of smart appliances that are compatible with smart meters will put the consumers firmly in charge of their energy consumption and will allow them to adjust their usage accordingly with an eye on cost. Development of smart homes will make them venues for clean energy generation especially in solar and wind energy, further ingraining the production and consumption of renewable energy within the EU.

Renewable energy has continued to grow across the EU. Akshat Rathi aptly summarizes this achievement in his assertion that, "in 2017, wind, solar, and biomass combined to produce 20.9% of all electricity in the EU, compared to 20.6% for coal and 19.7% for natural gas. (Hydro provided another 10.9% in 2017)" (Rathi, 2018). This is a rewarding development for a region keen on breaking away from its traditional consumption of carbon-emitting fossil fuels.

A good example of a new form of renewable energy is the production of batteries to power different means of transportation. The European Battery Alliance, an organization financed by several European countries, notably

Belgium, Finland, France, Germany, Italy, Poland and Sweden, was formally launched in October 2017. The organization's core mission is to manufacture clean energy based on high-performing battery cells. It further hopes to utilize the EU's integrated energy market to create cross-border linkages in its quest to supply batteries across the EU.[10]

Also beneficial is focused research on non-nuclear electricity in line with the EU's goal to produce at least 27 percent renewable energy as a percentage of total consumption in the region by the year 2030. While traditional industrial production has meant increasing emissions and an affront on the environment, the EU's Energy Union-driven innovations have seen increased industrial innovations and decreasing greenhouse gas emissions. Clean battery energy coupled with increased production of clean electricity, among others, are resulting in quantifiable benefits for greenhouse gas reductions.

THE ROAD TO 2030: THE EU'S ENERGY STRATEGY VERSUS THE REST OF THE WORLD

For a world caught up in an over-reliance on fossil fuels and a disjointed system of energy supply and consumption, the EU's path to affordable, clean energy is illustrative of policy makers taking steps in search of sustainable and affordable clean energy in line with the United Nations' SDG 7 stipulations. Not only has the EU through its Energy Union strategy managed to harmonize production and consumption activities for its member states, it is increasingly taking the lead in cutting greenhouse gas emissions through the production of welcome renewable sources of energy. The EU has also led the way in creating energy efficiency and tackling energy poverty as well as backing up progress in the production and sharing of renewable energy through huge financial investments.

At another level, the EU has taken a lead in setting global standards on climate change. Through such mechanisms as the Emissions Trading System, the EU has instituted a system of self-policing on the issue of harmful carbon emissions. This action is well in line with the Paris climate change agreement and serves as a beacon of responsibility for other countries across the world. Such regional organizations as the African Union, the Association of Southeast Asian Nations and Mercosur in South America can look up to the EU's firm progress towards achieving the goals set forth by SDG 7 as an example to emulate. Further, the EU's successful cap and trade principle through the Emissions Trading System could be widely expanded to help the world achieve set carbon-neutrality goals as part of the Paris Agreement.

But perhaps just as significant is the issue of technology transfer in the coming years. As the EU masters its renewable energy production skills and perfects industrial production of among others battery cells through research and innovation, other countries of the world stand to gain. Not only will the EU be able to export finished products to other countries, but also both private and public entities will be able to set up production plants across the world. By all accounts, this expansion of opportunities in the clean energy sector will allow for a host of benefits, including the spread of new technological knowhow along with offering ready employment and associated economic growth capabilities.

CONCLUSION

The question of how to achieve sustainable development continues to be at the heart of the EU's political entrepreneurship and remains a major headache for the region's policy makers and economic planners (Hąbek and Wolniak, 2016). A major sustainability concern is the issue of transforming the energy sector in order to achieve renewable and affordable clean energy. This issue has been a preoccupation of the EU for a long time and coincides with the EU's commitment in 2015 to achieving the stipulations of the UN's SDG 7 by the year 2030. Accessibility to adequate sustainable energy is at the heart of progress and can mean success or failure in economic growth. But equally important to a society's development is the need to ensure stability and good health for its people through responsible consumption behavior. Cutting greenhouse emissions talks directly to these twin aspects. Enhancing efficiency in energy use, the selective generation of only renewable clean sources of energy, as well as educating consumers and endowing them with smart technologies, are all great ways to ensure success in the energy sector. Further, these are also key elements of Agenda 2030's quest for reliable, affordable clean energy as enshrined in the stipulations of SDG 7. The EU has done a remarkable job to date in its quest for sustainability in the energy sector, but the journey to achieve its energy commitments by 2030 and beyond is just heating up.

NOTES

1.   The United Nations categorizes the world's most pressing needs and points to challenges related to poverty and inequality, climate change and environmental degradation, as well as the need for peace and justice as areas of urgent concern.
2.   In 1952, six European countries (Belgium, France, Italy, Luxembourg, the Netherlands and West Germany) ratified a treaty, initially signed in 1951, to create the European Coal and Steel Community, an administrative agency that served as the main agent for regulating and integrating the expansive coal and steel industries in Europe. The agency grew to include all members of the European Economic Community, later named the European Community and later again the EU. The agency was resolved in 2002 after the expiry of the original 1951 treaty.
3.   To break this down further, according to Eurostat, the EU's petroleum products (including crude oil) accounted for "almost two thirds of energy imports into the

EU, followed by gas (26 percent) and solid fossil fuels (8 percent)" (Eurostat, 2019b).

4. The Russian/Ukrainian conflict, sometimes referred to as the Russo-Ukrainian War, has been an absorbing, extended military conflict that dates back to February 2014 when Russia intervened in Ukraine's eastern and southern regions following a contested electoral outcome that led to violent protests and a political revolution. In March 2014, Russia annexed the autonomous region of Crimea and by early 2020 the conflict was still ongoing. Given Ukraine's historical position as the convenient pathway for a natural gas pipeline linking Russia and continental Europe, any violent confrontation between the two states has the potential of becoming very disruptive to Europe's power energy supply.

5. Equivalized income is a formula used to calculate poverty and social exclusion indicators. The formula measures a given household's income paying close attention to the household size and composition and seeking to equate that to other households based on the Organisation for Economic Co-operation and Development equivalence scale.

6. The EU Emissions Trading System utilizes what is referred to as the "cap and trade principle". A cap is the upper limit and details the sum total of particular greenhouse gases that an industrial plant can emit. This allowance is adjusted downwards to ensure reduction in emissions. Industries are allowed to buy and sell emission allowances and to trade with others as necessary.

7. The EU's "fair deal" legislation can best be described as a set of legal and ethical measures put in place by EU policy makers to facilitate the achievement of a higher level of consumer protection at different points of energy consumption.

8. In perhaps what is one of the best examples of the EU's political entrepreneurship, policy makers agreed to a set of eight new rules in clean energy policy, starting in mid-2019. The new rules set expectations to benefit consumers, the EU economies and the environment. The new rules further ingrain the role of the EU as a bona fide leader in dealing with global warming and achieving much sought-after carbon neutrality.

9. The Connecting Europe Facility is the EU's dedicated facility for the development of cross-border European infrastructure, with heavy investments in the transport and energy sectors as well as related digital bridging projects aimed at increasing connectivity among the EU's member states. The Facility relies on grants, financial guarantees and project bonds for its operations. For the 2014 to 2019 period, for example, a total of 23.3 billion euros was availed in terms of grants for the transportation sector.

10. In what is seen as a major challenge for Asia's hitherto dominance of battery cell production, the EU through the European Battery Alliance has moved to exponentially increase battery cell production and use it across its member states and beyond. The EU's can be seen as a bottom-up approach to enhance massive battery production by leveraging a totality of the EU's cross-border resources from available raw materials to labor, even financing through private–public relationship deals. Also important for this process is enhanced research and innovations in the search for the best technological solutions.

REFERENCES

Boersma, Tim and O'Hanlon, Michael E. (2016). *Why Europe's Energy Policy Has Been a Strategic Success Story*. Brookings Institute. Accessed on December 14, 2019 at www.brookings.edu/blog/order-from-chaos/2016/05/02/why-europes -energy-policy-has-been-a-strategic-success-story/

Department for Business, Energy and Industrial Strategy (2020). *Fuel Poverty Methodology Handbook*. Accessed on May 20, 2020 at https://assets.publishing .service.gov.uk/government/uploads/system/uploads/attachment_data/file/882233/ fuel-poverty-methodology-handbook-2020.pdf

European Commission (2015a). *A Fully-Integrated Internal Energy Market*. European Union. Accessed December 20, 2019 at https://ec.europa.eu/commission/priorities/ energy-union-and-climate/fully-integrated-internal-energy-market_en

European Commission (2015b). *Communication from the Commission to the European Parliament, the European Council, the European Economic and Social Committee, the Committee of the Regions and the European Investment Bank: A Framework Strategy for a Resilient Energy Union with a Forward-Looking Climate Change Policy*. February 25, Accessed on December 19, 2019 at https://eur-lex.europa.eu/ legal-content/EN/TXT/?uri=COM:2015:80:FIN

European Commission (2016). *Providing a Fair Deal to Consumers*. November. Accessed on December 20, 2019 at https://ec.europa.eu/commission/presscorner/ detail/en/MEMO_16_3961

European Commission (2017). *Clean Energy for all Europeans Package*. Accessed on January 10, 2020 at https://ec.europa.eu/energy/en/topics/energy-strategy/clean -energy-all-europeans

European Commission (2019). *Sustainable Development in the European Union: Monitoring Report on Progress towards the SDGs in an EU Context*. Accessed on January 7, 2020 at https://ec.europa.eu/eurostat/statistics-explained/index.php?title= Sustainable_development_in_the_European_Union

European Commission (2020). *EU Emissions Trading System (EU ETS)*. Accessed on January 15, 2020 at https://ec.europa.eu/clima/policies/ets_en

European Environment Agency (2019). *Final Energy Consumption in Europe by Mode of Transport*. Accessed on January, 10, 2020 at www.eea.europa.eu/data-and-maps/ indicators/transport-final-energy-consumption-by-mode/assessment-10

European Parliament (2019). *Directive (EU) 2019/2161 of the European Parliament and of the Council of 27 November 2019 Amending Council Directive 93/13/EEC and Directives 98/6/EC, 2005/29/EC and 2011/83/EU of the European Parliament and of the Council as Regards the Better Enforcement and Modernisation of Union Consumer Protection Rules*. Accessed on January 20, 2020 at https://eur-lex.europa .eu/eli/dir/2019/2161/oj

Eurostat (2018). *Eurostat Statistics Explained*. Accessed on December 22, 2019 at https://ec.europa.eu/eurostat/statistics-explained/index.php?title=Glossary: Equivalised_income

Eurostat (2019a). *Affordable and Clean Energy in the EU: Overview and Key Trends*. May. Accessed on January 7, 2020 at https://ec.europa.eu/eurostat/statistics -explained/index.php/SDG_7_-_Affordable_and_clean_energy

Eurostat (2019b). *Shedding Light on Energy in the EU: A Guided Tour of Energy Statistics. European Union*. Accessed on January 7, 2020 at https://ec.europa.eu/ eurostat/cache/infographs/energy/index.html

Eurostat (2019c). *Statistics Explained: Energy Production and Imports.* June. Accessed on January 10, 2020 at https://ec.europa.eu/eurostat/statistics-explained/pdfscache/1216.pdf

Eurostat (2020). *Renewable Energy Statistics.* Accessed on January 7, 2020 at https://ec.europa.eu/eurostat/statistics-explained/index.php/Renewable_energy_statistics

Evans, Simon (2014). *Who Is Donald Tusk and What Does He Think about Climate?* CarbonBrief. Accessed on December 22, 2019 at www.carbonbrief.org/who-is-donald-tusk-and-what-does-he-think-about-climate

Evans, Simon (2015). *What Is the EU's Energy Union?* CarbonBrief. Accessed on December 22, 2019 at www.carbonbrief.org/briefing-what-is-the-eus-energy-union

Hąbek, P. and Wolniak, R. (2016). Assessing the Quality of Corporate Social Responsibility Reports: The Case of Reporting Practices in Selected European Union Member States. *Quality and Quantity* **50**: 399–420.

Kottasová, Ivana (2018). *Europe Is Still Addicted to Russian Gas.* June 5. Accessed on January 8, 2020 at https://money.cnn.com/2018/06/05/news/economy/russia-europe-gas-dependency/index.html

Papada, Lefkothea and Kaliampakos, Dimitris (2018). A Stochastic Model for Energy Poverty Analysis. *Energy Policy* **116**(C): 153–64.

Raines, Thomas and Tomlinson, Shane (2016). *Europe's Energy Union: Foreign Policy Implications for Energy Security, Climate and Competitiveness.* London: Chatham House.

Rathi, Akshat (2018). *Two Countries Are the Reason the EU Is Hitting Its Ambitious Renewable Energy Targets.* Quartz, January. Accessed on January 22, 2020 at https://qz.com/1193603/two-countries-are-the-reason-the-eu-is-hitting-its-ambitious-renewable-energy-targets/

Renssen, Sonja Van (2015). *Brussels Tests Limits of Its Powers with Energy Union.* February 27. Accessed on December 28, 2019 at https://energypost.eu/brussels-tests-limits-powers-energy-union/

United Nations (2020). *Sustainable Development Goals.* Accessed December 3, 2019 at www.un.org/sustainabledevelopment/sustainable-development-goals/

9.   Agenda 2030 and the EU on sustainable cities and communities

Nino Berishvili

Ever increasing population size, growing rates of rural–urban migration and over half of the world's population living in urban areas have created the ultimate need of embedding urban spaces and cities in development agendas. The Sustainable Development Goals (SDGs) adopted in 2015, by United Nations (UN) member states, goals and targets grounded on the commitments of the Millennium Development Goals, expanded their scope to urban development. The UN refers to urbanization as a complex socio-economic process which transforms rural to urban settlements and shifts the populations' spatial distribution to urban areas (United Nations, Department of Economic and Social Affairs, Population Division, 2018: iii).

Due to tremendous growth in urban population, cities expand beyond their administrative boundaries, leading to unplanned urban sprawls. Such rapid increase in urban population can be explained by the Harris–Todaro model of urban migration as people are migrating away from rural areas in search of opportunities and a better quality of life (Harris and Todaro, 1970). It is projected that by 2030, six out of ten people will be urban dwellers. However, such brisk increase in urban population aggravates the issues of housing. Already in 2014, 30 percent of the urban population lived in slum-like conditions (United Nations, Department of Economic and Social Affairs, 2016). Densely populated areas and unplanned urban sprawls challenge other determinants of sustainable development, such as environment and health. For every 10 percent increase in unplanned urban sprawl there is a 9.6 percent increase in per capita pollution. It also leads to difficulties in management of irrigation and waste management systems leading to urban air pollution, in turn leading to illnesses (United Nations, Department of Economic and Social Affairs, 2016). This illustrates the interconnections across the SDGs and their targets. Nowadays, SDG 11, directly centering around urban development, represents an opportunity to improve living conditions of those residing in urban settlements, taking into account three dimensions of social, economic and environmental sustainability (Rozhenkova et al., 2019). Cities are central drivers of economic growth in the European Union (EU) as this is where the largest share of populations reside and the biggest share of gross domestic product is generated.

AGENDA 2030 ON SUSTAINABLE CITIES AND COMMUNITIES

The UN Sustainable Development Summit of 2015 played a pivotal role in acknowledging the relationship between socio-economic factors, human settlements, cities and sustainable development. This recognition has created the need to transform the way we plan and manage urban spaces and was entrenched in SDG 11: "Make cities and human settlements inclusive, safe, resilient and sustainable" (Al-Zu'bi and Radovic, 2018). The four pillars of the goal are interdependent and require an integrative approach.

In contrast with the Millennium Development Goals, "Transforming Our World: The 2030 Agenda for Sustainable Development" takes a more comprehensive stand towards embedding cities and human settlements, one of the key priority areas for development. Goal 11 directly targets sustainable cities and communities and focuses on making cities and human settlements inclusive, safe, resilient and sustainable. It contains ten targets and 15 indicators, adopted by the General Assembly in 2017 as part of a global indicator framework for the SDGs. Targets and indicators of goal 11 take a cross-sectoral and holistic approach with the aim of reaching the wider groups of stakeholders, and are directed towards calling on nations to improve inclusive access to safe housing and transformation, among other targets (Rozhenkova et al., 2019). They are based on the main building blocks of sustainability, taking into account social, economic and environmental factors. The targets and indicators of the goal address the pertaining issues of quality and availability of adequate housing, sustainable and accessible transport systems, protection of cultural and natural heritage, reduction of mortality rates and diminishing the impacts of natural disasters. Special focus areas also include attention to air quality and creation of green spaces, regional planning by supporting links between urban, peri-urban and rural areas and supporting countries in the global south by provisioning financial and technical assistance.

In 2016, acknowledging the peculiarity of each urban context and the importance of localizing the city-scale intervention, UN-Habitat pushed for the preparation of the National Urban Development plans as one of the tools of monitoring the progress towards achieving the goal, by preparing Habitat III (Parnell, 2016). The New Urban Agenda was adopted in 2016, at the UN Conference on Housing and Sustainable Urban Development. The document lays out the standards and guiding principles for urban areas against five key elements of implementation: it is available as a guiding resource for multiple levels of governance, from national and local governments to private-sector representatives. UN-Habitat has been reaffirmed as a focal point for sustainable urbanization and settlements. New Urban Agenda accentuates the connection between urbanization and livelihood, quality of life and economic opportunities highlighting the linkage between Agenda 2030 and the New Urban Agenda. The adoption of the Quito Declaration on Sustainable Cities and Human Settlement follows the interlinked principles of and commitments to leave no one behind, ensure sustainable and inclusive urban economies and environmental sustainability and to work towards transforming urban development by readdressing ways of planning and financing, recognizing the leading role of national governments and by adopting sustainable, people-centered integrated approaches to urban and territorial development. In order to ensure coherent implementation both on local and global levels, follow-up reviews will be conducted.

The New Urban Agenda encourages country-led, transparent and participatory follow-up and review, aimed at tracking progress and assessing the impacts to ensure effective coordination, implementation, transparency and inclusivity. It is centered around the acknowledgment of the pivotal role that local governments play as partners in the New Urban Agenda and the importance of effective coordination and importance of engaging relevant stakeholder groups including regional and sub-regional organizations (United Nations, Habitat III, 2017). In relation to paragraph 166 of the document, countries and relevant stakeholders are to report on the progress made on a quadrennial basis. In 2026, the quadrennial report is requested to include the challenges faced since the adoption of the New Urban Agenda, with the fundamental purpose of identifying further steps. Considering the variable factors affecting urban systems and the complexity of achieving sustainable urban development, the mandate of the New Urban Agenda encourages the General Assembly to hold Habitat IV, the next UN Conference on Housing and Sustainable Urban Development, in 2036. The conference is to be held within the context of new commitments to assess progress on the New Urban Agenda (United Nations, Habitat III, 2017). While UN agencies along with UN member states and relevant stakeholders have implemented initiatives directed towards realizing the anticipated outcomes of SDG 11 to meet its full potential, a Global SDG Indicators Database has been criticized for its generic approach to progress analysis. Although the database is being updated on a regular basis, the information provided is on the country/area level, not on the city level. This goes against the New Urban Agenda's principle of no one single solution to sustainable urban development and the antecedence of commitment from decision makers to localize the implementation strategies needed (Rozhenkova et al., 2019).

Despite the existing criticism, the review of SDG 11 in 2018, based on the data from 78 countries, demonstrates that over past years, significant progress has been made towards making cities and human settlements inclusive, safe and resilient. The proportion of the urban population living in slums and informal settlements had decreased, urban densities of cities had declined and 53 percent of urban populations had access to public transport. However, problems in achieving the desirable outcomes of Agenda 2030 still remain. In 2016, over 1 billion people globally resided in slums or informal settlements and over 3 billion people lacked access to waste disposal facilities. Urban air pollution still represents one of the principal challenges. In 2016, nine out of ten people in urban settlements breathed air that did not meet World Health Organization air quality guidelines (United Nations, Economic and Social Council, 2019).

EU POLITICAL ENTREPRENEURSHIP ON SUSTAINABLE CITIES AND COMMUNITIES IN EUROPE

The EU is one of the most urbanized areas in the world. Over 70 percent of its citizens reside in urban areas and it is projected that by 2050 this proportion will increase to 80 percent (Pact of Amsterdam, 2016). Urban areas can be engines of economic growth and play an important role in meeting the EU 2020 objectives. Thus, sustainable urban development can play a central role in solving many of the challenges pertaining to urban areas, including segregation, poverty and the refugee and asylum crisis.

Throughout the decades, challenges for EU political entrepreneurship in achieving sustainable urban systems and communities within Europe and globally have diversified. However, volatilities and oscillations in economic, political, social and environmental aspects have remained one of the constant and most referred-to adversities. Changes in each aspect have great influence on urban development and an implication for sustainable development. Given these strong interlinkages, possible measures and solutions are crucial for the social, economic and territorial cohesion of the EU.

CHALLENGES AND EU RESPONSES OVER TIME

The last decades of the twentieth century played a significant part in promoting sustainable urban development, marking a beginning for Europe-wide action. Lobbying for urban planning among EU member states started in the early 1980s. In 1980, the Council of Europe began the European Urban Renaissance Campaign which ran for two years and was followed by the Council's "Standing Conference of Local and Regional Authorities of Europe". In 1992 the Conference adopted a practical urban management handbook for local authorities, including urban environment issues along with economic and social aspects (CLRAE, 1992).

In 1993, the independent expert group on the urban environment, established by the European Commission, launched the Sustainable Cities Project and, in 1996, published a report on European sustainable cities. The report was focused on planning and management strategies critical to achieving urban sustainable development and highlighted the role of institutions as pivotal to achieving sustainability at all levels of the urban settlement hierarchy. It especially stressed the capacity of local governments to deliver coordinated planning and management essential to sustainability. The report also accentuated shared responsibility and the need to cooperate on different levels, even on cross-country levels. One of the core principles of the project indicated that member states and cities themselves can identify, develop and implement the most appropriate urban policies addressing needs in their local areas (European Commission, 1996). The report on European sustainable cities oversees the "Europe 2000+: Cooperation for European Territorial Development" as an imperative contribution to the central objectives of sustainable development of the European urban system.

The central purpose of "Europe 2000+" was to strengthen communication and cooperation among member states to achieve an effective spatial planning system in the region. The vision of spatial planning was related to political, social, economic and geographic development, which required cohesive planning of action. Thus, the initiative of strengthened communication among the member states was a valuable instrument. "Europe 2000+" viewed the communication not only between governments, but also among decision makers, policy advisers and other relevant stakeholders. It recommended setting up inter-regional and national information and consultation activities for effective decision making (Muller, 1995). "Europe 2000+" called for support of EU cooperation in managing the convergence of interests resulting from the growth of the community. The opening of the EU's internal borders, new member states and political shifts have intensified the pertaining issues of conflicts of interest. Thus, the "Europe 2000+" recommended participation of peripheral regions in cross-cooperation activities, new members to be directly engaged in the planning and cooperation relations and new initiatives to be developed to meet the concerns of the EU (Muller, 1995: 16). Five years later (in 2000) another document was developed, "Guiding Principles for Sustainable Spatial Development of the European Continent". It proposed measures to ensure cohesive socio-economic development and a responsible management of natural resources (Chistobaev and Fedulova, 2018).

In the most recent years, the Pact of Amsterdam, adopted in 2016, marked a milestone in the development of shared EU-wide approaches to urban challenges, through which the Urban Agenda for the European Union was established. The Agenda was adopted with the purpose of delivering the potential of urban areas by enhancing sectoral policies and improving coordination between different levels of government. It involves relevant authorities in urban development with the aim of improving knowledge sharing, enhancing funding and improving regulations (Pact of Amsterdam, 2016). The Agenda has been developed in line with the "New Urban Agenda" (Habitat III), presenting the key features for urban planning and calling for an integrated approach, which is essential in order to promote inclusive, safe, resilient sustainable urban development (European Commission, 2017). Twelve themes have been identified and prioritized in the Pact of Amsterdam: inclusion of migrants and refugees, housing, urban poverty, air quality, circular economy, jobs and skills in the local economy, climate adaptation, energy transition, sustainable use of land and nature-based solutions, urban mobility, digital transitions and innovative and responsible public procurement (European Commission, 2017: 4). Due to the cross-cutting nature of these themes, challenges within are to be addressed by the formation of partnerships and strong cooperation among and within countries, between governments and the private sector.

In the agenda framework, multi-stakeholder engagement and knowledge sharing is cited as one of the key principles, which provides important support to urban policy thinking and dialogues among stakeholders. "One Stop Shop for Cities" and "Urban Data Platform" provide a valuable impetus to dialogue in Europe (Pact of Amsterdam, 2016). Since the establishment of the Pact, a number of partnerships have been formed around the issues of urban poverty, inclusion of migrants, urban mobility, circular economy and climate adaptation. In 2016, four partnerships were formed, known as the Amsterdam Partnerships, followed by Bratislava Partnerships and Malta Partnerships. In early 2019, Vienna Partnerships was established addressing culture, cultural heritage and security in public spaces.

Vienna Partnerships was established after identifying the need for addressing the challenges with regards to security of public spaces and with culture/ cultural heritage. The challenges associated with public spaces include non-segregated access to quality, basic services, such as education, healthcare and law enforcement. They also include challenges associated with the protection of urban buildings and facilities, societal resilience and empowerment of communities. Culture and cultural heritage partnerships address cultural participation. They are vital for enabling local communities to benefit from culture (European Commission, Directorate General for Regional Policy, 2019). Presently, years after the initiation of the Pact of Amsterdam, actions are being implemented to address the cross-cutting challenges within the priority themes, contributing to the building of an effective and innovative governance.

The Urban Agenda for the European Union calls for the establishment of innovative and good governance practices. This has motivated a number of member states to apply innovative and integrative approaches at national levels. The case of Poland represents one such example. New approaches to urban planning were first initiated in 2015 when the "National Urban Policy" was launched. After two years, in 2017, the Ministry of Investment and Economic Development introduced the "Strategy for Responsible Development", which among other aspects of the strategy addresses the development of cities. One of the instruments addressing the cities is the "Partnership Initiative of Cities" which applies working processes and approaches of the Urban Agenda for the European Union. Poland has been successful in piloting strengthened cooperation and engagement of stakeholders in decision-making processes. Regular meetings are attended by local stakeholders of municipalities, where innovative ideas, actions and projects are explored to be implemented. This approach leads to more inclusive decision-making systems in the country. Moreover, Poland has achieved progress towards the "New Urban Agenda" by implementing concrete actions through programs such as the "Human Smart Cities Programme" (European Commission, Directorate General for Regional Policy, 2019). The Polish government coordinates and monitors the implementations in order to ensure consistency of national projects with global priorities and challenges.

Circular economy is one of the 12 priority themes identified within the framework of the Urban Agenda for the European Union. During the last decade the EU has promoted the delineation of governance approaches to a circular economy, through numerous implementations. One such initiative included reducing the generation of waste. Urban areas account for the generation of approximately 50 percent of global solid waste, and this is projected to grow as a result of increased consumption of goods and services in urban areas (McKinsey Global Institute, 2016). The increase in urban sprawls, excessive consumption of land and of goods and waste production are prevalent in peri-urban areas of urban regions (European Commission, Directorate General for Regional Policy, 2011). These issues are generally caused by fragmented local governance systems. Three key dimensions of governance that need to be considered towards understanding concrete, cross-cutting challenges are: multi-level governance, cross-sectoral governance and multi-actor governance. Within the EU, the Netherlands is one of the most successful countries in terms of waste management. The country has founded its waste management on the principles of circular economy by promoting cooperation among stakeholders. Amsterdam Metropolitan Area is one of the frontrunners in shifting waste management systems towards the circular economy. The city of Amsterdam has adopted a circular city policy which guides decision-making processes in the area. Furthermore, private-sector actors involved in the formation of circular development initiatives set the objective for the sectoral performance (Obersteg et al., 2019). Some of the principal objectives for the circular economy include the redevelopment of wastescapes, reusage of airport waterscapes, reduction in food waste and reduction in bio-waste from agricultural production (Obersteg et al., 2019: 22). Many partnerships established within the Urban Agenda for the European Union are fostering actions to make EU funding more accessible for cities. Guidelines have been developed for EU funding programs, supporting cities in implementing innovative projects and embedding long-term solutions.

A number of European cities have managed to participate in European programs and have been successful in acquiring funding for their projects. Rotterdam has implemented an integrated territorial investment project supported by the European Regional Development Fund. The development addresses the challenges of job creation by connecting neighborhoods with high unemployment rates with the areas of the city with economic opportunities. Furthermore, in order to minimize existing skill gaps within the city, Rotterdam has introduced career and talent-orientation programs. With the support of European Structural and Investment Funds, Barcelona has piloted a multi-solution project to tackle climate change. One of the innovative solutions supported by the EU programs targets the transformation of school playgrounds into climate shelters. With the purpose of raising awareness of climate change the city is piloting an initiative to strengthen cooperation with school communities that includes teacher training (European Commission, Directorate General for Regional Policy, 2019).

Multi-level governance and effective partnerships are at the core of the Urban Agenda for the European Union. The European Commission, other EU institutions, member states, private-sector actors and cities are working together towards transformative change to ensure a more sustainable urban development. The Urban Agenda for the European Union has engaged approximately 100 cities in projects contributing to global, regional and local urban challenges. The Urban Agenda for the European Union is grounded on international commitments and dimensions. Thus, actions of the member states and their urban policies need to respond to global challenges and be in line with international agreements such as the UN SDGs. Most of the actions within the Urban Agenda for the European Union are linked to SDG 11. All partnership responses of the member states under the agenda are addressing relevant SDGs. Partnerships on jobs and skills in the local economy and on the inclusion of migrants and refugees addressing the challenges of socio-economic disparities are directly targeting SDG 10, reducing inequalities. The impetus to urban development has not only been within the EU, but also globally, where the EU and its member states have been conducive to promoting principles of urban planning.

EU POLITICAL ENTREPRENEURSHIP ON SUSTAINABLE CITIES AND COMMUNITIES GLOBALLY

The EU's external actions on urban development intend to integrate and address the challenges recognized by the 2030 Sustainable Development Agenda. The EU has supported the implementation of these actions through EU-funded actions, policies and partnerships.

The European Neighbourhood Policy (ENP), launched in 2004, is instrumental in linking the EU with its southern and eastern neighbors. It was implemented to govern the EU's relations with its 16 neighbors to work jointly on common priority interests, including the promotion of human rights, social cohesion, democracy and the rule of law. Global changes in socio-economic conditions have created the need to review the initial policy. Thus, in response to these fluctuations the ENP has evolved significantly. The revised policy is directed towards building effective partnerships to build more stable EU neighborhood socio-economic, political and socio-economic terms. The actions towards urban issues, within the context of the ENP, include the implementation of infrastructure interconnection projects in partner countries, such as new gas networks, electricity interconnections, improved transport networks and rail infrastructure, addressing the pertaining challenges of cities and communities (Commission of the European Communities, 2004). The EU is actively engaged in responding to environmental challenges in partner countries. Cooperation on environmental policy issues is achieved by addressing best practices on regional and sub-regional levels. Furthermore, EU representation in ENP partner countries is actively participating in environmental campaigns, such as global clean-up campaigns (European External Action Service, 2019).

The EU has committed to allocating resources to address the challenges of informal settlements and slums. The participatory slum upgrading program is a joint effort by the EU, UN-Habitat and the African, Caribbean and Pacific Group of States countries. The program is active in 35 countries, covering 160 cities and serving to improve millions of lives (European Commission, International Cooperation and Development, 2019a). The initiative embodies a human rights approach, embedding the recognition of the right to adequate housing into participatory decision-making processes. In Kenya, over 15,000 households have benefited from the implementation of a slum-upgrading program. The program targets the empowerment of most vulnerable community members by allocating 10 percent of the budget for community-led initiatives (UN Habitat, n.d.).

Numerous EU policies and actions supporting SDG 11 are directed to improved access to water and sanitation, energy efficiency, housing and land access and disaster prevention and preparedness. The EU has adopted policies, established cooperative, financed programs and provided humanitarian aid as its contributions to SDG 11. The EU invested 30 million euros in the AfricaConnect project, aimed at establishing a regional data network for research and education in Eastern and Southern Africa (European Commission, International Cooperation and Development, 2019b). Another project funded by the EU is the Milange–Mocuba road project, implemented by the government of Mozambique, to improve the road infrastructure between rural and urban areas. The EU allocated 150 million euros for the project, which has significantly enhanced regional integration and a reduction of poverty by opening up the Milange–Mocuba corridor (European Commission, International Cooperation and Development, 2019c). While EU institutions and its member states channel resources towards global sustainable urban development and have made significant progress in the delivery of the Agenda 2030, several EU member states have the highest negative spillovers vis-à-vis the delivery of the goals externally (Kettunen et al., 2018). This indicates a clear need for the EU to address the aspects of delivering SDGs globally and to review the internal policies that can have a negative effect in the global context.

CONCLUSION

During recent decades, urban sustainable development has become an integral part of development strategies for many countries, which was mostly as a result of an expansion in urban growth. It has been widely disputed that, despite approaches being fostered by countries to reach inclusive and sustainable urbanization, there are still problems in understanding which specific policies are effective and which policies need to be amended across SDG 11.

Being one of the wealthiest regions globally, the EU has lots to contribute to the realization of SDGs both internally and externally. Annually, EU institutions and its member states invest around 75 billion euros in global sustainable development initiatives (Kettunen et al., 2018). EU political entrepreneurship towards urban development is centered around the principles of good governance and partnership. Approximately 5 percent of the European Regional Fund is dedicated to cities and integrated urban strategy developments. Through the European funding programs cities have adopted actions contributing to global challenges. Post-2020, allocation of budgets by the European Regional Fund is expected to increase to 6 percent. It is now, as the world is in a constant state of flux, that the EU has to adopt indicators for global SDG delivery to decrease negative spillover effects of EU internal policies.

REFERENCES

Al-Zu'bi, M. and Radovic, V. (2018). Cities and Key Interactions, *SDG11 – Sustainable Cities and Communities: Towards Inclusive, Safe, and Resilient Settlements (Concise Guides to the United Nations Sustainable Development Goals)*, Bingley: Emerald Publishing, pp. 3–20.

Chistobaev, A. and Fedulova, S. (2018). Spatial Planning in the European Union: Practices to Draw on in Russia. *Baltic Region*, 10(2), 86–99.

CLRAE (1992). *The European Urban Charter. Standing Conference of Local and Regional Authorities of Europe.* Strasbourg: Council of Europe.

Commission of the European Communities (2004). *Communication from the Commission: European Neighbourhood Policy.* Working Paper. Brussels. Available at: https://ec.europa.eu/neighbourhood- enlargement/sites/near/files/2004_commu-nication_from_the_commission_-_european_neighbourhood_policy_-_strategy_paper.pdf

European Commission (1996). *European Sustainable Cities.* Brussels: Expert Group on the Urban Environment.

European Commission (2017). *Report from the Commission to the Council: On the Urban Agenda for the EU.* Brussels: European Commission. Available at: https://ec.europa.eu/regional_policy/sources/policy/themes/urban/report_urban_agenda2017_en.pdf

European Commission, Directorate General for Regional Policy (2011). *Cities of Tomorrow: Challenges, Visions, Ways Forward.* Luxembourg: Publications Office of the European Union.

European Commission, Directorate General for Regional Policy (2019). *Urban Agenda for the EU: Multi-Level Governance in Action.* Regional and Urban Policy. European Commission. Available at: https://ec.europa.eu/regional_policy/sources/docgener/brochure/urban_agenda_eu_en.pdf

European Commission, International Cooperation and Development (2019a). *On the Implementation of the European Union's Instruments for Financing External Actions in 2018.* Annual Report. Luxembourg: European Union. Available at: https://ec.europa.eu/international-partnerships/system/files/devco-annual-report-2019-en-web.pdf

European Commission, International Cooperation and Development (2019b). (2019). *AfricaConnect.* Available at: https://ec.europa.eu/international-partnerships/projects/africaconnect_en

European Commission, International Cooperation and Development (2019c). *Milange Mocuba Road to Success: International Cooperation and Development European Commission.* Available at: https://ec.europa.eu/international-partnerships/projects/milange-mocuba-road-success_en

European External Action Service (2019). *European Union in Jordan Participates in Global Clean-Up Campaign.* Available at: https://eeas.europa.eu/diplomatic-network/european-neighbourhood-policy-enp/68129/european-union-jordan-participates-global-clean-campaign_en

Harris, J. and Todaro, M. (1970). Migration, Unemployment and Development: A Two-Sector Analysis. *American Economic Review*, 60(1), 126–42.

Kettunen,, M., Bowyer, C., Vaculova, L. and Charveriat, C. (2018). *Sustainable Development Goals and the EU: Uncovering the Nexus between External and Internal Policies.* Think 2030. Brussels: IEEP. Available at: https://ieep.eu/uploads/

articles/attachments/8399886b-8e29-43f7-b98c-4a714a0f0cc8/t2030-ieep_sdg
_globaldimension_final-1.pdf?v=63711750136
McKinsey Global Institute (2016). *Urban World: The Global Consumers to Watch.*
New York: McKinsey & Company.
Muller, E. (1995). *Europe 2000+: Cooperation for European Territorial Development.
1996.* EU Economic and Social Committee. Available at: http://aei.pitt.edu/41761/
Obersteg, A., Arlati, A., Acke, A., Berruti, G., Czapiewski, K., Dąbrowski, M.,
Heurkens, E., Mezei, C., Palestino, M., Varjú, V., Wójcik, M. and Knieling, J.
(2019). Urban Regions Shifting to Circular Economy: Understanding Challenges for
New Ways of Governance. *Urban Planning,* 4(3), 19.
Pact of Amsterdam (2016). *Urban Agenda for the EU: Pact of Amsterdam.* Amsterdam:
European Commission. Available at: https://ec.europa.eu/regional_policy/sources/
policy/themes/urban-development/agenda/pact-of-amsterdam.pdf
Parnell, S. (2016). Fair Cities: Imperatives in Meeting Global Sustainable Developmental
Aspirations. In D. Simon, ed., *Rethinking Sustainable Cities: Accessible, Green and
Fair.* Bristol: Policy Press.
Rozhenkova, V., Allmang, S., Ly, S., Franken, D. and Heymann, J. (2019). The Role of
Comparative City Policy Data in Assessing Progress toward the Urban SDG Targets.
Cities, 95, 1023–57.
UN Habitat (n.d.). *Participatory Slum Upgrading Programme Empowers Women and
Girls through Community-Managed Funding: Office of the Secretary-General's
Envoy on Youth.* United Nations. Available at: www.un.org/youthenvoy/2017/
03/participatory-slum-upgrading-programme-empowers-women-girls-community
-managed-funding/
United Nations, Department of Economic and Social Affairs (2016). *The Sustainable
Development Goals Report 2016.* Available at: https://reliefweb.int/report/world/
sustainable-development-goals-report-2016
United Nations, Department of Economic and Social Affairs, Population Division
(2018). *World Urbanization Prospects 2018: Highlights.* United Nations. Available
at: https://population.un.org/wup/Publications/Files/WUP2018-Highlights.pdf
United Nations, Economic and Social Council (2019). *Report of the Secretary-General
on SDG Progress 2019.* Special edition. Available at: https://sustainabledevelopment
.un.org/content/documents/24978Report_of_the_SG_on_SDG_Progress_2019.pdf
United Nations, Habitat III (2017). *New Urban Agenda.* Quito: Habitat III Secretariat.
Available at: http://habitat3.org/wp-content/uploads/NUA-English.pdf

10. Agenda 2030 and the EU on climate action

Daniel Silander

Realizing the goal of peaceful, just and inclusive societies is still a long way off. In recent years, no substantial advances have been made towards ending violence, promoting the rule of law, strengthening institutions at all levels, or increasing access to justice. Millions of people have been deprived of their security, rights and opportunities.

(UN, 2015: SDG 16)

The Sustainable Development Goal (SDG) 16 addresses the important work of promoting inclusive societies based on strong institutions and the rule of law. It includes providing access to justice for all citizens around the world, developing solid, effective, accountable and inclusive political institutions and providing for peaceful and free societies. Although the concept of democracy is not mentioned in goal 16, democracy is clearly stated in the political declaration of the Agenda and the fundamental norms and values embedded in democracy are strictly pointed out as necessary to fulfil sustainable development. Democracy is both a fundamental goal and a means for sustainable development. A democracy must protect and promote the fundamental values of equal access to political participation, equality before the law and accountability from decision makers (UN General Assembly, 2015b: 4). Building democracy is about institutionalizing transparent and accountable political institutions, effective state administration and the rule of law, all core aspects of goal 16, as illustrated in Table 10.1.

On July 15, 2019, the deputy secretary-general Amina Mohamed addressed the importance of stepping up global engagement on goal 16 by highlighting the importance of democracy in United Nations (UN) activities and promoting sustainable development in our contemporary world. Although it was stated that democracy may have different shapes of governance, based on countries' history and culture, democracy is about free and fair elections, state institutions representing the will of the people, fair and balanced rules for people/state relations, checks and balances and inclusive and citizen-responsive institutions. As argued, 'Democracy is therefore a political system that is not just built on public participation and representation alone, it is also built on the equal treatment and respect for all. It needs a commitment to safeguard people's rights and human dignity' (UN Secretary-General, 2019).

The UN has stated how goal 16 calls for inclusive and non-discriminatory state institutions, justice and the rule of law. Today, the UN identifies several hindrances to the achievement of goal 16. Such hindrances are primarily ethno-nationalism, authoritarianism, suppressed civil society, violence, limited freedom of expression, societal inequalities and corruption, among many other things. There is an urge for a global commitment and response to such challenges to promote and revitalize our democracy through improved representation and participation to improve relations between decision makers and citizens, to build and strengthen trust to improve social cohesion for all groups of society and finally to ensure that democracy delivers more effectively on peace, prosperity, security and freedom.

This chapter focuses on democracy in Europe by exploring the status of political rights and civil liberties in the EU member states. By using the Freedom House Index, the analysis explores the status of freedom among European states regarding political rights and civil liberties and identifies changes and challenges within the European democratic landscape. In addition, this chapter focuses on the institutionalized role of the EU in promoting and protecting democratic institutions and the rule of law regionally as well as globally. Overall, despite existing and alarming European challenges to freedom in rights and liberties, the EU, with its member states, is a global frontrunner on the Agenda 2030 on peace, justice and strong institutions and is a unique example of how peace and democratic governance are related.

AGENDA 2030 ON PEACE, JUSTICE AND STRONG INSTITUTIONS

The Agenda 2030 and goal 16 specifically address the importance of peace, justice and strong institutions in providing for sustainable development. The UN declares that sustainable development requires peace and stability, good governance and human rights based on the rule of law. The aspects of goal 16 are, however, in great need of promotion and protection around the world. The UN member states are highly divided regarding peace, justice and strong institutions. While some regions are mostly free from violence and challenges to the rule of law and human rights, other regions and states are constantly undermined by conflict and violence, as well as democratic and human rights abuses. By the end of 2017, the UN estimated that about 68.5 million people were forcibly displaced due to persecution, conflict and violence. About 10 million people were declared stateless, without any protection of rights, and about 1 billion were legally 'invisible' due to a lack of documentation of where they came from (UNDP, 2019). At the same time, authoritarianism has had a recent resurgence, with declining scores on freedoms of rights and liberties around the world. Fragile and authoritarian states are today two major challenges to goal 16 and a world of states with peace, justice and strong institutions delivering upon the will of the people (Freedom House, 2019c). The lack of justice and stable and accountable institutions is a hindrance to social and economic development, leading to social exclusion and exploitation. The work on promoting peaceful and inclusive societies for sustainable development, providing access to justice for all and building effective, accountable and inclusive institutions at all levels, is an ambitious, complex but highly needed effort in the world.

The goal set by the UN includes a wide range of targets to be met in 2030. These targets are summarized in Box 10.1 and highlight the different pillars of the goal in building strong, transparent, accountable and inclusive political institutions for improved representation based on the rule of law.

BOX 10.1 SUMMARY OF TARGETS IN GOAL 16

- Reduce all forms of violence and related death rates.
- End abuse, exploitation, trafficking and violence against and torture of children.
- Promote the rule of law and ensure equal access to justice.
- Reduce illicit financial and arms flows, strengthen the recovery and return of stolen assets and combat organized crime.
- Reduce corruption and bribery.
- Develop effective, accountable and transparent institutions.
- Ensure responsive, inclusive and participatory and representative decision making.
- Broaden and strengthen the participation of developing countries in global institutions.
- Provide legal identification for all, including birth registration.
- Ensure public access to information and protect fundamental freedoms.
- Strengthen national institutions to prevent violence and combat terrorism and crime.
- Promote and enforce non-discriminatory laws and policies for sustainable development.

Source: UN Goal 16 (2019).

The UN stresses that the wide range of targets under goal 16 can only be met through peaceful, just and inclusive societies with effective and inclusive public institutions that can provide sustainable development in quality education, healthcare, fair economic policies and inclusive environmental protection. Such public institutions require accountability where government, civil societies and communities work together based on the freedom to express views, engage in decision-making processes and be treated as citizens without discrimination or exclusion. As stated by the UN, 'Institutions that do not function according to legitimate laws are prone to arbitrariness and abuse of power, and less capable of delivering public services to everyone' (UN, 2019b).

One of the UN member states' visions addressed in the Political Declaration of 2015 is to 'envisage a world of universal respect for human rights and human dignity, the rule of law, justice, equality' (UN General Assembly, 2015b: 3). It is further stated that such a world is 'one in which democracy, good governance and the rule of law, as well as an enabling environment at the national and international levels, are essential for sustainable development' (UN General Assembly, 2015b: 4). The declaration also stresses how the UN emphasizes 'the responsibilities of all States, in conformity with the Charter of the United Nations, to respect, protect and promote human rights and fundamental freedoms for all' (UN General Assembly, 2015b: 6). It focuses on ensuring the 'agenda recognizes the need to build peaceful, just and inclusive societies that provide equal access to justice and that are based on respect for human rights (including the right to development), on effective rule of law and good governance at all levels and on transparent, effective and accountable institutions' (UN General Assembly, 2015b: 9). Finally, the political declaration addresses the key role of the people:

> What we are announcing today – an Agenda for global action for the next 15 years – is a charter for people and planet in the twenty-first century. Children and young women and men are critical agents of change and will find in the new Goals a platform to channel their infinite capacities for activism into the creation of a better world...
>
> Our journey will involve Governments as well as parliaments, the United Nations system and other international institutions, local authorities, indigenous peoples, civil society, business and the private sector, the scientific and academic community – and all people. Millions have already engaged with, and will own, this Agenda. It is an Agenda of the people, by the people and for the people – and this, we believe, will ensure its success. (UN General Assembly, 2015b: 12)

Democracy is a fundamental value underlying all work assigned by the UN. The words 'We the people' (UN Charter, 1945: 1) introduce the UN Charter, and they express the core value of goal 16. Since 1945, the UN has embarked on a path to protect and promote democracy, human rights, development, peace and security. For about 75 years, this path towards universal freedom has embedded activities that include providing for accountable institutions, free and fair elections, strengthening an independent and dynamic civil society and the rule of law. Such work has been institutionalized through the

United Nations Development Programme, the United Nations Democracy Fund, the Department of Peace Operations, the Department of Political and Peacebuilding Affairs, the Office of the High Commissioner for Human Rights and the United Nations Entity for Gender Equality and the Empowerment of Women, etc. (UN Democracy, 2019).

Although the UN Charter of 1945 does not mention democracy, due to international politics, the rights and liberties embedded in the notion of democracy are the cornerstones of the UN system. Opening the Charter with 'We the people' symbolizes how the people are the legal and legitimate source for member states and the UN as a whole. The principles, rights and liberties inherent in a democracy are necessary for the development and protection of people's empowerment, participation, equality, security and human dignity. As stated by the UN, 'Democracy provides an environment that respects human rights and fundamental freedoms, and in which the freely expressed will of people is exercised. People have a say in decisions and can hold decision-makers to account. Women and men have equal rights and all people are free from discrimination' (UN Democracy, 2019). The Universal Declaration of Human Rights and the International Covenant on Civil and Political Rights have also reaffirmed democratic values, and the General Assembly has adopted resolutions on democracy for decades. In addition, the UN Commission on Human Rights and the Office of the High Commissioner have supported national governments in promoting and protecting peace, the rule of law and institutions in transitional democracies. In 2012, the Human Rights Council decided on *Human Rights, Democracy and the Rule of Law*, a resolution confirming the importance and interdependent nature of funda-mental freedoms, democracy, human rights and development (UN General Assembly, 2012). This was followed by a 2015 resolution institutionalizing a forum on human rights, democracy and the rule of law for discussion and cooperation on these areas (UN General Assembly, 2015a). Today, the UN engages as an impartial actor providing electoral assistance in about 60 coun-tries every year. This engagement promotes transparent and accountable insti-tutions and peace through programs/funds in the Under-Secretary-General for Political and Peacebuilding Affairs, the Electoral Assistance Division within the Department of Political and Peacebuilding Affairs, the United Nations Democracy Fund and the United Nations Development Programme, in addi-tion to partnerships with regional, international and governmental organiza-tions. In March 2015, the UN General Assembly decided on the *Education for Democracy* resolution, stressing that in their relations to member states all UN agencies should promote education as a tool for peace, democracy and human rights around the world. Since 8 November 2007, the UN has recognized the International Day of Democracy, decided by the General Assembly to declare how peace, human rights, the rule of law and development are best promoted and protected in democratic societies and how democracies are a solid platform for a strong and dynamic civil society in which people participate. As the UN stated on International Day of Democracy, 15 September 2019:

> This year's International Day of Democracy is an opportunity to recall that democracy is about people. Democracy is built on inclusion, equal treatment and participation – and it is a fundamental building block for peace, sustainable development and human rights... This International Day of Democracy, is an opportunity to urge all governments to respect their citizens' right to active, substantive and meaningful participation in democracy. (UN, 2019a)

THE EU CHARTER OF FUNDAMENTAL RIGHTS

The nature of goal 16 is largely embedded in the *EU Charter of Fundamental Rights*. It addresses the importance of dignity, freedoms, equality, solidarity and citizens' rights and justice. The Charter consists of shared European norms and values and provides a platform for European integration and individual states' development. It is stated that the EU 'is founded on the indivisible, universal values of human dignity, freedom, equality and solidarity: it is based on the principles of democracy and the rule of law' (EU Charter, 2012). Box 10.2 summarizes and explains these fundamental values.

BOX 10.2 SUMMARY OF THE EU CHARTER OF FUNDAMENTAL RIGHTS

1. Dignity
   a. Human dignity
   b. Right to life
   c. Right to integrity
   d. Prohibition of torture and inhumane treatment and punishment
   e. Prohibition of slavery and forced labour
2. Freedoms
   a. Right to liberty and security
   b. Respect for private and family life
   c. Protection of personal data
   d. Right to marry and found a family
   e. Freedom of thought, conscience and religion
   f. Freedom of expression and information
   g. Freedom of assembly/association
   h. Freedom of the arts/sciences
   i. Right to education
   j. Freedom to choose an occupation and right to work

    k.   Freedom to conduct business
    l.   Right to property
    m. Right to asylum
    n.   Protection in the event of removal, expulsion or extradition

3. Equality
    a.   Equality before the law
    b.   Cultural, religious and linguistic diversity
    c.   Gender equality
    d.   Rights of children
    e.   Rights of older people
    f.   Integration of persons with disabilities

4. Solidarity
    a.   Workers' right to information and consultation
    b.   Right to collective bargaining and action
    c.   Right of access to placement services
    d.   Protection of unjustified dismissal
    e.   Fair and just working conditions
    f.   Prohibition of child labour and protection of young people at work
    g.   Protection of family and professional life
    h.   Social security and social assistance
    i.   Health care
    j.   Access to services of general economic interests
    k.   Environmental protection
    l.   Consumer protection

5. Citizen rights
    a.   Right to vote and stand as a candidate to European Parliament
    b.   Right to vote and stand as a municipal-level candidate
    c.   Right to good administration
    d.   Right to access documents
    e.   European Ombudsman
    f.   Right to petition
    g.   Freedom of movement/residence
    h.   Diplomatic/consular protection

6. Justice
    a.   Right to remedy and fair trial
    b.   Presumption of innocence and right of defence
    c.   Principles of legality/proportionality of criminal offences/penalties
    d.   Right not to be tried or punished twice in criminal proceedings for same offence

The European Commission has promoted and highlighted the democratic community of European norms and values over time. The Charter sets out the cornerstones of European integration in dignity, freedoms, equality, solidarity, citizen rights and justice. In 2019, the European Commission addressed the EU's normative community by addressing the EU's core norms and values. As stated,

> We Europeans can be proud of our track-record. Through integration and close cooperation, we have created unprecedented wealth, high social standards and great opportunities for our citizens. We have anchored our common principles and values of democracy, human rights, and the rule of law in our Treaties, and built a European Union, whole and free. This success is due to the fact that Europeans set the bar high. Our strong democratic culture spurs on fierce debates, and rightfully so. (European Commission, 2019: Foreword)

The European Commission shed light on the fact that the EU is a solid democratic union, including member states with free and fair elections, the rule of law and extended rights and liberties. In a global comparison, the EU has become a collaborative political project by like-minded states that has developed democracy, human rights standards, freedoms and the rule of law within individual member states and common European institutions based upon such norms and values. Today, the EU is unique in international politics – a regional project that has come to serve the many norms and values within the UN goal 16 very well.

Table 10.1 illustrates the high democratic status within EU member states. The EU member states provide a regional score on freedom among a large number of states that has no global comparison.

All of the EU member states, except Hungary, are assessed as free states with high levels of political rights and civil liberties. Freedom House uses a methodology derived from the Universal Declaration of Human Rights adopted by the UN General Assembly in 1948. The Freedom in the World Index explores universal values inherited in the UN Charter by focusing on freedoms. The focus on political rights refers to aspects such as whether an electoral process, political pluralism and participation and functioning government exist. The focus on civil liberties refers to freedom of expression and belief, associational and organizational rights, rule of law and personal autonomy and individual rights (Freedom House, 2019b). Box 10.1 on the summary of goal 16 provides an overview that shows Freedom House's assessment is very important to understanding the EU member states' stand on goal 16. Goal 16 refers to rule of law, the functioning of government in accountable and transparent institutions, political pluralism and participation in responsive and participatory representative decision making, freedoms of expression, beliefs, association and personal autonomy in protecting fundamental freedoms. The

Table 10.1   Status of political rights and civil liberties among EU member states

EU member state	Political rights	Civil liberties	Freedom rate
Austria	1	1	1.0 FREE
Belgium	1	1	1.0 FREE
Bulgaria	2	2	2.0 FREE
Croatia	1	2	1.5 FREE
Cyprus	1	1	1.0 FREE
Czech Republic	1	1	1.0 FREE
Denmark	1	1	1.0 FREE
Estonia	1	1	1.0 FREE
Finland	1	1	1.0 FREE
France	1	2	1.5 FREE
Germany	1	1	1.0 FREE
Greece	1	2	1.5 FREE
Hungary	*3*	*3*	*3.0 PARTLY FREE*
Ireland	1	1	1.0 FREE
Italy	1	1	1.0 FREE
Latvia	2	2	2.0 FREE
Lithuania	1	1	1.0 FREE
Luxembourg	1	1	1.0 FREE
Malta	2	1	1.5 FREE
Netherlands	1	1	1.0 FREE
Poland	2	2	2.0 FREE
Portugal	1	1	1.0 FREE
Romania	2	2	2.0 FREE
Slovakia	1	2	1.5 FREE
Slovenia	1	1	1.0 FREE
Spain	1	1	1.0 FREE
Sweden	1	1	1.0 FREE
United Kingdom	1	1	1.0 FREE

Source: Freedom House (2019a).

European scores on freedoms regarding rights and liberties shed light on a region of consolidated democratic states.

In a global comparison, the 2019 Freedom House Index[1] identifies the 13th consecutive year of decline in global freedom regarding rights and liberties. The decline of freedom has spread globally, leading to greater repression in consolidated authoritarian states such as China and Russia and declining freedoms in consolidated democracies such as the United States. While authoritarian states have stepped up repression against citizens and civil society activists and become internationally active in putting counter-pressure on democratic norms and values in diplomacy, trade and within international organizations, some consolidated democracies have also faced challenges stemming from corruption, economic inequalities, anti-liberal populist movements, hindrances to the rule of law and discriminatory treatment of minorities, etc. In democracies around the world, mostly right-wing populist politicians have challenged the protection and promotion of individual rights and liberties by invoking the notions of unique and traditional national values, limiting the freedom of information and expression by putting pressure on civil society activists, academia and journalists, and challenging the principle of checks and balances (Freedom House, 2019a).

Today, 44.1 per cent of countries are free, 30.3 per cent are partly free and 25.6 per cent are not free. This is an increase of freedom rates around the world compared to 1988 (35.8 per cent free, 26.7 per cent partly free and 37.6 per cent not free) but a decline compared to 2008 (46.1 per cent free, 32.2 per cent partly free and 21.8 per cent not free) (Freedom House, 2019c). In a time of democratic recession, Europe continues to be the foremost democratized region in the world with peaceful relations between EU member states. The development of democracy and the rule of law has served individual European states very well. Nevertheless, challenges within Europe need to be addressed. The global resurgence of authoritarianism, populism and anti-liberal norms and values have spilled over to the European landscape in many EU member states. Foremost in Central Europe and the Balkans, democracies are influenced by anti-democratic leaders pushing for power beyond the constitutional limits, criticizing institutions that protect freedom of expression and association, questioning in actions the rule of law and oppressing civil society activities sceptical to the regime. The worst Central European case has been Hungary, which under prime minister Viktor Orbán has faced serious declines of freedom, based on the Freedom House Index. In Hungary, any opposition within the civil society of organizations and associations, the media and academia has met right-wing nationalist oppression. In Poland, the conservative Law and Justice Party led by Jarosław Kaczyński has challenged the rule of law by invoking political control over judicial branches, including the Supreme Court. Austria has also faced democratic challenges due to a new right-wing government restricting public broadcasting. In the Czech Republic, prime minister Andrej Babiš influences the media to make political scandals disappear, and in Slovakia corruption links politicians to organized crime and the killing of reporter Ján Kuciak (Freedom House, 2019c).

Today, Hungary is the only EU member state that is defined as partly free, based on freedoms regarding rights and liberties (Freedom House, 2019a).

The Hungarian case is, however, a larger symbol of a democracy in crisis in a European context. Although the EU consists of democratized states that take political rights and civil liberties as universal freedoms for granted, some of the anti-democratic tendencies have also been seen in other European states such as Poland. The anti-democratic tendencies have led the EU to trigger the use of Article 7 against both member states due to the suspicion that both member states did not fully commit to Article 2 of the EU's fundamental norms and values. The European Parliament has the right to trigger Article 7 based on a two-thirds majority of the parliamentarians, and it called upon the Council to act based on Articles 7(1) and 7(2). Article 7(1) allows the EU to take action if there is suspicion that a member state does not adhere to the EU's fundamental norms and values and requires an absolute majority of four fifths of the Council, whereas Article 7(2) includes possible sanctions on a member state, although requiring unanimity among members in such cases (Treaty of Lisbon, 2007).

THE DEMOCRACY–PEACE NEXUS IN EUROPE

The European striving for democracy has attracted scholarly attention for decades. Studies on the European integration of additional member states and more in-depth policy areas have paid attention to how European democracies have developed peaceful relations in the region. Based upon an old scholarly tradition of democratic peace theories, scholars of international relations in general and European politics in particular have acknowledged the European democratic peace order (see Chapter 3). Scholars have explained the peaceful relations among EU member states in many ways, pointing out important hindrances for democracies to engage in war against each other (see Russett & Oneal, 2001; Russett, 1993; Ray, 1995, 1998). One such hindrance has been that democratically elected leaders may not engage in war without public support. The democratic mechanism of free and fair elections is therefore a hindrance for elected leaders to jeopardize people's safety. A second hindrance is the establishment of checks and balances within democratic systems. The separation of powers may be an obstacle for individual leaders to engage in war. A third possible hindrance to war is the political culture of democracies in allowing for competing political ideas and discussions and the readiness to negotiate and seek compromises with like-minded states. Fourth, democracies are also politically transparent regimes that minimize political and military surprises, misunderstandings and misperceptions in political relations with other states. A fifth mentioned hindrance to war in democracies is that many democratic states are also wealthy societies that strive to avoid conflicts and wars that could challenge and destroy integration, welfare and infrastructure. The well-being of many democracies also makes them less likely to engage in war over scarcity of resources, which otherwise is an important explanation of inter-state conflict. Sixth, democracies are often free and open economies with multiple trade relations, foreign investments and dependent markets, which are economic factors that could be destroyed by war. Finally, democracies as like-minded states are also often open for international collaboration with other democracies, providing a platform for shared institutions, common laws and treaties. This has been the obvious case with the EU in European affairs (Ray, 1995; Weart, 1998).

All these factors seem to have played a pivotal role in European integration for decades, comprising the widened and deepened integration within the EU. In the autumn of 2012, the Norwegian Nobel Committee declared its announcement to award the Nobel Peace Prize to the EU. The committee stated how European integration over time facilitated peace, stability, democracy and human rights in Europe. From the ashes of World War II, the integration of Southern Europe in the 1980s and Eastern Europe in the 1990s and thereafter were a major symbol of the power behind democratic collaboration on the European scene. In the early 2000s, such democratic force led to democracy and reconciliation in the southeast of Europe, which had suffered war and devastation. In 2020, there are no signs of war between EU democracies. As stated by the Norwegian Nobel Committee in 2012,

> The Norwegian Nobel Committee wishes to focus on what it sees as the EU's most important result: the successful struggle for peace and reconciliation and for democracy and human rights. The stabilizing part played by the EU has helped to transform most of Europe from a continent of war to a continent of peace. The work of the EU represents 'fraternity between nations', and amounts to a form of the 'peace congresses' to which Alfred Nobel refers as criteria for the Peace Prize in his 1895 will. (Nobel Prize Organization, 2012)

In the early 2000s, the academic world referred to the European project and the EU as a normative power in international politics (see Chapter 2) (Manners, 2002; Pace, 2007). This was a result of a historical democratic project in the European Coal and Steel Treaty (1951), the Treaty of the European Community (TEC, 1957), the Treaty of European Union (TEU, 1992) and the EU treaties thereafter. These treaties acknowledged that the founding ideas of peace and security were linked to liberty, democracy, rule of law and human rights. As stated in the TEU of 1992 in a post-Cold War context: 'The Union is founded on the principle of liberty, democracy, respect for human rights and fundamental freedoms, and the rule of law, principles which are common to the Member States' (Maastricht Treaty, 1992, article 6:1).

Over time, the democratic norms in European politics have guided European states on how to pursue the political game both domestically and internationally regarding rules, procedures and behaviour. The democratic norms have also established political expectations regarding appropriate international behaviour (Pace, 2007). In the early 2000s, the European Council stressed in the Charter of Fundamental Rights of the European Union that EU external relations were also founded on democratic norms and values. Already in the 1990s, such a notion had been institutionalized, such as in the TEC development cooperation policy (article 177), the TEC common foreign and security provisions (article 11), and the Copenhagen criteria (membership requirements of 1993) (Manners, 2002: 242; Laffan, 2001). It was clearly stated that the EU's external actions had to be guided by the fundamental norms and values underpinning the European project. The EU's role in international politics was to promote collaboration to safeguard democracy, the rule of law, human rights and international law (TEU, 2007: article 21). In the TEU of 1992, it was stated that 'The Union shall define and implement a common foreign and security policy covering all areas of foreign and security policy, the objectives of which shall be... to develop and consolidate democracy, rule of law, and respect for human rights and fundamental freedoms' (Maastricht Treaty, 1992: article 11:1).

BUILDING JUST AND DEMOCRATIC INSTITUTIONS ABROAD

The EU has pursued a role in international politics based on an exclusive strategy that has implied the use of conditional cooperation towards other states using a carrot-and-stick approach to promote democracy and peace (Schmitter, 2001: 29–30). The conditional cooperation approach has embedded EU support with the aim of establishing democratic norms and values, but neglect of democratic reforms in targeted states has led to cancelled cooperation. In many cases, the democratic clause in all external aid and trade relations has resulted in an asymmetrical relationship between the EU and targeted states (Schimmelfennig, 2002; Smith, 2008).

The Enlargement Policy

The EU's most efficient foreign policy tool has been its enlargement policy. The EU has offered membership after absorption of European norms and values domestically. The Copenhagen criteria of 1992 have been cornerstones of the enlargement procedures and have guided potential member states towards democracy, the rule of law and economic and judicial integration based on EU political and financial support. The EU applied such conditionality to post-communist states in the 1990s, using reaccession processes from 1999 onwards, to promote reforms and progress candidate states (Commission of the European Communities, 2001). The addition of new member states in

2004 and 2007 was then based on the adoption of democracy, liberty, human rights, the rule of law and a market economy with the sudden disappearance of former dividing lines between West and East (Bosse, 2009; Dannreuther, 2006).

Although the Treaty of the EU declares that all European countries may become member states, such opportunity comes with EU demands regarding specific norms and values that must be in place before being accepted. The Copenhagen criteria demands the following:

- Stable institutions guaranteeing democracy, the rule of law, human rights and respect for minorities.
- A functioning market economy and the capacity to handle competition and market forces within the EU.
- The ability to absorb and implement EU membership obligations, including following the aims of the political, economic and monetary union.

When it comes to goal 16 on peace, justice and strong institutions, the first criterion addresses the importance of new member states fully embracing stable democratic institutions and the rule of law. The European Commission handles negotiations with potential EU member states and acts as the monitor, but before a new member state is accepted all other member states need to agree. The Commission's role is to inform the Council and the European Parliament of progress made through annual strategic reports. More recently, the membership criteria has developed beyond the Copenhagen criteria to include regional collaboration and peaceful neighbouring relations as a direct result of the Balkan countries' great interest in joining the EU. The so-called Stabilization and Association Process regarding these countries has included fostering good relations with neighbouring states due to the civil war in the former Yugoslavia. In practice, the accession process has come to focus on the status of the candidate country and the adoption and implementation of EU norms, values and regulations. The rules and regulations refer to the accumulated legislation, including 35 different regulatory policy areas that need to be addressed (e.g., transport, energy and environment). In addition, negotiations between the Commission and the candidate country also concern financial arrangements in economic costs and benefits to become a member state and transitional arrangements on a time plan to have fully adapted to EU rules and regulations.

The European Neighbourhood Policy

A second mechanism for the promotion and protection of the European democracy–peace nexus has been the European neighbourhood policy (ENP).

The idea behind the ENP was launched at the European Council Meeting in Copenhagen of 11–12 December 2002, discussing upcoming enlargements and how to approach future neighbours. It was stated that enlargements would expand EU territory and thereby create new union borders. In the Presidency Conclusion, it was stated that the EU 'wishes to enhance its relations with Ukraine, Moldova, Belarus and the southern Mediterranean countries based on a long-term approach promoting democratic and economic reforms' (Council of the European Union, 2003: 7).

The term 'ENP' was published in 2003 in the Commission Communication on Wider Europe (Commission of the European Communities, 2003). The result was the Strategy Paper on European Neighbourhood Policy of May 2004 (Commission of the European Communities, 2004). The ENP objective was to promote peace in neighbouring states by building partnerships with them to socialize neighbours into becoming 'like us, but not one of us' (Avery, 2008: 194). The ENP never promised membership, but rather 'a mutual commitment to common values' (Commission of the European Communities, 2004) in four identified core areas of cooperation: (a) democracy, rule of law and human rights; (b) market economic reforms; (c) employment and social cohesion; and (d) security in foreign policy cooperation, counter-terrorism, non-proliferation of weapons of mass destruction and the reinforcement of security in neighbouring states.

The group of partner states within the ENP framework were identified as Armenia, Azerbaijan, Belarus, Georgia, Moldova and Ukraine in the east and Algeria, Egypt, Israel, Jordan, Lebanon, Libya, Morocco, the occupied Palestinian territory, Syria and Tunisia in the south. In 2007, the EU initiated the European Neighbourhood and Partnership Instrument as the primary funding mechanism for ENP, but the European Neighbourhood Instrument (ENI) replaced it in 2014. The ENI has been the financial instrument for implementation, including a budget of €15.4 billion between 2014 and 2020 (European Union External Action, 2016). The financial requirements have foremost addressed joint priorities for cooperation in good governance, democracy and the rule of law, human rights, economic development, security and migration and mobility (EU, ENP). The structure of collaboration within the ENP is mostly bilateral, with tailor-made assistance to partner states based on their societal challenges and overall relations with the EU. The bilateral ENP action plans are a shared commitment by the individual partner state and the EU, including the official agenda of objectives to be met and reforms to be taken. In addition, the ENP also includes regional programmes that complement the individual Action Plans for each partner state. Although the EU and state governments in each partner state agree on the ENP with action plans and regional programmes, the ENP has also focused on support to the civil society to promote development from the bottom up. EU officials have stated that a strengthened and dynamic civil society is crucial for democracy building and societal development in partner states. Civil society is an important part of the action plans and regional programmes and has been the focus of other EU instruments, such as the European Instrument for Democracy and Human Rights (EIDHR), further discussed below (European Union External Action, 2016).

The European Instrument for Democracy and Human Rights

The EIDHR is a thematic funding instrument for democracy and human rights that has global reach. The European Parliament and the Council decided on regulation (EU) No 235/2014 in 2014, for the period of 2014–20 (European Parliament & Council, 2014). The regulation replaced the previous EIDHR for 2007–13, and before that the European Initiative for Democracy and Human Rights between 2000 and 2006. The main objective of this EU instrument is to promote democracy and human rights projects worldwide with a particular focus on a bottom-up approach by favouring a dynamic civil society as a driving engine for democratic reforms and human rights protection (European Parliament & Council, 2014).

The EIDHR complements other EU external actions, but with a direct focus on the civil society organizations engaged in democracy and human rights and without consent from state authorities. It allows the EIDHR to work for reforms in areas that many times are politically sensitive to authorities, such as torture, human rights abuses by state actors and political, economic and social discrimination of ethnic minority groups and other marginalized groups. Based on the last regulation of 2014, the main focus between 2014 and 2020, with a budget of €1,332.75 million, was to promote and project human rights and human rights defenders at risk, complement and support other crucial EU-identified human rights issues, favour democracy and EU Election Observation Missions and finally promote important human rights actors and processes within international and regional bodies (European Parliament & Council, 2014).

To achieve these priorities, the EIDHR channels support in different ways; for example, grants to local civil society organizations and Human Rights Defenders under the EIDHR Country Based Support Scheme via the formal EU call for proposals process. These grants are advertised each year and handled by EU delegations within partner states; as stated above, they focus on civil society organizations.

With Agenda 2030 and goal 16 in mind, the EIDHR not only focuses on democracy and human rights globally, but also on providing for peace and conflict management. The Instrument Contributing to Stability and Peace (IcSP) addresses the importance of the EU's coherent external actions in the areas of security threats, conflict prevention and management and peace. The main objective of this instrument is to provide rapid help in times of man-made and natural crises and disasters, providing support to existing humanitarian assistance and actions taken through the Common Foreign and Security Policy and the European Security and Defence Policy. The overall budget for the IcSP between 2014 and 2020 was €2,338,719,000 (European Commission, International Cooperation and Development, n.d.).

Development Cooperation Instrument

The EU constitutes the largest aid donor in the world, accounting for more than 50 per cent of all aid. The aid policy is based upon EU treaties, the 2006 European Consensus on Development and the 2017 New European Consensus on Development (Council & Representatives of Member States, 2017), titled *Our World, Our Dignity, Our Future*, which is based upon the objectives and priorities set out in the UN Agenda 2030. It is the responsibility of the Commission and the Directorate-General for International Cooperation and Development to structure the development policy to target developing states around the world. The 2006 European Consensus on Development set out the EU vision on development and the structures for EU cooperation with developing states around the globe. As stated, 'the "European Consensus on Development" provides, for the first time, a common vision that guides the action of the EU' (European Parliament, Council & Commission, 2006: 1–2). The joint statement identified the common EU development objectives by highlighting the importance of sustainable development, and in the partnerships and dialogues with third-state and developing actors, promoting European values of human rights, fundamental freedoms, peace, democracy, good governance, gender equality, the rule of law, solidarity and justice (European Parliament, Council & Commission, 2006: 2–3). In paragraph 86, the European Consensus on Development explicitly stated, 'Progress in the protection of human rights, good governance and democratisation is fundamental for poverty reduction and sustainable development' (European Parliament, Council & Commission, 2006: 13).

The statement aligns with the UN Agenda 2030 and the four cornerstones of people, planet, prosperity and peace. The EU development approach of 2017 onward also focuses on the integrating dimensions of economic, social and environmental development for sustainability. It addresses the importance of a global commitment to sustainable development and how a multilateral approach of various partners is needed to achieve development in developing states. The EU also states its active role in the political dimension of sustainable development in promoting and protecting good governance, democracy and the rule of law, human rights and sustainable development, in addition to fighting hunger and inequality, conserving natural resources and mitigating climate change impact. It is stated that the EU's response to the 2030 Agenda includes the importance of the development policy addressing the complex challenges in the world, but where the EU stands on development in external actions is always founded on democracy, the rule of law, human rights and dignity and fundamental freedoms (Council & Representatives of Member States, 2017: 5–7).

On 11 March 2014, the European Parliament and the Council decided on Regulation (EU) 235/2014 establishing a financing instrument for democracy and human rights worldwide. The Development Cooperation Instrument focuses on developing countries worldwide through geographical programmes including about 47 countries in Latin America, South Asia and North and South East Asia, Central Asia, the Middle East and Southern Africa. The Regulation referred to Article 2 of the Treaty of the EU by highlighting that the Union is based on the shared values of respect of human dignity, freedom, democracy, equality, the rule of law and respect of human rights and how development cooperation with developing states embeds such values (European Parliament & Council, 2014: 1).

The programmes targeted many aspects of the Agenda 2030 and goal 16 by including inclusive and sustainable growth for human development and justice, human rights, democracy, the rule of law, good governance, anti-corruption measures and equality. In addition to the geographical programmes, there are also thematic programmes that fall into two categories. First is 'Global public good and challenges', which addresses climate change, environment, energy, human development, food security and migration. Second is 'Civil society organisations and local authorities', which promotes civil society and local authorities for societal development. There is also a newly established Pan-African Programme to promote a specific and strategic partnership between the EU and Africa. Overall, the Development Cooperation Instrument budget for 2014–20 was €19.6 billion (European Parliament, 2017).

The Global Strategy on Foreign and Security Policy

In June 2015, the European Council called upon the High Representative to develop a Global Strategy on Foreign and Security Policy. The strategy was to identify important changes and challenges in European security, initiate a revision of the 2003 European Security Strategy and develop a framework of available tools to pursue European security in a global world. The work on a global strategy included various actors within the European governance setting, including member states, the European Parliament, experts and think tanks. The High Representative, Federica Mogherini, argued that 'The crises within and beyond our borders are affecting directly our citizens' lives. In challenging times, a strong Union is one that thinks strategically, shares a vision and acts together... None of our countries has the strength nor the resources to address these threats and seize the opportunities of our time alone' (Mogherini, 2016: 3).

In this process, the European Parliament debated and spoke out on an EU global strategy in a Resolution, *The EU in a Changing Global Environment – a More Connected, Contested and Complex World* (European Parliament, 2016), and pinpointed ideas on an EU security strategy. On 28 June 2016, the High Representative finally launched the *Global Strategy for the European Union's Foreign and Security Policy*, foremost identifying five objectives for EU foreign policy and security (Mogherini, 2016). These five objectives were as follows: (1) the security of our Union's democracy and prosperity; (2) state and societal resilience to the east and south through enlargement procedures and neighbourhood policies, etc.; (3) an integrated approach to conflicts focusing on prevention with all necessary means; (4) cooperative regional orders where the EU is guided by its shared norms and values, and (5) global governance for the twenty-first century promoting international law, sustainable development and a strong UN (Mogherini, 2016: 10).

The High Representative stated the need for new thematic/geographic strategies, and in November 2016, the High Representative released an implementation plan on defence and security issues focusing on responding to external conflicts and crises, capacity building of partners and protecting the EU and its citizens. The implementation plan also included proposals on how to meet the demands set out in the Global Strategy on Foreign and Security Policy by proposing a Coordinated Annual Review of Defence Spending, a reformed EU Rapid Response with EU Battle groups and permanent structured cooperation for member states with a willingness to deepen collaboration on security and defence. In addition, the Commission also produced *Launching the European Defence Fund*, which set out a proposal on how to increase and structure investment within EU member states' defence sectors by highlighting the importance of innovative research, co-financing framed by the European Defence Industrial Development Programme and support of the development of defence capabilities.

The Global Strategy of 2016 was a complex strategy addressing numerous EU security challenges, but also the many tools available for the EU to handle such threats together. The strategy addressed the importance of EU collaboration on building military capabilities and anti-terrorism procedures, as well as mechanisms for peace building and human rights protection, in addition to using the EU's soft power and civilian capacities together with hard power. 'For Europe, soft and hard power go hand in hand' (Mogherini, 2016: 4). Mogherini further stressed that a wide range of soft- and hard-power capacities would serve European security and stability well, but also that such capabilities are essential to promote and protect European needs, hopes and aspirations, as well as the peace that has developed among European states for about 70 years (Mogherini, 2016: 5).

The global strategy embedded an assumption that European and global security are intertwined and that European norms and values regarding security, prosperity and democracy are only safeguarded by an internal and external security approach. Such efforts were to be built upon to promote and fulfil the UN SDGs worldwide, by pushing for a rule-based international order of multilateralism and to secure European unity (Mogherini, 2016: 8, 13–16).

CONCLUSION

The European project, creating over decades what we today refer to as the EU, is a result of more than a half a century of European political entrepreneurship. The growing number of member states has expanded a zone of democracy and peace not seen elsewhere in international politics. The contemporary EU with member states has fostered a political culture of promoting and protecting democracy to seek freedom and peace. Out of the ashes of Nazism and World War II – and strengthened during the Cold War by the threat of fascism and communism – Western European states (with United States alliance) saw the promotion and protection of democracy as a political vaccine for a better world. The notions of goal 16 on peace, justice and strong institutions in the UN Agenda 2030 have been institutionalized in European politics through democratic governments. The democratic regimes have provided integration, shared institutions, the rule of law and common norms and values of freedom leading to a zone of democratic peace. In addition, today the EU symbolizes not only a democratic peace project, but also a global force for freedom through a democracy clause in its external relations. Europe continues to be the symbol of regional peace and democracy in the world, however, serious challenges to Europe exist due to the severe hindrances to peace, justice and strong institutions in the world. Today, European peace and democracy are under severe challenges due to migration, terrorism and authoritarianism rooted externally, but pulling for European disintegration.

NOTE

1. Freedom in the World assesses the state of freedom in 195 countries (and 14 territories) annually using scores between 0 and 4 points on 25 indicators, with an aggregate score of up to 100. These scores reflect (a) political rights and (b) civil liberties where 1 represents the freest conditions and 7 the least free. There are three categories of countries' freedom – an overall status of 1 = free, 2 = partly free or 3 = not free. The methodology used is based on the Universal Declaration of Human Rights (Freedom House, 2019b).

REFERENCES

Avery, G. (2008). 'EU expansion and wider Europe'. In E. Bomberg, J. Peterson & A. Stubb (eds) *The European Union: How Does It Work?* New York: Oxford University Press, 161–84.

Bosse, G. (2009). 'Challenges for EU governance through neighbourhood policy and eastern partnership: The value/security nexus in EU–Belarus relations'. *Contemporary Politics*, 15(2): 215–27.

Commission of the European Communities (2001). *COM 2001: 700 Final – Making a Success of Enlargement. Strategy Paper and Report of the European Commission on the Progress towards Accession by Each of the Candidate Countries.* Brussels: European Commission.

Commission of the European Communities (2003). *COM 2003: 104 final-Wider Europe— Neighbourhood: A New Framework for Relations with our Eastern and Southern Neighbours.* Accessed January 15 2020 at https://library.euneighbours.eu/content/communication-commission-wider-europe—-neighbourhood-new-framewo rk-relations-our-eastern-and

Commission of the European Communities (2004). *COM 2004: 373 Final – European Neighbourhood Policy – Strategy Paper.* Brussels: European Commission. Accessed 15 January 2020 at https:// ec.europa.eu/neighbourhood-enlargement/sites/near/files/2004 _communication_from_the_commission_-_european_neighbourhood_policy_- _strategy_paper.pdf

Council & Representatives of Member States (2017). *The New European Consensus on Development 'Our World, Our Dignity, Our Future'.* Brussels: European Commission.

Council of the European Union (2003). *Copenhagen European Council 12 and 13 December 2020: Presidency Conclusions.* Brussels: Council of the European Union. Accessed 9 September 2019 at www.consilium.europa.eu/media/20906/73842.pdf

Dannreuther, R. (2006). 'Developing the alternative to enlargement: The European Neighbourhood Policy'. *European Foreign Affairs Review*, 11: 183–201.

EU Charter (2012). *Charter of Fundamental Rights of the European Union.* Accessed 11 September 2019 at www.europarl.europa.eu/charter/pdf/text_en.pdf

European Commission (2019). *Reflection Paper: Towards a Sustainable Europe by 2030.* COM(2019) 22 final, 19 January. Brussels: European Commission.

European Commission, International Cooperation and Development (n.d.). *International Cooperation and Development: Funding.* Accessed 5 January 2020 at https://ec.europa.eu/international-partnerships/funding

European Parliament (2016). *Report on the EU in a Changing Global Environment: A More Connected, Contested and Complex World.* Accessed 5 January 2020 at www.europarl.europa.eu/doceo/document/A-8-2016-0069_EN.html#title1

European Parliament (2017). *Briefing How the EU Budget Is Spent: Development Cooperation Instrument.* Accessed 5 January 2020 at www.europarl.europa.eu/ RegData/etudes/BRIE/2017/608764/EPRS_BRI(2017)608764_EN.pdf

European Parliament & Council (2014). *Regulation (EU) No 235/2014 of the European Parliament and of the Council of 11 March 2014 Establishing a Financing Instrument for Democracy and Human Rights Worldwide.* Brussels: European Union.

European Parliament, Council & Commission (2006). *The European Consensus: Official Journal of the European Union*, 24 February. Brussels: European Union.

European Union External Action (2016). *The European Neighbourhood Policy*. Accessed 18 January 2020 at https://eeas.europa.eu/diplomatic-network/european -neighbourhood-policy-enp/330/european-neighbourhood-policy-enp_en

Freedom House (2019a). *Freedom in the World, Countries*. Accessed 20 November 2019 at https://freedomhouse.org/report/countries-world-freedom-2019

Freedom House (2019b). *Methodology*. Accessed 15 January 2019 at https:// freedomhouse.org/report/methodology-freedom-world-2019

Freedom House (2019c). *Democracy in Retreat*. Accessed 7 January 2019 at https:// freedomhouse.org/report/freedom-world/freedom-world-2019/democracy-in-retreat

Laffan, B. (2001). 'The European polity: A union of regulative, normative and cognitive pillars'. *Journal of European Public Policy*, 8(5): 709–27.

Maastricht Treaty (1992). *Treaty on European Union*. Accessed 5 October 2019 at https://europa.eu/european-union/sites/europaeu/files/docs/body/treaty_on _european_union_en.pdf

Manners, I. (2002). 'Normative power Europe: A contradiction in terms?' *Journal of Common Market Studies*, 40(2): 235–58.

Mogherini, F. (2016). *Shared Vision, Common Action: A Stronger Europe – A Global Strategy for the European Union's Foreign and Security Policy*. Brussels: European Union.

Nobel Prize Organization (2012). The Nobel Peace Prize.

Pace, M. (2007). 'The construction of EU normative power'. *Journal of Common Market Studies*, 45(2): 1041–5.

Ray, J. (1995). *Democracy and International Conflict*. Columbia, SC: University of South Carolina Press.

Ray, J. (1998). 'Does democracy cause peace'. *Annual Review of Political Science*, 1: 27–46.

Russett, B. (1993). *Grasping the Democratic Peace*. Princeton, NJ: Princeton University Press.

Russett, B. & J.R. Oneal (2001). *Triangulating Peace: Democracy, Interdependence, and International Organizations*. New York: W.W. Norton.

Schimmelfenning, F. (2002). 'Introduction: The impact of international organizations on the Central and Eastern European States – Conceptual and Theoretical Issues'. In H.R. Linden (ed.) *Norms and Nannies: The Impact of International Organizations on the Central and East European States*. Lanham, MD: Rowman & Littlefield.

Schmitter, P.C. (2001). 'The influence of international context upon the choice of national institutions and policies in non-democracies'. In L. Whitehead (ed.) *The International Dimensions of Democratization: Europe and the Americas*. Oxford: Oxford University Press, 4–25.

Smith, K. (2008). *European Union Foreign Policy in a Changing World*. Cambridge: Polity Press.

Treaty of Lisbon (2007). *Amending the Treaty on European Union and the Treaty Establishing the European Community* (2007/C 306/01). Accessed 5 September 2019 at http://publications.europa.eu/resource/cellar/688a7a98-3110-4ffe-a6b3 -8972d8445325.0007.01/DOC_19

UN (2015). SDG 16. 'Promote peaceful and inclusive societies for sustainable development, provide access to justice for all and build effective, accountable and inclusive institutions at all levels'. Accessed 5 November 2019 at https://unstats.un.org/sdgs/ report/2019/goal-16/

UN (2019a). *International Day of Democracy – September 15*, 19 September. Accessed 14 January 2019 at www.un.org/en/events/democracyday/

UN (2019b). 'Peace, justice, and strong institutions: Why they matter'. Accessed 9 January 2019 at www.un.org/sustainabledevelopment/wp-content/uploads/2018/09/16.pdf

UN Charter (1945). *UN Charter*. Accessed 16 October 2019 at www.un.org/en/sections/un-charter/un-charter-full-text/

UN Democracy (2019). *Shaping Our Future Together*. Accessed 14 January 2019 at www.un.org/en/sections/issues-depth/democracy/index.html

UN General Assembly (2012). *Human Rights Council 19th Session, Promotion and Protection of All Human Rights, Civil, Political, Economic, Social and Cultural Rights, Including the Right to Development*, 19 April. New York: United Nations.

UN General Assembly (2015a). *Human Rights Council Twenty-Eighth Session Agenda Item 3 Promotion and Protection of All Human Rights, Civil, Political, Economic, Social and Cultural Rights, Including the Right to Development*, 23 March. New York: United Nations.

UN General Assembly (2015b). *Transforming Our World: The 2030 Agenda for Sustainable Development*. New York: United Nations General Assembly, 25 September. Accessed 16 October 2019 at www.un.org/ga/search/view_doc.asp?symbol=A/RES/70/1&Lang=E

UN Goal 16 (2019). 'Promote just, peaceful and inclusive societies'. Accessed 9 January 2019 at www.un.org/sustainabledevelopment/peace-justice/

UN Secretary-General (2019). *Deputy Secretary-General's Remarks at ECOSOC Side Event 'What Is Democracy? Stepping Up Engagement around Goal 16'*, 15 July. Accessed 17 October 2019 at www.un.org/sg/en/content/dsg/statement/2019-07-15/deputy-secretary-generals-remarks-ecosoc-side-event-what-democracy-stepping-engagement-around-goal-16-prepared-for-delivery

UNDP (2019). *Peace, Justice and Strong Institutions*. Accessed 9 January 2019 at www.undp.org/content/undp/en/home/sustainable-development-goals/goal-16-peace-justice-and-strong-institutions.html

Weart, S.P. (1998). *Never at War*. New Haven, CT: Yale University Press.

11. The EU and Agenda 2050: New political entrepreneurship in its making

Daniel Silander

On 28 November 2018, the European Commission called for a climate-neutral Europe by 2050. The Communication *A Clean Planet for All: A European Strategic Long-Term Vision for a Prosperous, Modern, Competitive and Climate Neutral Economy* was sent to the European Parliament, the European Council, the Council, the European Economic and Social Committee, the Committee of the Regions and the European Investment Bank. The Communication aimed at setting out a European vision for a green, sustainable continent. Taking Europe 2020 into account and the endorsed United Nations (UN) Agenda 2030, which the European Union (EU) played a pivotal role in shaping and making, the EU Commission has with Agenda 2050 continued to be an active political entrepreneur in European politics. In a time of recent economic and financial crisis, migration challenges, Brexit and right-wing populism, creating disintegration and polarization, the Commission has continued to strive for European integration as a driving engine for unity. The Commission has a unique formal role within the EU with no global equivalent: the Commission is a political entrepreneur in European politics striving for unity through diversity, a whole and free Europe and a peaceful, prosperous, powerful and pro-climate continent.

Agenda 2050 is a bold vision for a climate-neutral European continent. The Commission pursues the role of political entrepreneur by setting out an important path for all of Europe, but also a possible EU model for the rest of the world to follow to provide for a clean planet for everyone. The Commission calls upon all actors in political, economic and civil society to commit to such a path and collectively work for a prosperous and cleaner Europe. As stated in the Communication, 'Overall, failing to take climate action will make it impossible to ensure Europe's sustainable development and to deliver on the globally agreed UN Sustainable Development Goals' (European Commission, 2018a: 3). The Commission sets out seven strategic areas to engage in: (i) deployment of renewables; (ii) clean, safe and connected mobility; (iii) a competitive industry and a circular economy; (iv) infrastructure and interconnections; (v) bio-economy and natural carbon sinks; (vi) carbon capture and (vii) storage to address remaining emissions. As stated in the Communication:

> The threats and risks of climate change are known, and so are many ways to prevent them. This Strategy provides a number of solutions that could be pursued for the transition to a net-zero greenhouse gas emissions economy by mid-century. These options will radically transform our energy system, land and agriculture sector, modernize our industrial fabric and our transport systems and cities, further affecting all activities of our society. (European Commission, 2018a: 6)

The Communication identifies seven crucial strategic areas in which development must occur to achieve a climate-neutral Europe (see European Commission, 2018a: 9–16). The seven areas are:

1. Maximize the benefits from energy efficiency.
2. Maximize the deployment of renewables and the use of electricity to fully decarbonize Europe's energy supply.
3. Embrace clean, safe and connected mobility.
4. Move toward competitive EU industry and the circular economy to reduce greenhouse gas emissions.
5. Develop an adequate smart network infrastructure.
6. Reap the full benefits of the bio-economy.
7. Tackle remaining CO_2 emissions with carbon capture and storage.

First, Agenda 2050 addresses the interlinked and contemporary challenges of climate change and socioeconomic growth by focusing on the importance of a European transformation based on technological solutions to provide for a dynamic and greener economy and a sustainable and prosperous European society. As stated by the vice-president in charge of the EU Energy Union, Maroš Šefčovič:

> We cannot safely live on a planet with the climate that is out of control. But that does not mean that to reduce emissions, we should sacrifice the livelihoods of Europeans. Over the last years, we have shown how to reduce emissions, while creating prosperity, high-quality local jobs, and improving people's quality of life. Europe will inevitably continue to transform. Our strategy now shows that by 2050, it is realistic to make Europe both climate neutral and prosperous, while leaving no European and no region behind. (European Commission, 2018b)

To achieve these goals, the Communication includes the proposal to increase climate mainstreaming to reach about 25 per cent in the next Multiannual Financial Framework, making the EU the driving engine for change, but also a triggering factor for private and public investments. The Commission calls for reorienting private capital to sustainable investments, unifying a classification system on sustainable economic activities, legislating on low-carbon benchmarks, setting up a carbon pricing system, taxing environmental impacts and investing in research and innovation to develop zero-carbon solutions for a new green economy (European Commission, 2018a: 16–19).

The climate-neutral approach highlights the Commission's commitment to address the goals in Agenda 2030, such as goal 6 on clean water and sanitation and sustainable management of water to provide safe water and sanitation, and goal 7 on sustainable energy and sustainable energy services and access to affordable, reliable and modern energy, but also goal 8 on works and growth to promote decent work and full employment through inclusive and sustainable economic growth, as well as goal 9 on industries and innovation and sustainable industrialization and fostered innovation. However, the ambitious vision set out by the Commission in Agenda 2050 is also strictly connected to goal 12 and responsible consumption and production and responsible supply chains and business practices, as well as the promotion of the green economy, goal 13 on climate action and combatting climate change and its impacts, goal 14 on life below water and the sustainable use of oceans, seas and marine resources, as well as goal 15 on life on land to protect and promote sustainable terrestrial ecosystems on land and combat unsustainable management of forests, desertification and land degradation. The ambitious nature of the Communication by the Commission was restated by the commissioner for climate action and energy, Miguel Arias Cañete, who said:

> The EU has already started the modernization and transformation towards a climate neutral economy. And today, we are stepping up our efforts as we propose a strategy for Europe to become the world's first major economy to go climate neutral by 2050. Going climate neutral is necessary, possible and in Europe's interest. It is necessary to meet the long-term temperature goals of the Paris Agreement. It is possible with current technologies and those close to deployment. And it is in Europe's interest to stop spending on fossil fuel imports and invest in meaningful improvements to the daily lives of all Europeans. (European Commission, 2018b)

Second, the impact of climate change on resources is another dimension raised in the Agenda 2050 and which is linked to the EU Commitment to the UN Agenda 2030. The Communication highlights how climate change has a negative impact on goal 1 on ending poverty and the reduction and eradication of poverty, goal 2 on food security and the ending of hunger and promotion of sustainable agriculture, as well as goal 3 on health and well-being and health systems, health coverage and countermeasures for diseases. It is clearly stated in the Communication how ongoing climate change is a major risk to the production of food and the promotion of public health.

Third, Agenda 2050 also addresses the impact such transformation might have on citizens and societies in Europe. Although a greener economy will bring new employment opportunities, the transformation will also challenge and change societies that have been dependent on coal and carbon-intensive growth. Industrialized regions in Europe will transform and such changes will impact citizens. It is therefore important that the EU is prepared to mitigate negative effects on citizens and societies during the transformation towards a green economy. This requires the provision of support to social protection systems, education, training and lifelong learning, as new types of jobs will require new skills and know-how. This also highlights goals in the Agenda 2030 such as goal 4 on quality education to provide for inclusive and equitable education and life-long learning opportunities, as well as goal 5 on gender equality and girls' and women's empowerment and social and economic participation. In addition, Agenda 2050 has obvious links to Agenda 2030's goal 10 on reduced inequalities and the importance of structural transformation to address income inequalities and goal 11 on sustainable communities and the aspect of sustainable urbanization to provide for effective local development.

Fourth, Agenda 2050 stresses how crucial it is for the EU to engage European citizens in the process and to make citizens see the positive effects a green transformation will bring. Citizens are consumers and as such powerful actors in providing for a net-zero greenhouse gas economy by purchasing sustainable products and services and putting pressure on companies to be part of the climate-adjusted changes (European Commission, 2018a: 23). As stated by the Commission:

> Climate change is a global threat, and Europe alone cannot stop it. Cooperation with partner countries will therefore be essential to reinforce greenhouse gas reduction pathways that are consistent with the Paris Agreement. Nevertheless, the EU has a vital interest in working towards a net-zero greenhouse gas emissions economy by mid-century and demonstrating that net-zero emissions can go hand in hand with prosperity, having other economies follow its successful example. It should be based on the empowerment of all citizens and consumers in making change possible and proper information to the public. (European Commission, 2018a: 23)

Such awareness touches upon Agenda 2030 and goal 12 on responsible consumption and production and the importance of responsible supply chains and business practices for a green economy. Overall, the Agenda 2050 on a climate-neutral Europe addresses many of the Sustainable Development Goals in the UN Agenda 2030 and is a result of the European Commission perceiving climate change as a risk to survival and prosperity, but also and importantly as a window of opportunity for change. The Commission acts upon the climate change crisis as a political entrepreneur addressing challenges as opportunities in building a better, more prosperous Europe where the

EU could become a driving engine for global change. Such Commission work has a solid track record over the last two decades (see Silander, 2016, 2018; Nilsson, 2018).

This study has focused on European political entrepreneurship in the EU's approach towards the Agenda 2030 strategy. It has analysed the 2030 Agenda and the role of European political entrepreneurs in shaping, influencing and realizing the Agenda. The EU consists of many different actors. One driving agenda and political entrepreneur in European politics is the European Commission on Europe 2020, UN 2030 and EU 2050. On 12 December 2019, the European Council endorsed the Commission Communication on Agenda 2050 and stated its commitment to make the EU climate neutral by 2050. The European Council[1] stressed the importance of a climate-neutral Europe and how such a transformation will provide for new jobs and sustainable growth, but also how such a transformation requires taking into account the social and economic impacts on citizens and societies. The Commission was called upon to develop a proposal on the EU's new climate strategy to be presented to the UN in 2020 (Finnish Government, 2019).

NOTE

1.   Only Poland did not sign up for the Agenda 2050 commitment.

REFERENCES

European Commission, 2018a. *Communication from the Commission to the European Parliament, the Council, the European Economic and Social Committee, the Committee of the Regions and the European Investment Bank: A Clean Planet for All: A European Strategic Long-Term Vision for a Prosperous, Modern, Competitive and Climate Neutral Economy.* Brussels, 28 November. COM(2018) 773 final.
European Commission, 2018b. *The Commission Calls for a Climate Neutral Europe by 2050.* Press release, 28 November. Accessed 5 February 2020 at https://ec.europa .eu/commission/presscorner/detail/en/IP_18_6543
Finnish Government, 2019. *European Council Agreed: EU to Become Climate Neutral by 2050.* 13 December. Accessed 7 February at https://valtioneuvosto.fi/en/article/ -/asset_publisher/10616/eurooppa-neuvosto-sopi-eu-sta-ilmastoneutraali-vuoteen -2050-mennessa
Nilsson, Martin, 2018. The European Union and Global Climate Change. In Donald Wallace & Daniel Silander (eds), *Climate Change, Policy and Security: State and Human Impacts.* New York: Routledge.
Silander, D., 2016. The Political Entrepreneur. In Charlie Karlsson, Charlotte Silander & D. Silander (eds), *Political Entrepreneurship: Regional Growth and Entrepreneurial Diversity in Sweden.* Cheltenham, UK and Northampton, MA, USA: Edward Elgar Publishing, pp. 7–20.
Silander, Daniel, 2018. The European Commission and Europe 2020: Smart, Sustainable and Inclusive Growth. In Charlie Karlsson, Daniel Silander & Brigitte

Pircher (eds), *Smart, Sustainable and Inclusive Growth: Political Entrepreneurship for a Prosperous Europe*. Cheltenham, UK and Northampton, MA, USA: Edward Elgar Publishing.

Index

to facilitate orderly and safe
migration and mobility
of people 84–8
recommendations for 93–4
European neighbourhood 175–7
foreign and security, global strategy
on 179–81
gender equality 54–6, 61–4, 69–70
critique against 71–2
policy entrepreneurs 7–8
policy learning 65
political entrepreneurship
Agenda 2050 towards new 185–9
aim and structure of study 10–11
conceptualization 7–10, 54
and EC 36, 37–8, 39, 51
EU
achieving sustainable
development at heart
of 146
on Agenda 2030 4–7
on climate change globally
125–6
on climate change in Europe
116–25
equity in energy affordability
138
on industry, innovation and
infrastructure globally
107–9
on industry, innovation and
infrastructure in Europe
102–7
initiatives in relation to energy
142–3, 147
on migration and integration in
Europe 83–4
on sustainable cities and
communities globally
158–9
on sustainable cities and
communities in Europe
153, 159
political rights and civil liberties 169–72
protective Europe 48
Ps, four (people, planet, prosperity and
peace) 2–3, 99, 109, 178

recession

Agenda 2030 as opportunity to
reverse damage 14
economic progress since 46
funding implementation of climate
action policies 123
infrastructure system affected by
105
MDG progress halted by 15
political entrepreneurship protecting
from deeper 36, 51
variety of consequences 5
as window of opportunity for
integration 6
regional actors (Agenda 2030) 27–8
research, instituting 141
resilience
climate change reform 118–19
Sendai framework 117, 119–20
Rio+20 Conference on Sustainable
Development 1, 15, 16–17, 24, 27,
99, 133

Schengen cooperation 6–7, 84, 95
Sendai Framework for Disaster Risk
Reduction 1, 115
Sendai resilience framework 117, 119–20
smart growth 5, 11, 36, 39–40, 51, 102
social dimension of SDGs 21–2
soft policy 73
solidarity
achieving 136–7
cementing case for 143
clause 84, 87
in EU Charter of Fundamental
Rights 168
lack of among some member states
87–8, 93
principle of 107
social, as European norm 38
UN to emphasize importance of
global 1
as value 167
sovereignty 99–100
State of the Union 43–9
*Strategic Engagement for Gender
Equality* 70
*Strategy for Equality between Women
and Men* 69
strong institutions
Agenda 2030 on 163–7